D0722413

BEYOND THE MIRACLE WORKER

BEYOND THE MIRACLE WORKER

The Remarkable Life of
Anne Sullivan Macy
and
Her Extraordinary Friendship
with Helen Keller

KIM E. NIELSEN

BEACON PRESS, BOSTON

Beacon Press
25 Beacon Street
Boston, Massachusetts 02108-2892
www.beacon.org

Beacon Press books
are published under the auspices of
the Unitarian Universalist Association of Congregations.

12 11 10 09   8 7 6 5 4 3 2 1

This book is printed on acid-free paper that meets the uncoated paper
ANSI/NISO specifications for permanence as revised in 1992.

Text design by Susan E. Kelly at Wilsted & Taylor Publishing Services

Library of Congress Cataloging-in-Publication Data
Nielsen, Kim E.
Beyond the miracle worker : the remarkable life of Anne Sullivan Macy and
her extraordinary friendship with Helen Keller / by Kim E. Nielsen.
p. cm.
Includes bibliographical references and index.
ISBN-13: 978-0-8070-5046-0 (hardcover : alk. paper)
1. Sullivan, Annie, 1866–1936. 2. Teachers of deaf-blind people—
United States—Biography. 3. Keller, Helen, 1880–1968. I. Title.
HV1624.S84N54 2009
371.91'1092—dc22
[B]   2008036689

Materials from Perkins School for the Blind are courtesy of the Perkins School
for the Blind, Watertown, Massachusetts. Copyright for the Alexander Graham
Bell Family Papers in the Library of Congress, Manuscript Division, is held by
the Library of Congress. All letters by Helen Keller copyright © 2009 American
Foundation for the Blind, Helen Keller Archives. Parts of chapters 5 and 6 are
based on material in "The Southern Ties of Helen Keller," Kim E. Nielsen,
Journal of Southern History, LXXIII, No. 4 (November 2007), 783–806,
and are used courtesy of the *Journal of Southern History*. Excerpts from
Arthur Keller and Kate Keller collections are courtesy of Keller Johnson
Thompson, Helen Keller Foundation for Research and Education.

Frontispiece: Photograph of Helen Keller and Anne Sullivan courtesy of
Thaxter Parks Spencer Papers, R. Stanton Avery Special Collections Department,
New England Historic Genealogical Society, Boston, Massachusetts.

TO THOSE WHO HAVE GONE BEFORE:
Elijah Samuel Tuff, who continues to teach me;
Ken Cmiel, to whose scholarship, humanity,
and mentoring skills I aspire; and
Susan Durrant, whom we miss immensely.

A PROBLEM historians encounter while writing about women is that female subjects often change their names. In *Beyond the Miracle Worker* I've chosen to refer to my historical subject according to her changing last name. She was Annie Sullivan (sometimes Annie Mansfield Sullivan) until her 1905 marriage and then became Annie Sullivan Macy. Thus I refer to her first as Sullivan, then Macy. I tend to use her and Helen Keller's first names when referring to their private lives, and last names when referring to public life.

CONTENTS

Introduction

IT'S TEMPTING to begin this book like a fairy tale. *Once upon a time a poor, blind, and orphaned child named Annie magically grew into a happy, sighted, and successful adult woman. She became a miracle worker, lighting the intellectual fire and imagination of the deaf-blind girl Helen Keller at a water pump in the wilds of Alabama.* We know this kind of story. Many of our books and movies, the morality tales and parables we tell, even the heroes we've created, are versions of the same inspirational tale. The cheerful and uplifting message is that yes, you too can conquer anything in order to do the impossible.

But I won't.

"Any book about me," Anne Sullivan Macy reflected near the end of her life, "must be full of contradictions."[1] *Beyond the Miracle Worker* is a book that reflects these contradictions—the contradictions of a delightful, gloomy, charismatically fascinating, and annoying woman who was neither blind nor sighted. Though she was born in 1866, her life is a surprisingly contemporary tale. It is the story of a caring, fiercely proud, and intelligent woman trying to forge meaningful human relationships despite her own ingrained flaws and wounds. It is the story of a woman deeply frightened of depending upon anyone else for emotional, economic, or social sustenance.

And yet—in one of those contradictions that Macy warned us

about—she made one notable exception: she did not hesitate to lean on her famous student, and later friend, Helen Keller. While the whole world assumed that Keller's deaf-blindness forced her to depend on her teacher, Anne Sullivan Macy, my research suggests that the reverse more accurately characterizes their relationship of nearly fifty years. Macy leaned on Keller, juggling her uneasy combination of emotional vulnerability and a fierce desire for independence. Her lifelong struggle with chronic illness and depression was far more debilitating than Keller's deaf-blindness. Keller provided love, acceptance, daily assistance, an income, and a home. Their deep friendship, and Macy's willingness to allow herself to be dependent on Keller, gave meaning to Macy's life. Macy regarded herself as a "badly constructed human being," perceptively providing a way to understand the complex adult that the orphaned and deserted child of the Tewksbury Almshouse became. Yet, we shouldn't confine her to that characterization. As she herself admitted, "some of us blunder into life through the back door." Though it may have been through the back door, and blunder she did, she entered into life fully.

Indeed, she saw the benefits of blundering, and faltering through life didn't bother her. "If all people knew what was good for them and acted accordingly, this world would be a different world, though not nearly so interesting. But we don't know what's good for us, and I'm spending my days in experimenting. The experiments are amusing—and sometimes costly, but there's no other way of getting knowledge."[2]

This remark characterizes Anne Sullivan Macy perhaps better than anything else. From childhood on, many others had held firm opinions about what was good for her. Those opinions could amuse her, wound her, or strengthen her, but in the end her determination to discover her own life path lay at the very core of her character. She knew she had made mistakes—some of them profoundly painful. Whatever the benefit, whatever the cost, she had to discover for herself what was best. The marvel is the ferocity with which she thirsted to discover life, in its pains and its joys, for herself. As she said in concluding one of her 1916 letters to Helen, "We have only to keep a stiff upper lip and do our damnedest."[3]

* * *

AFTER COMPLETING two previous books on Helen Keller I swore I would never again write anything even remotely related to her. I started a project far removed from Keller. I informed everyone in my professional circle about that far-removed project in order to commit myself to it.

Then I reread Anne Sullivan Macy's 1916 letters to Helen Keller. Macy had written them as she dealt with the illness that she thought would kill her. The letters reveal an introspective woman trying to understand her life. Vacillating between urgency and detachment, she reflected on pleasure, anger, complacency, and amazement. It struck me that her life embodied both contradictions and intensity: physical pain, emotional pain, isolation, friendship, joy, intellect, tenacity, success, and near constant self-doubt. Yet, as she thought about death, as she pondered her life, she took immense joy in the daily life of the Puerto Rican countryside where she was staying.

As I reconsidered Macy, I became convinced that I, and nearly everyone else, had shortchanged the woman known only as the teacher of Helen Keller. A new biography of Anne Sullivan Macy is greatly needed, not only to do justice to her and to provide a peephole into Keller and Macy's multifaceted, and often surprising, friendship, but also because our cultural memory mythologizes and simplifies Macy as a straightforward educational superhero. She deserves more.

In addition, the increasing but still slow integration of people with disabilities into education, the workplace, and the public world makes this project significant. Macy's disability did not occur in a vacuum, isolated and abstract. Her daily experience of it was often defined by context—by institutions, by the expectations of others, and by the lack of social welfare support. Her life story, particularly when placed alongside that of Keller, reminds us of the diversity of disability experiences historically and today—and of the multiple ways that we, as individuals, as institutions, and as a country, contribute to the disabling nature of physical and mental impairments.

Surprisingly, telling the life story of Anne Sullivan Macy with her as the central figure is a markedly new strategy. Numerous Keller biographies, both older and more recent, discuss Macy but primarily as an ancillary figure to the real star of the story. These include Joseph P.

Lash's *Helen and Teacher: The Story of Helen Keller and Anne Sullivan Macy* (1980) and Dorothy Herrmann's *Helen Keller: A Life* (1998). *Helen and Teacher* provides the most complex analysis of Macy but retains a nearly exclusive focus on her development and life as a teacher. The most comprehensive biography of Macy is that of Nella Braddy Henney, *Anne Sullivan Macy: The Story Behind Helen Keller* (1933). Endorsed by Keller, approved by Macy, and written by an intimate friend of both women, this book sought to establish Macy as a pedagogical hero. Macy's most recent adult biography, published over forty years ago by Lorena Hickok, also defines her only according to Keller—even in its title: *The Touch of Magic: The Story of Helen Keller's Great Teacher, Anne Sullivan Macy* (1961). Macy was Keller's teacher, and proud of it, but her life story is so much more complicated and interesting than that single-minded characterization.

The goal of *Beyond the Miracle Worker* is to present Anne Sullivan Macy in all of her complexity. First and foremost, by telling and analyzing Macy's life as *her* story—not Helen's—this biography tells a new tale. *Beyond the Miracle Worker* follows the accidental and unexpected path an orphaned asylum child took to become a world-famous educator. This includes an intimate depiction of growing up amidst the horrors of a mid-nineteenth-century asylum, a rarely if ever told story in U.S. history. It chronicles a tumultuous marriage. It analyzes the adult life of a chronically ill, disabled woman whose public identity excluded nearly all acknowledgment of her disability. It follows a smart and ambitious woman trying to make a professional life in a patriarchal society. And it traces the ever-changing friendship between Macy and Keller, in which the deaf-blind Keller eventually cared for and became the personal aid of her former teacher.

In many ways, Macy resembles an archetypal American figure—the self-made man. As a young orphan housed in Massachusetts's Tewksbury Almshouse, she pleaded her way out with single-minded determination by literally pulling on the sleeves of touring philanthropists and begging for an education. Later on in her life, she exercised further determination and retained control of the child Helen Keller—and thus of her own professional life—despite the machinations of numerous others who were far more powerful. With intense purposefulness, she repeatedly created herself. The obvious complication, however, is that though a "self-made man," she was female, disabled, and of (to her) shameful beginnings. Her life raises questions about the opportunities available to women to reinvent themselves in turn-of-the-century America.

A related theme is that of the narrow but changing economic and professional opportunities available to women. Macy is contemporary with the first generation of female college students who embraced pivotal and important roles in U.S. social reform, education, and civic life. She is a contemporary of those who—like Jane Addams, Julia Lathrop, and Florence Kelley—developed and energized the settlement house movement. She is, however, dramatically different. Though an extremely brilliant woman, she lacked any educational training or advanced degree, came from a family with no connections to wealth or prestige, was deeply ashamed of her past, and had little involvement in broad social reform. Other than her relationship to Keller, she had few opportunities to build on for personal advancement. Those she had came from flirtatious relationships with older men. From the time of Keller's college graduation in 1904 until the early 1920s the two constantly sought new economic opportunities and stability as various money-making attempts failed. While she and Keller clearly valued one another, Macy clung to the relationship with such tenacity partially because of the narrow options available for a woman of her class and background, let alone one with a disability.

Also important to this biography and Macy's life is the theme of education. As a child, Macy grasped for an education as an escape, and a redemption, from poverty and the almshouse. As an untrained, inexperienced, and isolated young woman she accomplished a task many had thought impossible: teaching language to the almost seven-year-old deaf-blind Helen Keller. Though not a Radcliffe student, she attended the prestigious female college alongside Keller, fingerspelling for her all lectures and books. Ironically, the woman who became one of the world's most famous educators had no educational training, and did little regarding the education of others after her one student became an adult.

The teacher and student were only fourteen years apart in age.

Helen Keller and Anne Sullivan Macy cared deeply for one another and enjoyed the excitement of each other's company. The relationship is both more and less significant to Macy's life than historians have recognized. It's more significant because it's a vastly more complex and profound relationship than the common teacher–student story of the miraculous water pump at which Macy taught Keller. It's less significant, because as one recasts the story with Macy herself as the focal point, the biography becomes a much broader and wide-ranging story than that of just one relationship.

The relationship between the two women raises questions about autonomy, independence, and friendship. While a child and student, Helen depended greatly on Macy; as both grew older the teacher became increasingly dependent upon her student. Their intense and multifaceted relationship contributed to the deterioration of the Macys' marriage—John Macy was not only Anne's husband but also Keller's editor and political mentor. Even public perception of Keller and Macy was contradictory, haunted by the question of which woman enabled and created the other. Many credited the teacher with crafting her student's personhood; but as Keller grew to adulthood, others dismissed Macy as a low-status assistant.

Since first meeting in 1887, the two women had quickly become the central persons in each other's lives—but in profoundly and significantly different ways. Though publicly perceived to be the teacher and able-bodied one, Annie depended on Helen. Helen felt immense friendship, gratitude, and love for Annie, but she did not *need* Annie in the same way that Annie needed her. Annie's emotional, financial, and physical dependence on Helen thus raises questions about the meanings of disability. In some ways, Macy lived a life far more vulnerable than that of Keller.

For me, the process of telling Macy's life has raised ethical and practical questions about my role as a biographer and historian. Were Macy alive today, she might be diagnosed with depression or post-traumatic stress disorder, complicated by frequent or chronic pain. Diagnosing the dead, however, is difficult and perhaps even unethical, and Macy left inadequate materials for us to do so even if we wanted to. Most significantly, however, I am a historian and not a psychologist or physician. Nor do I want to medicalize or make deviant what does not need to be. Throughout this book I sometimes use *depression* to characterize Macy's emotional well-being or lack thereof, but this does not imply a clinical diagnosis.

Macy's life also raises questions about the writing of biography. The source material that remains is in complex and contradictory layers. At least once Macy burnt letters and memoir materials in order that others not read them. And at least once she kept letters for a future biographer, contrary to Helen's wishes. She tried to write an autobiography but couldn't complete it. She never published much of the autobiographical material she wrote, and some of what she left is in a lightly fictionalized form. She remained deeply ambivalent about how she wanted to be remembered—sometimes seeking to shape and control those remembrances, at other times paying them no heed. Near the end of her life she cooperated with, even encouraged, the biographical efforts of her friend Nella Braddy Henney, and took joy in the positive reviews of the resulting biography. For decades Keller tried to write Macy's life story, completing and publishing it twenty years after Macy's death. Both Henney and Keller considered their biographical efforts to be labors of love, expressions of gratitude and praise. The resulting books must be read as homage. *Beyond the Miracle Worker* is not homage, but it is my hope that if Macy were still alive, this biography would earn a wry nod of approval from her.

Near the end of Macy's life, after the death of her husband, John, from whom she had been estranged for decades, she wrote, "Deep in the grave our dust will stir at what is written in our biographies."[4] I hope *Beyond the Miracle Worker* will continue to stir the dust—for Anne Sullivan Macy, and for those asking questions about childhood trauma, the contradictory consequences of intelligence and drive for turn-of-the-century American women, the meanings of friendship, the nature of teaching, and the complexities of disability.

CHAPTER I

Feeding Hills, 1866–1876

THE ROLLING COUNTRYSIDE of Anne Sullivan Macy's childhood in Feeding Hills, Massachusetts, always haunted her. Her early life there haunted her so deeply, in fact, that when she returned for the first time decades later, she traveled anonymously. So surreptitiously did she return that we don't know exactly when the trip occurred—likely in the early 1900s. While there she hid her fame and identity from the Sullivan clan still in Feeding Hills, and hid her past from nearly all of those in her present.

Had she not become the famed teacher of Helen Keller, we would know nothing about the woman who became Anne Sullivan Macy. The first years of her life are largely undocumented and remain obscure. The poverty of her immigrant parents, her mother's death from tuberculosis, and her father's reputed alcoholism and abandonment of his children contribute to a lack of the substantial sources from which historians traditionally build a life narrative, leaving behind a limited story. The bare bones can be found in the census and the basic records of birth and death. Going beyond the bare bones is more difficult.

It is perhaps fitting that one of the first times Annie's parents, Thomas and Alice (nee Chloesy) Sullivan, appear in the historical records is when they brought her, their firstborn child, to St. Michael's Cathedral in Springfield, Massachusetts, for baptism. They baptized her into a distinctly Irish Catholic community. Like many others, the young, illiterate parents had left Ireland for what they hoped would be a better life in the United States. Recording her memories in her early sixties, Macy did not know when her parents had come to the country, where they landed, how they met, or when or where they married.[1]

If her memories and family tales were correct, her father followed already settled siblings from County Limerick, Ireland, to the Feeding Hills neighborhood of Agawam, Massachusetts (just outside of Springfield), where he worked as a farm laborer. The census doesn't tell us who came first, and the myriad Sullivans entering the United States, Boston, and even Agawam make it difficult to discern whether those found in the historical materials are the correct Sullivan clan. It appears that by 1860 some of Thomas's siblings lived in Agawam. His brother John owned land valued at $250. He and his wife, Mary, had three children, all born in Massachusetts, thus indicating that he had arrived in the United States by 1853. As with so many Irish immigrants, the chain of sibling migration appears to have led the Sullivan siblings to emigrate and settle near one another.[2]

We know little about Macy's paternal family, and nothing about her mother's. The census indicates both parents were born in Ireland. Thomas had two brothers named John—Mary's John and Anastasia's John, as Annie distinguished them, according to their wives. Why the brothers shared the same first name is unknown. Family stories document that another brother, James (or Jimmie, a name also given to Annie's brother), drowned in Feeding Hills. By 1870 the Sullivan men—John, Thomas, and John—had populated the countryside with fourteen children. The value of the land owned and farmed by Mary's John had jumped to an impressive $3,000. In the census, each man called his first daughter Anna, a derivative of Johanna, perhaps the name of the mother they left in Ireland. Baptismal records list Bridget Sullivan as Annie's baptismal sponsor, suggesting that Thomas had a sister.[3]

Although we don't know which years the Sullivan siblings left Ireland, we can assume that the family was affected by the Irish famine. Between 1846 and 1855, during what is known as the Famine Decade, over 1.8 million Irish arrived in North America. Considering that Thomas was born in approximately 1840, it's likely that he crossed the

Atlantic after the apex of migration that had included his siblings John and John—probably after 1860, since he doesn't appear in the 1860 Agawam census like his siblings—but certainly before Annie was born in 1866. The worst years of the famine were over, but the economy of Ireland remained dire.

If Thomas and Alice knew each other in Ireland, in order for them to marry it would have been almost necessary for them to leave County Limerick. Marriages in the post-famine years were generally based not on romance but, as historian Hasia Diner explains, "on economic calculation with parents figuring and weighing the financial benefits and liabilities of their children's marital futures." Land was a near prerequisite for marriage, and most likely none of the Sullivans had any. In one County Limerick parish, the marriage rates had fallen by half from 1840 to 1880; the marriage rate decreased as the age at time of marriage increased.[4]

For Thomas's sisters and perhaps for his wife, Alice, emigration was thus a near necessity. With marriage and employment unlikely, Irish women had few options for economic survival. As historian Janet Nolan puts it, women "had grown ever more superfluous." The resulting emigration was a "massive female exodus," and "in the decades after the famine more Irish women than Irish men immigrated to the United States." Among immigrant populations in the United States, the Irish were in this way unique. Whether the Sullivan men and their eventual wives married before they left Ireland is not clear, although one family story indicates that they did. If so, they were in the minority. Irish immigrants were primarily single men and women in this period. From Munster, the province containing Limerick, 85.5 percent of the female emigrants aged fifteen to thirty-five were single.[5]

For reasons unknown the extended family chose to settle in the Feeding Hills neighborhood of Agawam, Massachusetts. Few Irish immigrants in this period settled in rural areas; even fewer went into farming. Those Catholics who came to the region in this period came largely as laborers. They built canals on the Connecticut River or worked in cotton or paper mills. The region flourished economically, in great part due to the canals, on which construction had begun in the 1790s. Rich farmland, paper mills, cotton mills, textile plants, and an armory that later became Smith & Wesson provided employment for many and wealth for some. The elite colleges of Smith, Amherst, and Mount Holyoke were not far away; nor were Emily Dickinson and the intellectuals of the transcendentalist movement. Abolitionist John Brown lived in nearby Springfield.

During the 1850s and 1860s, when the extended Sullivan family was slowly arriving in Agawam, the small town already housed a paper mill, broadcloth and cotton mills that employed area women, and the distillery that made the famous Old Agawam gin. The Feeding Hills neighborhood they settled in was largely agricultural, named Feeding Hills in 1638 when the Springfield voters agreed to allow area men to graze their horses and cows on the then-unoccupied land. The population officially incorporated in 1855.

Arriving around the tumultuous time of the Civil War, the extended Sullivan clan members were outsiders. They had little money and lived away from major Irish settlements. Histories of Hampden County published in 1902, 1936, and 1991 list no Sullivans among the region's important figures, though many Irish-immigrant Sullivan family groups lived in the region.[6]

Thomas and Alice Sullivan carried their firstborn the four miles to Springfield for her baptism at St. Michael's Cathedral on April 22, 1866. The baby, born April 14, was baptized "Johanna Sullivan." Bridget and John Sullivan served as her baptismal sponsors. The young parents must have felt proud of the nearly new church. The Catholic community of Boston and the entire Springfield region contributed funds to build it, and it had been consecrated in 1861. The brick building was impressive, its spire rising far above the street. On the outside of the tower stood a life-sized St. Michael with a spear in one hand. The local priest encouraged Irish Catholics to take up the spear and enroll in the Union Army, perhaps in part to prove their loyalty to their new country, but none of the Sullivan brothers did so. Agawam got its own Catholic Church in 1874, but it was a reminder of the Irish community's marginality. This church served the French Catholics who had come to the region from Canada to work in the mills.[7]

The young parents must, at first, have been optimistic. In an undated and lightly fictionalized account of her life, Annie wrote that her father was "poor, but he was young and he believed that American fortune would smile upon him and his family." By 1870 the new immigrants Thomas and Alice had three children—Anna (1866), Ellen (1867), and James (1869), as they were listed in the 1870 census. Between 1870 and 1872, Ellen, or Nellie, died, and infant son John was born and died, on dates that remain uncertain.[8] In 1873, Alice gave birth to Mary, who was also carried to the Catholic cathedral in Springfield for baptism.

Embedded in the memories Macy left us of her childhood are the cycles of agriculture and community. She remembered hog killings and the crowds of people—adults and children—who gathered to labor. In one place this seems a fond memory of games, chaos, cousins, and neighbors; in another her "horror of dead things" causes her to "hide all day" during the "repulsive performance." Her cousins, she remembered, "took fiendish delight" in chasing her while dangling recently decapitated chickens. An "old, gnarled golden-sweet apple-tree at the end of the house" provided pleasure. Barns were places for children to play, with ladders, lofts, and horses. "We children," she remembered, "could tie ourselves up in the stalls and play that we were horses." She also loved riding horses: "I would climb on the back of any horse, holding on to the harness until I was up, and this was when I was so small that my bare feet rested on his back, and I had no hold with my knees."[9] Pastures were places where one forgot to mind the cows, and instead daydreamed.

Neighbors were to be envied. Next door lived a girl with "red hair and a blue parasol," presumably part of the Taylor family, for which Annie's father did farm labor. To the young Annie, "I could have fallen down and worshipped [her] . . . she was so beautiful." Her home had a parlor with a "huge, shiny" piano that tantalized the eldest Sullivan child. She remembered sneaking into the room, touching the piano keys in order to make sound, and being caught and exiled from the beautiful home, for "bad children were not to come to the person's house." The Taylor children attended school and Annie did not, though she remembered one of the women in the Taylor household taking her to visit the local school.[10] This must have made the curious child more envious than ever.

Annie's memories indicated that her family's cottage served as part of her father's salary. According to the 1870 census, the native-born Taylor household consisted of what seems to have been two elderly parents (Sophia and Rufus Taylor); a widowed daughter-in-law, Eliza, who at forty-five is listed as the legal owner of the farm, valued at over $10,000; her twenty-four-year-old son, John, and his twenty-year-old wife, Mary; young children of both Eliza and Mary; and a domestic servant and a single farmer laborer. The census lists John as head of household. One wonders whether John or his mother, Eliza Taylor, directed the farm labor, and what the landless immigrant Thomas Sullivan thought of working for the Taylor family.[11] Clearly his daughter beheld the household with awe.

Annie's eyes may have been a reason she did not attend school. She had acquired trachoma, a highly contagious disease most prevalent in impoverished communities, where personal hygiene is difficult. Exposure to the bacterium causes inflammation and scar tissue to develop in the eye, generally on the inside of the eyelid, the blinking and rubbing of which then create additional scar tissue. Impaired eyesight and discomfort, often severe pain, result. Annie's first memory of herself was hearing someone say, "She would be so pretty if it were not for her eyes." As one historian put it, "Trachoma victims wore their stigma on the most prominent part of the face—the eyes."[12] In the 1870s doctors had few options for treating the disease (today's treatment is simple antibiotics), but the Sullivan household could not have afforded much anyway. Annie's mother followed the ineffectual advice of a neighbor to wash Annie's eyes in geranium water.

Sometime during the two years following her mother's death, her father took her to see an oculist in Westfield. The doctor apparently did little or nothing, but Macy later remembered the event as a special outing—during which her father, of whom she had few fond memories, bought a beautiful white hat with a blue ribbon and pink rose for the girl who'd been told she wasn't pretty.[13]

Fear and death, however, dominated her memories of her family. The birth of a child that must have been her sister Mary was a time of screams, and strangers in the house: "I was terribly frightened. I wanted to get out of bed; but I was afraid." She remembered the death of her infant brother, Johnny, and how she hid in a tobacco shed when her mother asked her to look at him. Her feelings, she remembered, were pleasure at her "best dress and shoes and stockings" and relief that he had finally stopped crying. She later told her friend Nella Braddy Henney that her only memory of him was in his coffin on her father's knees in the carriage on the way to the funeral. To a child the carriage ride simply meant "ever changing fields and my heart fairly danced when the horses clattered over the bridge."[14]

Overshadowing everything about these years and those that followed, however, was the 1874 death of Alice Sullivan. Family stories indicate she had tuberculosis, and Annie's memories of her cough agree with that: "Mother had always awakened us in the morning, calling our names and telling us it was time to get up. The effort made her cough, and we used to take advantage of the coughing paroxysm to lie in bed a little longer."[15]

Annie was eight when her mother died. As an older woman, Macy said that the memories of her mother never "faded with all the years. Every detail remains distinct, and they are all vivid, and even to this day perturbing and unpleasant." She remembered her mother as slender, with dark eyes and dark brown hair, and a hip injury that had occurred not long after she gave birth to Annie. She also remembered her mother's caretaking: a refusal to help her father catch her when he thought she deserved a whipping. What could have been a happy memory of her mother in a beautiful dress, "what I now know to be a wine color, with black velvet trimmings and large black, shiny buttons" was spoiled by a memory of her own bloody arm, hurt by someone holding her back from grasping the shiny buttons. Further spoiling the memory was the image of her mother falling, the cookstove toppling, and the spilling of soot as her mother attempted to reach her. Macy told Henney that she remembered her mother ill and in bed, all of them desperately poor in a dark place with lots of steps.[16]

Tuberculosis was the leading cause of death in the United States through the nineteenth and into the twentieth century. The disease that ignored geography, class, race, and age caused an astounding one out of every five deaths from 1800 to 1870. Alice Sullivan could have acquired the tubercle bacillus in Ireland, for it was as common there as in the United States; aboard ship while en route to the United States; or once she arrived in Massachusetts, where Boston health officials blamed Irish immigrants for the disease. Death came slowly. As historian Sheila Rothman says, "Acute attacks alternated with remissions; the process of wasting and dying could take a few years or span several decades." Because there was no way of knowing how long someone with tuberculosis would live, and one could live for a substantial period, women in Alice's situation were expected to proceed with marriage and children even if they knew they had the disease.[17]

In tuberculosis, then known as consumption, "the body was literally consumed by the disease." Even if the Sullivans had been able to afford quality medical care, treatment in the 1870s and the 1880s was what historian Katherine Ott calls "virtually a free-for-all." Of all the treatments offered, whiskey might have been the only one available, as the inhalers doctors began to use in the 1870s were prohibitively expensive. The first stage of the disease would have been hard to notice. Eventually Alice would have likely experienced night sweats, a cough, pain, persistent diarrhea, and perhaps the loss of her voice. Nearer her death all symptoms would have become much more severe, and the fatigue would have been relentless. As Ott describes it, "By the time death was at hand, emaciation was so complete that it appeared as if a cadaver had already replaced the human form."[18]

Alice Sullivan's life had not been easy, but nor was it substantially different from the lives of many women in the United States at that time. She had been born in the midst of the Irish famine, survived emigration to North America, lived in poverty with a man who apparently drank substantially, and had lost two of her five children to death. In her last years, she likely knew the imminence of her own death. Presumably, but perhaps not, she and her husband spoke of her death and what would happen to her surviving children. Deborah Fiske, a middle-class, literate New Englander living not that far from the Sullivans, died of tuberculosis at approximately the same time as Alice. Knowledge of her coming death prompted her to talk with her children about it, to involve relatives in the care of her children, and to leave letters for her children. Like Alice, she had multiple pregnancies while tubercular, each of which likely weakened her and exacerbated the tuberculosis. Though not literate, Alice probably adopted similar strategies to mother her children while dying.[19]

In 1874 children such as Annie Sullivan grew up with death as an "expected part of their lives." She routinely saw the slaughtering and death of farm animals, had already experienced the death of two of her siblings and possibly several cousins, and undoubtedly knew of death among neighboring adults and children. This knowledge, however, would not have shielded her from trauma. The memories she shared of her mother's death were of the evening of death and the funeral that followed: being woken in the night by "someone we called 'Auntie'" in order to view the body; ever-present people preparing the body and attempting to care for her, Jimmie, and Mary; being given a penny and told to buy herself candy at the local store. Those who study bereavement characterize its initial period as one of denial, numbness, and a feeling of being on "automatic pilot," and these same feelings emerge even in the multiple memoirs written by Macy nearly sixty years later. In one place she wrote, "I do not remember what my feelings were, I know I did not cry. . . . Jimmie put his arms around me, and we both cried, I do not think from grief, but because of the strangeness and stillness everywhere."[20]

The most detailed visual memories recorded by Macy were those of her mother's body being laid out. Hiding in a corner of the room where her mother lay, the eight-year-old had watched the dismantling of a trundle bed and the construction of a casket. Discovered, she was "jerked out of the room" and let in again only when the body was prepared. Her mother had likely made preparations for her death with area priests. In two separate places Macy described the brown gown used to cover her mother's body; it had been brought to the house by priests before her mother's death, wrapped in tissue paper, and placed in a bureau drawer. Written in white letters across the front was the word *Jesus*.[21]

"I looked and looked at her and wondered," Macy later wrote. "I saw Mary and Jimmie sobbing, and Mary was sitting on my father's knee. I didn't cry or move. Somehow they didn't seem to belong to me, or I to them. They seemed more like the other people who were sitting around—strangers. I don't remember any one speaking to me, or anything that happened afterwards." Just as at the death of her infant brother, Johnny, the funeral meant a carriage ride for the young children, who presumably got few of them. "I was furious with Jimmie because he wouldn't give me his place by the window so that I could watch the horses. He began to cry, saying I hurt him, and my father struck me sharply on the side of my head. A fire of hatred blazed up in me which burned for many years." That night she woke to the food, singing, alcohol, and crowd of an Irish wake.[22]

Alice's death left Thomas Sullivan, an illiterate hired hand, with three children eight years and under. Two of his children had already died. Eight-year-old Annie's trachoma meant her eyes often caused her pain and her sight was increasingly limited. Five-year-old Jimmie's hip caused him pain and mobility problems. Mary was probably just over a year old. The children had lost not only a parent, but the parent who provided most of their caretaking. And at a time when his children needed him desperately, he likely had few personal resources to draw on to offer them support. As Macy wrote in one version of her life story, "fortune seldom smiled upon the poor and the ignorant."[23]

Blue-eyed and red-haired, Thomas Sullivan left his daughter a strong sense of being Irish. "My coleen bawn," she recollected hearing him say, "you can't hear the little people in this new land, but in Ireland the brake is full of voices, lowlike, and many are the time I heard them meself." The fairies and Irish ghosts of his stories were so real that as a child she searched for them under the stones around her house. Annie remembered fond, intimate moments: "After the evening meal and on rainy Sundays," he sat her on his knee and shared "tales of the little folk who lived in Ireland far, far away. I never wearied of these stories, and I loved the broad accents of the Irish tongue." The stories he told were repeated so often that near the end of her life she could still write many down. "Some of the tales," she wrote, "linger on in my brain. A word, an inflection starts vague, disturbing clues. They unravel a little way, then I lose the thread, and all is blank."[24]

Unlike her father, however, Annie grew up as an American—or, at least, running from Irishness. Once she became conscious of the "critical attitude of others" toward the Irish brogue, her attitude toward her father changed: "Then I often vexed my father and spoilt a tale by correcting him and reminded him that he talked like the other field hands. . . . When I sneered at one of his truly engaging Irishisms, he would look at me wistfully, as a dog looks at a child who has beaten him, wondering at the meaning of the unkind treatment." She wrote that "stupid people" had turned her "against the speech of poetry and taught me to hold to the thorn and fling away the rose."[25] Such comments not only turned her away from the lyricism of the Irish tongue, they also turned her away from her father.

Thomas drank, and after Alice's death it appears that he fell apart. He lost his job, and thus their house. Annie's memories from this time included unmade beds, her father's failure as a cook, and an empty house. She wrote that they moved many times before going to live with her uncle John (Anastasia's John), but that she couldn't remember "anything connected with our migrations downward."[26] Relatives in Springfield took in three-year-old Mary. Annie and Jimmie remained with John and Anastasia, but at some point Thomas and the extended family decided that they could no longer care for the two disabled children. In February of 1876 the extended family delivered them to the state almshouse in Tewksbury, Massachusetts.

Annie believed herself to have been a difficult child and her family spoke of her in that way. In the early 1900s, when she and her dear friend John Hitz traveled incognito through Feeding Hills and spoke with one of Annie's aunts, probably Anastasia, they heard "legends of her intractability." The aunt told the supposed strangers that she would have kept the Sullivan children after Alice died, except that they were poor and challenging children. She reported that Annie had been a disobedient child with bad eyes.[27] By the early 1900s Annie was famous. Reconciling the famous woman with the child of these memories and placing her in the framework of family lore may have been difficult, perhaps even impossible, for family members who had chosen not to embrace her years before. One wonders if they even knew that the famous teacher Anne Sullivan was the daughter of Thomas and Alice.

During the last half of her life Macy had few sympathetic words or memories to share about her Sullivan relatives. In the lightly fictionalized, unpublished version of her life story, she wrote, "So far as

Johannah can ascertain, the birth roll of her branch of the Dunnivan [Sullivan] genealogical tree bore no dilectible [*sic*] fruit in art, literature, or science. The generation did not endow a single birth with genius. Of intellectual lineage, Johannah had none." None of them had visited her in the almshouse, and she believed none had ever written to inquire after either her or Jimmie. To her knowledge, they told those who asked that the two children were dead.[28]

The little information Macy left behind about the first ten years of her childhood, those essential years that construct us as human beings, is anguished and disjointed. Her biographer, Nella Braddy Henney, wrote that in 1928, on the first day they ever discussed those years, "she talked all afternoon about the part of her life which no living being knows."[29] To her these were shameful years for which she had no adequate language. There was little available cultural framework to describe the disintegration of her family and her separation at the age of ten from what remained of them. Nor was there language to lay out sporadic happiness, the confused memories of a child, and the realities of poverty and death. The difficulty of separating myth, nostalgia, a child's misinterpretation, and wishful thinking from her lived experience was exacerbated by her steady efforts to diminish those years in her life story.

CHAPTER 2

Tewksbury Almshouse, 1876–1880

MOST ASSUREDLY terrified and bewildered, ten-year-old Annie and four-year-old Jimmie arrived at the Massachusetts State Almshouse at Tewksbury on February 22, 1876. The rest of her life Anne Sullivan Macy said virtually nothing of her years at Tewksbury—less publicly, and even privately, than the limited amount she said about her family and life at Feeding Hills. As an adult, she characterized these years as "a crime against childhood." After interviewing her about these years, Nella Braddy Henney wrote, "she has spent her life since the age of fourteen trying to forget what happened up to that time."[1]

Perhaps not surprisingly, most of the material Macy later wrote about these years was unpublished and fictional. All of it is incomplete, undated, and unordered. It ranges in length from a sentence to several pages and appears in multiple but unnumbered revisions. Some memories may have been easier to relive as fiction. Rather than confront or acknowledge her own trauma, she wrote of trauma that occurred to the child "Johannah Dunnivan," who grew up in "Seeding Hills, Massachusetts" and was interred in "Dookesbury Asylum" after the death of her mother and desertion of her father. Though Sullivan could acknowledge that Johannah Dunnivan's "character was formed of those terrible experiences in that tragic place," fiction may have allowed her to distance herself from the fact that such experiences had formed

The Tewksbury Almshouse, erected circa 1854–1858. Image (circa 1890) courtesy of the Public Health Museum, Tewksbury, Massachusetts.

her own character. In an era before tell-all talk shows, fiction allowed her to credit experiences to Johannah Dunnivan that no reputable and educated woman of her social standing ever would have had.[2]

The Massachusetts social welfare system Annie Sullivan entered led the nation in size, institutional development, and bureaucracy. In what one historian has called a "major landmark in the history of American welfare," in 1863 the state had brought numerous almshouses, residential schools for blind and deaf children, asylums for those considered insane, state prisons, and public hospitals under the direction of the Massachusetts State Board of Charities.[3] Led by reformer Franklin B. Sanborn, the Board sought to centralize the system's bureaucracy and make its goals and practices consistent. Two of its members—Sanborn and Samuel Gridley Howe—would play pivotal roles in Sullivan's life.

The Massachusetts State Almshouse at Tewksbury was one of several founded in the state in the 1850s. Public almshouses, intended to provide refuge and labor for those unable to provide for themselves, had grown in number across Massachusetts throughout the nineteenth century. Their "eclectic" admissions policies meant that the institutions "accepted the very young, the aged, the infirm, and the mentally ill, among others." In this case, concerns about foreign-born Irish paupers were entangled with rhetoric about the state's moral obligations to its indigent citizens. On May 1, 1854, the almshouse at Tewksbury opened with a planned capacity of five hundred people, fueled by anti-Irish sentiment and intended primarily for indigent immigrants. Within three weeks it housed more than eight hundred. Though not markedly dissimilar from other almshouses, it was not a pleasant place. As historian Gerald Grob characterized it, "Conditions at the Tewksbury almshouse . . . deteriorated rapidly; its only redeeming virtue was that its cost per patient per year by 1861 was $52, as compared with $130 at the three state hospitals." In 1866 the state legislature and board of charities expanded the institution's scope to include the Tewksbury Asylum for the Chronic Insane.[4]

Of the fictional Dookesbury, Macy wrote that it "sheltered the vilest, the most degraded, the most abandoned human being[s] at that time." In that context, "Johannah Dunnivan was forgotten." She was only one of many: "Into these houses of woe are thrown tramps who prey upon the public, prostitutes who are no longer able to ply there [sic] trade, heaps of maniacs, destitute women who are about to become the mothers of illegitimate children, innocent paupers, tubercular people from the slums, foundlings, cripples, blind people and forsaken people."[5]

In 1876, the year that the Sullivan children arrived at Tewksbury, the institution's inspectors optimistically wrote that it was "never in a better condition than it is to-day." Just a year earlier the institution's superintendent had invited "all who have the welfare and comfort of this class of people at heart" to tour the facility, which was only forty-five minutes and sixty cents away from Boston by train. He assured the public that "We shall be happy to welcome and show through the institution all who may wish to come, on Tuesdays, Wednesdays, Thursdays, and Fridays, holidays excepted." How many visited that year is unknown. The 1877 annual report noted that "750 visitors have entered their names in the register provided for that purpose." The superintendent estimated that people came in equal numbers as "critics, philanthropists, or simply out of curiosity."[6]

Though the 1876 annual report cautioned that having more than nine hundred residents in an institution built for five hundred would "increase the sickness and mortality, and endanger the health of all," the average weekly number that year was 918. In February of 1876, Annie and Jimmie arrived with 143 other new residents. They were not the only children. Like Annie, twelve were between ten and twenty years of age; like Jimmie, twenty-two were under ten years of age. Nor were they the only Irish: 40 percent of those admitted were either Irish immigrants or their children. Their brief intake records specify that their father, Thomas Sullivan, held no estate and was born in Ireland; also noted was a lack of information about his naturalization, his service in the Union Army, and his tax status. Their mother, Alice, had been dead for two years. Sister Mary, just three, lived in Agawam with an aunt. Of the children, it only said, "Sore eyes and James has hip complaint. Neither ever went to school."[7]

At the age of four, Jimmie was too old to be placed with the foundlings—the very young. Bureaucracy and common practice dictated that the two siblings were to be separated and placed in the general populations of the men's and women's wards.

Already, at this pivotal moment, hints of Anne Sullivan Macy's tenacity and potential fury emerged. As an adult, Macy wrote of Johannah Dunnivan that "All the love and tenderness her nature was capable of were lavished upon her little brother, Jimmy."[8] The ten-year-old had already experienced much separation. Death had taken her mother and two siblings. Relatives had taken her sister, but had rejected her and Jimmie. She had little information about her father and whether or not she would ever see him again. She knew virtually nothing of this loud, large, and frightening institution into which they had just stepped after what must have been one of their first train rides. Her younger brother was all she had.

Whether it was a tantrum she or both children threw, words they said, or copious tears, something convinced Tewksbury administrators to allow them to stay together. For three months, the children lived together in the women's ward of the hospital. Perhaps administrators chose the hospital because of Annie's eyes; perhaps it was simply the easiest place to put them. Jimmie wore a pinafore to aid the pretense.

The Sullivan children sought to make a life and establish community at Tewksbury as successfully as they could. In his pivotal 1961 book *Asylums*, sociologist Erving Goffman asserted that "any group of persons—prisoners, primitives, pilots, or patients—develop a life of their own that becomes meaningful, reasonable, and normal once you get close to it." The "dead house" became the site of Annie and Jimmie's efforts to create normality. This space was partitioned off from the main room of the ward. "When any of the patients died," she wrote, "they were rolled in there. They were not prepared for burial, but were hurled into pine boxes." The children apparently spent their first night there, and claimed it as their own play space; one can assume they were successful because no one else wanted to be among the dead bodies. The children spent much of their time cutting pictures of criminals and fashion plates from the *Police Gazette* and *Godey's Lady's Book* in order to paste them on the walls of the dead house. The decorations were allowed to remain, the pictures of fashion and crime in jarring juxtaposition to the dark space and dead bodies. "Our artistic efforts were encouraged by the doctors and attendants," Macy wrote as an adult. "They would show the exhibition to visitors with great gusto." Jimmie took over the cutting tasks, performed with tools appropriated from the hospital doctors, after Anne's limited eyesight caused her to cut too many heads off.[9]

Like everyone else in the women's ward, the children slept on iron cots lined up in rows that extended the length of the building. Iron pipes that also ran the length of the room provided heat. As Macy described it, "The head of the cots were kept away from them by a wooden track, about a foot from the wall." Rats easily came in and out of the holes made by the pipes. This served as entertainment for the fictional Johannah and Jimmie. The two children "teased the rats with sticks which they made by rolling paper. They laughed with glee when the rat jumped at the stick or ran under the bed which made the occupant scream." A dispensary in which doctors saw and treated patients sat between the women's ward and the men's ward. Frosted windows let in daylight, but could not be opened for ventilation and were hard to see through.[10]

The fictional Johannah and Jimmie sometimes saw patients "set nearly crazy," and would hide their heads under their pillows futilely trying to escape the shrieks. Soon, however, curiosity would overcome the two children and their heads came up in time for them to see straightjackets used. Johannah once saw a woman attack an attendant with an iron bar she had torn from a bed; the attendant then "pounced upon her and beat her with the bar which had been wrenched out of her hand."[11]

Asylum residents had to walk halfway down the yard to use the toilet facilities. The women's toilet, Macy remembered, contained three well-fought-over seats. To the child Annie, this was sometimes fascinating: "The conversation that went on as they squatted longer than necessary would not pass even an indifferent censor." The stench was the "subject of unprintable remarks."[12]

Residents knew in advance when state officials or otherwise esteemed personages were expected, for the "toilet was renovated as far as could be." Macy remembered that residents shared "a standing joke" about how the attention of visitors was "invariably diverted when they reached the toilet." As one employee later remembered, "When the trustees were coming we got up at 4 o'clock in the morning so that the trustees would find everything in order; the trustees would be all right and come there and get their dinner and go away."[13]

At some point in those first three months Thomas Sullivan traveled from Agawam to Tewksbury to visit his two children. Macy noted the visit in her story of the fictional Johannah. Thomas brought candy, as well as his half brother. The men shared their plan to go west, toward Chicago, in order to find employment building canals and railroads. Presumably he came to say goodbye. Macy left no direct or fictionalized record of her emotions regarding the visit. It was, however, the last time she saw her father.[14]

Separation and death were painfully omnipresent throughout Annie's early years. It must have been not long after her father's visit that Jimmie died, on May 31, 1876. At Tewksbury he was only a number. The institution's records indicate that 21 residents died that month and 238 that year. Like Jimmie, 208 of them had been at Tewksbury less than a year; and 99, almost half of them, were children five or under. The bodies of all of them, presumably, went through the death house. As Macy later wrote, "I was perfectly familiar with the idea of death. I had seen my mother lying cold and still and strangely white, and I had seen women die in the ward where we were."[15] Jimmie's death, however, affected her more than any other. Almost fifty years later she wrote of it in greater detail than any other life event.

She woke one morning to find him in more pain than normal— standing and dressing caused him to fall, screaming in pain. The "bunch on his thigh," Macy wrote, "seemed larger than I had ever seen it." His now eleven-year-old sister knew what was coming: "An indescribable feeling of terror swept over me. It was as if sharp cruel fingers gripped my heart." It was only a day or two more before she woke to a "black, empty space" where Jimmie's bed had been.[16]

Once again, the death house played a prominent role in her life narrative. She snuck in.

It was all dark inside. I couldn't see the bed at first. I reached out my hand and touched the iron rail, and clung to it with all my strength until I could balance myself on my feet. Then I crept to the side of the bed—and touched him! Under the sheet I felt the little cold body, and something in me broke. My screams waked everyone in the hospital. Someone rushed in and tried to pull me away; but I clutched the little body and held it with all my might.

Pulling her away from the body, attendants dragged her back to the ward.

But I kicked and scratched and bit them until they dropped me upon the floor, and left me there, a heap of pain beyond words. After a while the first paroxysm subsided, and I lay quite still. One of the women—a poor cripple—hobbled to me, and bent down as far as she could to lift me up; but the effort hurt her so that she groaned. I got up and helped her back to her bed. She made me sit beside her, and she petted me and spoke tender words of comfort to me. Then I knew the relief of passionate tears.[17]

The next morning she once again went to the dead house. Once she had dressed, washed her hands and face, and promised to "behave," the attendant let her in. The description Macy gave as an older adult is of an angelic dead child: "The light from the half-window fell upon the bed, and Jimmie's little white face, framed in dark curls, seemed to lift from the pillow." She "kissed and kissed and kissed his face—the dearest thing in the world—the only thing I had ever loved." Ordered by a staff member to leave, she did, recording years later her hatred of the one who ordered her to do so. Alone, she "wished to die with an intensity that I have never wished for anything else."[18]

Macy's memories contrasted her hatred for this staff member with the kindness of others. The "poor cripple" woman tried to soothe her. One matron invited her onto the hospitals grounds to pick lilacs and allowed her to pick "an armful" that she then placed on her brother's body. The men carrying the casket did so "very gently." The intervention of a doctor allowed her to accompany the body to the burying ground outside the hospital gate. As she collapsed "in a heap on the sand, and lay there with my face in the weeds" alongside Jimmie's grave, another man brought her geraniums to place on the grave.[19]

When she returned to the ward Jimmie's bed had been restored to its place, awaiting another individual. As she wrote years later, "I sat down between my bed and his empty bed, and I longed desperately to die. I believe very few children have ever been so completely left alone as I was."[20]

As Nella Braddy Henney wrote, "Annie never went into the dead house again."[21]

Despite her intense feelings of loneliness, Annie entered into a community of almshouse women who, in their own ways, cared for her while she was at Tewksbury. Many of them told stories of immigration and the Irish famine, like her mother, even in her mother's brogue. Years later, when she was in her early sixties, she wrote in great detail of individual women, illustrating their significance in her formation and memories. Their stories, and the stories read to her, became life lessons and the models of womanhood available to the young girl moving into adolescence. They were cautionary tales that warned her about men, sexuality, and reproduction, and presented education and economic independence as the solution to women's problems.

Delia Atwood (O'Connor), for example, she liked "best of all the young women." Delia's childhood was spent in England, where her Irish immigrant family dwelt in crowded poverty: "the almshouse was a palace compared to where she had lived." Numerous and frequent childbirths, constant labor, poverty, and a violent husband meant a wretched life for Delia's mother: "Delia's mother seldom spoke. Delia said she couldn't remember her mother's voice; but her face haunted her always. It was so white and thin and troubled!" A sister worked in a laundry and "made some money on the side from men." She earned Delia's admiration, for economic independence and for not letting "any one boss her about." Delia told young Annie that prostitution "'wasn't much different from the way other women got their living,' by marrying men—and she thought the wives got the worst of it." Knowledge "about how babies come" was routine to Delia, and Annie's later words indicate that she may have passed some of that knowledge to her young friend: "She said she had seen her father and mother and other men and women in the most intimate embrace, and had thought nothing of it." After her mother's death and more violence from her father, Delia found a man to finance her trip to America. Soon left pregnant and alone, she ended up at Tewksbury.[22]

At Tewksbury, Delia provided support to Annie: "We were both hungry for affection. The absence of love in our childhood drew us together." Annie cared for Delia's child while Delia labored in the alms-house laundry. The lessons about having children were complex. Delia told Annie she loved the child, but "she told me she regretted bringing it into the world to suffer as she had suffered." After Delia was removed from the almshouse to a workhouse, Annie "grieved bitterly, and was lonelier than ever." Delia soon wrote her of the baby's death and prom-ised to visit. Annie's lack of education, her limited eyesight, isolation, and the destitution of the almshouse conspired to end the relationship: "I did not answer her letter because I could not write myself, and I was too sensitive to get another person to write for me. I never heard from Delia again."[23]

In her fictionalized story of Dookesbury as well as her unpublished memoir, another favorite of Annie's emerged as an angelic and mater-nal figure. Maggie Hogan came to Tewksbury as a young adult, hunch-backed after a childhood accident and later orphaned. Just as in the life tales of many others, the death of a father had left Maggie and her mother economically vulnerable. For Johannah, Maggie "moved in the blackness of the almshouse like sunlight." She grew flowers in a shelf near her bed, and prepared a pristine altar when priests visited. She protected the young girl "as far as it was in her power . . . from the evil that surrounded her," and also protected other vulnerable females. Ob-scene language drew fierce rebukes from her, but her voice was sweet and soothing as she reassured young women fearful of giving birth in the almshouse. Maggie frequently sat with women near their time of delivery, all night if needed, and served as godmother at baptisms.[24]

Maggie also taught Annie and others important lessons about themselves. "You can't help being poor," she told them, "but you can help poverty from eating the heart out of you." Their misery was not their fault, but they themselves held responsibility for the state of their spirit.[25]

Annie's memories leave the impression of a child left unsupervised to wander freely through the chaos of the almshouse. The fictional Johannah wandered "from dormitory to dormitory, seeking knowledge and diversion." Constantly listening, Johannah "meditated and learned." There was much to see and listen to. In the almshouse hospital lay a "half-crazy bed ridden woman" who sang lamentations. In the dormitory lived a woman named "Lost." As others explained to Johannah, a "frightful accident" had caused her "to forget even her name."[26]

The dormitory across the hall served as Johannah's favorite place. Always full of twenty-five women in various stages of pregnancy, it "interested Johannah more than anything else in the world." Despite Maggie's instructions to stay out, the stories of these young women fascinated her. "It was often course [coarse] in the extreme, but Johannah did not mind at all. She took them at their own valuation, which meant that they were heroines quite as romantic as some of the heroines in the books."[27]

The tales of the women at Tewksbury, as Annie remembered them, repeat classical themes of respectable but poor women seduced and then ruined by men, and generally left pregnant. Their gender and resulting economic vulnerability left them virtually no options but Tewksbury. Sophia, the "exceedingly beautiful" daughter of an Irish immigrant washerwoman, fell in love with a banker's son. Dying of tuberculosis, she was "waiting for the end" while she served as Johannah's first confidante. Bertha Maitre, an orphan from Quebec, came to Boston with a man who deserted her once she became pregnant. Kicked out of her boardinghouse, she was sent to Tewksbury by the courts. Molly from Cork, Ireland, told a similar story. Sally Stacy warned Annie that "kisses lead to other things [which] are no end of trouble." The daughter of a Presbyterian pastor and Irish immigrant mother, she dared not tell her parents after her brother's best friend rejected her once she became pregnant with his child. She fled to Boston, thought of killing herself, but heard of a refuge for "fallen women." Police sent her to Tewksbury. Born "horribly deformed" and with tuberculosis, her child died soon after birth. "That's my story," she told Johannah. "It's a hard world for poor girls. It isn't true that God is merciful."[28]

Annie recorded both empathy for and impatience with the repeated story of seduction, sex, and desertion. As a child, she seems to have been both tantalizingly confused and bored by these tales with their oft-repeated narrative themes and styles. At some point in the story, the narrator almost always paused. At this point the fictional Johannah knew "the next words would be, 'Then it happened. . . . I could not help myself. . . . I couldn't help giving in.'" Curiosity and forbidden knowledge pulled her in, yet the stories were "vulgar." What really bothered Johannah was the lack of thought and analysis behind so many women's stories. "They were forever explaining," she wrote, "how some male creature had robbed them of their virtue. . . . Their tirades against their suitors seemed hollow."[29] And their biggest complaint was always about the poor food at the institution.

Tewksbury exposed Annie not only to the pregnant women of the "lie-in ward," but also to the infants of the foundling house. One wonders what the young adolescent, who had already seen several siblings die as infants, thought of the scene. As the fictional Johannah described it, it usually held about thirty babies. "Most had sores and boyles [boils] which were not protected from flies and mosquitoes. All of them were pale from not being properly nourished. They were cared for by old women, or rather they were neglected by them." In 1876, the year Annie and Jimmie entered Tewksbury, the institutional physician reported that the "number of motherless and deserted infants sent to us of late has been unusually large." Throughout the decade institutional administrators repeatedly warned the state that they had more foundlings than they could handle, and expressed continual frustration and embarrassment about the nearly 100 percent death rate among the children under one year of age. Undoubtedly residents at Tewksbury, and particularly the pregnant woman, were profoundly aware of this mortality rate.[30]

Macy's memoirs leave evidence that mothers at Tewksbury sought to do all they could to care for their infants. For example, the fictional Johannah's friend Molly from Cork worked in the superintendent's house after delivery. She often brought food to those inmates who cared for her baby during the day. To Johannah, this often meant "cakes, roast chickens, pies, etc. and other delicacies."[31]

Stories, however, seem to have been the most constant currency at Tewksbury. The older women of the dormitory and the younger women of the maternity ward competed for Johannah's stories. With her "excellent memory and a pleasant voice," she bartered stories for companionship, community, and purpose. When she failed to complete her end of the bargain, the other women "would grieve, they would weep, and beg her please to finish the story."[32]

Many of the stories read among the women at Tewksbury were from the weekly Irish American newspaper the *Pilot*. Weekly, inmates read aloud each and every page. Irish dissident Charles Stewart Parnell was a hero, as was abolitionist Wendell Phillips. As an adult Macy credited the newspaper's reportage and "the eloquence of great dissidents such as Phillips and Parnell" with protecting her "as by holy flame from the insidious poison of my environment."[33] Annie and the women at Tewksbury undoubtedly followed the *Pilot*'s reports on Parnell's 1879 visit to Boston. There he was received as a king, welcomed by Boston's mayor as well as Annie's hero Wendell Phillips.

Annie also collected many of her stories from the news and literature of the time period, although her limited eyesight and lack of education meant she couldn't read and needed to have someone read to her. In the lightly fictionalized story of Dookesbury, this is where Tilly Delaney stepped in—a "mildly crazy girl subject to epileptic fits" who also held hopes of escaping from the almshouse. Maternal Maggie Hogan made a deal with Tilly—if Tilly read to Johannah, Maggie would help Tilly escape. The educated and adult Maggie chose the books. Even listening became an adventure. Sometimes Tilly skipped paragraphs or larger sections. Tilly's seizures and the sleep that followed frequently interrupted the reading, and Johannah had to be patient. If a fictional event suggested new means of attempting escape, Johannah had to help Tilly plan the effort before they could go on.[34]

Annie lived at Tewksbury between the ages of ten and fourteen, an age at which respectable girls of her era were supposed to know little about seduction, sex, and desertion. She, however, clearly knew something. In her personal notes on Tewksbury she conceded her knowledge of sex at a young age, but insisted that it did not besmirch her. Everything she knew, she insisted, came through "talk" but not experience. "From my earliest days I listened to talk upon every subject by persons whose experience had been such that they blasphemed against every respectability—talk which reached the climax in disgusting sex revelations." She heard about "the bawdy house," about seduction, about brothels and police corruption. The "glimpses of promiscuity" she gained from those conversations "sickened one,—trysting in dark courtyards, love-making in closets, drunkenness, amours of people that frequented sinister alleys like cats, and children begotten and abandoned on door-steps, or otherwise disposed of. There was nothing I did not hear broadly discussed in gutter-language."[35]

As an adult Macy always maintained in her memoirs and fictional accounts, perhaps in self-defense, that the knowledge of sex she gained as a child did not corrupt her. She insisted that "there are nascent in the child mind countless pure immunities that prevent it from being harmed." Much of what she remembered of the almshouse was "indecent, cruel, melancholy, gruesome in the light of grown-up experience; but nothing corresponding with my present understanding of these ideas entered into my child mind."[36]

Though it is likely that Macy's adult understanding of sex and sexuality did not correspond with the confused impressions of childhood, her insistence that "immunities" protected her child mind from "harm" is barely credible—particularly given contemporary insights into psychology and trauma. Perhaps at Tewksbury she saw men and women engaged in sexual behaviors, coerced or willing. Contemporary statistics reveal that institutionalized women and girls experience far more sexual assault and harassment than the already high rates females experience outside of institutions.

That Annie left Tewksbury with direct knowledge or experience of sexual contact is not impossible. Indeed, it is sadly probable that the young adolescent experienced sexual assault.

The fictional Johannah, for example, feared the kitchen boss, who gave the women extra food "if they allowed him to handle them." She "shivered like a dog about to be whipped" when near him, but still felt capable of vengeance. One day Sadie Sullivan, "one of the boldest of the pregnant women," rebuked him. He attacked Sadie and "Johannah jumped on the table and tumbled the bucket of hot tea all over him." With a harsh blow he swept Johannah off the table. In less than a week both Sadie and her baby had died.[37] Women resisted men and their harassment, but the cost was high.

In another part of Macy's fictionalized memoir a young Jimmy Burns initially charmed the adolescent girl, but also represented danger. Maggie warned Johannah away from him, but "it was sweet to hear his pleasant masculine voice speaking to her." The young man, "one of the insane who was trusted to run errands for the asylum," called her Jennie, spoke sweet words, and caressed her cheek. Breaking her vow to Maggie not to see him again, she met him once more: "Alas Johannah did and said the foolish things that other girls did and said in similar situations." When she attempted to leave, "there arose cunning of madness in his voice. He caught her around the waist with one arm and forcibly pressed her head against his shoulder." He insisted she'd never get away this time, that he knew she (Jennie) had always loved him. When he "saw the fright in Johannah's face," he drew a long knife. Macy refused to allow her fictional self to be sullied: a mysterious man knocked Jimmy down from behind, telling Johannah to run. Of Johannah, Macy wrote, "Somehow Johannah got the idea that men are terrible beasts. And did something awful to girls who loved and trusted them."[38] Johannah, and likely Annie, knew of both the appeal and the danger of men.

Nowhere else in her fictionalized story of Johannah does Macy mention Johannah's future, but in this section she does. Johannah, she wrote, "tried to think out some terrible vengeance upon men. That idea continued until she was married herself. Then she learned that there are compensations which she had never expected, and there was never any reason for things to be half as bad as she thought, but the scar remained on her soul." Macy wrote this while in her early sixties, thinking back perhaps on her own tumultuous marriage and the previous two decades, during which she'd rarely spoken to the man she had refused to divorce. She'd learned that sex could be pleasurable and that relationships with men could be enjoyable, but, as she went on, "the scar remained on her soul." However confusing the messages Annie received at Tewksbury about sex and relationships with men, they taught her that women—and she specifically—should be incredibly wary of men.[39]

As an adult, Macy wrote several unpublished versions of a Tewksbury event she called "the procession of the horribles." In this narrative of life at the almshouse, the women of her community appear as watchers. As the whistle blew three times a day to call men to meals, the women would "rush to the windows crying 'The Horribles! The Horribles!'"

> It was indeed a sight to rouse interest and horror. On it flowed like a noisome river—this procession of the disinherited—deformed in every degree of ugliness, bent almost double, limping on one leg, a trunk without legs wriggling along on its arms, one with his neck twisted so that he seemed to be going backwards, occasionally a young man carrying on his arm a shard that had once been young like himself, white faces, yellow faces, black faces, bearded faces, faces distorted by cancer or goiters, their throats sagging with the weight of the growth, faces with inflamed, swollen eyelids—on they came hurrying, doggedly determined to get to their feed, like animals, the blind bumping into the fence and each other, the epileptics dropping down in their tracks—and pushed aside by the oncoming mob—hundreds of them, and in winter-time more than a thousand!

Accompanying the parade was a "strange, irregular sound, broken by the taps of canes, crutches and other contrivances for support and locomotion." The women would "laugh boisterously when a cane descended upon some one's head, or a crutch dug into a fellow's back."[40]

Then came the running commentary as the women assessed each man: "'Do you see him with the twitching mouth?' 'Do you see him—the fellow with the bulging eyes?—they look as if they were on the ends of sticks!' 'There's a dummy! That's the way they talk with their arms—signs for words. You've got to be one of them to understand.' 'That little fellow with the hump is new.'"[41]

As Macy remembered it, men constituted the "procession of the horribles." One assumes that the men watched the women in a similar

fashion. Yet, in Macy's description, the disabled, the monstrous, the in-
human, the disturbingly contorted bodies were male. She remembered
the community of women—who presumably embodied the same vari-
ety of humanity—as watchers, removed from the horribles, and thus
not part of the monstrosities of Tewksbury.

Macy's unease and sometimes disgust toward people with disabilities in her description of the "procession of the horribles" is disturbing. Her face presumably mirrored those of the men she described as
having "faces with inflamed, swollen eyelids . . . like animals, the blind
bumping into the fence and each other." She does not seem to have
drawn connections between her own disability and those of other
Tewksbury residents; nor does she seem to have drawn connections
between the needs of Tewksbury residents and the educational and
employment needs of blind people, for which she advocated through
much of her adult life. Her reflections on Tewksbury moved back and
forth between blaming poverty for the erosion of the human body
and spirit, and blaming each individual for his or her circumstances.

Annie's own blindness, as well as her age, profoundly shaped her
life at Tewksbury. Her variable eyesight and the physical pain of trachoma meant that she encountered doctors, religious figures, and institutional administrators frequently, and it presumably made her
more vulnerable amidst the almshouse population. The year before
she entered Tewksbury, a doctor from nearby Lowell had volunteered
to spend one day a week at the institution performing eye and ear
surgeries. Institutional officials described Moses G. Parker, M.D., as
"a promising and enterprising young man, who has spent more than
a year in the medical schools in London, Paris and Germany in per-
fecting himself in the science of surgery, especially of the eye and ear."
Parker performed the surgeries for free. One wonders if he needed the
practice; though Tewksbury reports indicate "his operations have been
performed with neatness, skill and dispatch." Between October 1, 1874,
and September 30, 1875, he performed fifty-eight eye operations on
Tewksbury residents aged two through eighty-seven. The year Annie
entered the institution he continued his work. In her 1934 biography
of Macy, Henney reports that the young Annie had two eye surgeries
while at Tewksbury. Presumably Moses Parker operated.[42]

Presumably, however, Parker's surgeries were unsuccessful. At the instigation of a Jesuit priest named Father Barbara, Annie left Tewksbury on February 13, 1877, almost exactly a year after she arrived and nine months after Jimmie's death. At the hospital of the Sisters of Charity (Soeurs de la Charité) in Lowell, a Dr. Savory operated. After her recovery Father Barbara took her to Boston, where she served briefly as a domestic servant at the home of a family named Brown. Having scarcely arrived there, she was taken on July 16, by whom is not clear, to the city infirmary, where doctors performed two more surgeries. Afterward, with her eyesight apparently unchanged, she had nowhere to go. Father Barbara had left the city and the Browns did not want her. The only ones willing to claim the now eleven-year-old were once again the Commonwealth of Massachusetts and Tewksbury Almshouse.[43]

The materials that remain from Macy's life do not mention this brief respite from Tewksbury. The only information available is what Henney compiled for her biography. Henney presents Father Barbara, the nuns of Lowell, and the city infirmary staff (Dr. Wadsworth, Dr. Williams, and head nurse Miss Rosa) as kind, compassionate individuals who treated the girl child respectfully. The Sisters of Charity were particularly "lovely," and Henney describes Anne's life there in great detail.[44] Perhaps this brief respite made the return to Tewksbury even more painful; perhaps the trauma of Tewksbury was simply too overwhelming. Whatever the case, Macy made little if any reference to this approximately six-month departure from Tewksbury.

While Annie appreciated Father Barbara and the Sisters of Charity, her intellectual and emotional wrestling with the teachings of religion followed her from Tewksbury to the Perkins Institution and beyond. Her parents, Thomas and Alice, had brought her to the Catholic cathedral for baptism, as they had all her siblings, but that was not enough for an easy relationship with religion. As an adult Macy wrote about the fictional Johannah, "I am afraid she was a pagan in her cradle. All the gods they had brought to her had clay feet, and they never impressed her impatient spirit." The fictional Johannah refused to go to confession even before she was nine, approximately the same age Annie was when her mother, Alice, died. For Johannah, the refusal to believe was "a shield against suffering"—for to acknowledge the good-ness of God would have meant also acknowledging that the evils of poverty and the almshouse existed nonetheless. Jimmie's death left her "emotionally dead," fearing "neither God nor man." She wasn't sure she wanted to believe in a God who knew all things and was all powerful, but did not "destroy the wicked."[45]

Macy recorded frustration and anger at the evangelists who visited Tewksbury during her stay. When they visited the women's ward, the women apparently ridiculed them, shouting curse words and sexual innuendos. Macy recorded her childlike excitement that the women "were rude to the 'nice people,'" though she liked the singing and en-tertainment the visitors provided. Although she may have experienced them as benign at Tewksbury, as she grew older her analysis of evange-listic do-gooders grew sharper. To her, they epitomized hypocrisy. She once told a teacher at Perkins that "the Beatitudes . . . are sweet," but that they "sounded like the purring of a cat" when read by evangelists at Tewksbury: "That is what good people with plenty of money sound like. . . . They are drowsy like cats, they purr and purr and purr! But if you try to take a part of the sunny door-sill from them, their soft paws unfold, and you get a scratch on your nose that you won't forget."[46]

Ironically, however, Annie ended up owing her education and final departure from Tewksbury to the wealthy do-gooders with the hidden claws. At Feeding Hills she had wanted, but been denied, an educa-tion. The fictional Johannah shared her yearning for an education with her confidante Sophia Starkey as she died of tuberculosis. Johannah learned about an unnamed school for blind students in South Boston, presumably Perkins, from another blind inmate. At that point, "she knew sometime she would leave the almshouse and go to school." For Johannah, however, the reality was that "there was not one man or woman in authority there who cared enough for Johannah to try to get her sent to school."[47]

The do-gooder in whom Annie placed her hopes was Franklin B. Sanborn, in 1881 the inspector for the Massachusetts State Board of Charities, the bureaucracy that oversaw all state almshouses, asylums, and hospitals. Sanborn had been involved with the State Board of Charities since its creation in 1863, serving also as secretary and chair.

How much Annie knew about Sanborn is unclear, but he knew many of the pivotal figures of U.S. culture and politics in the nineteenth century. He was active in the transcendentalist circles of Concord, Massachusetts, that included Ralph Waldo Emerson, Henry David Thoreau, and Louisa May Alcott. Years earlier he had become a controversial national figure as one of the Secret Six conspirators who had supported antislavery agitator John Brown.

For the young Annie Sullivan trying to get out of Tewksbury, Sanborn's importance lay in his position as General State Inspector of Charities. Like other dignitaries, as Annie explained it later, "at regular intervals affable officials from the State-house made their appearance. Most of the men had impressive beards. The women wore trains which they held up with their right hands."[48] Her only hope lay in reaching Sanborn during one of his tours of the institution and convincing him to take her away from Tewksbury.

Sanborn's life was intricately entwined with that of Samuel Gridley Howe, who, as the founder of the Perkins Institution and Massachusetts Asylum for the Blind, would posthumously play a pivotal role in Annie's future life. Howe and Sanborn both supported John Brown as members of the Secret Six, and both emerged relatively unscathed by the association, compared with the other four. Howe also sat on the State Board of Charities, and the men shared similar philosophies about education, the role of the government, and the state's responsibilities for the poor. Amidst rumors of atrocities and inappropriate spending, Howe had recommended an investigation of Tewksbury Almshouse before he died in January of 1876. Sanborn carried out that investigation.

The story of young Annie's successful contact with Sanborn was related not by Macy herself as an adult, but only by Henney. In Henney's version this is a dramatic story: Sanborn arrived, and when the news reached Annie, she pursued his group from ward to ward, following the noise of their conversation and footsteps. At the very last possible moment, not knowing which blurry body was his, she hurled herself forward into the group of well-dressed men and women. "Mr. Sanborn, Mr. Sanborn, I want to go to school!"[49]

Whether the event was this dramatic or not, we'll never know. In this version, the now fourteen-year-old bore sole responsibility for her salvation from Tewksbury. However it happened, the meeting required initiative and action from Annie. In an institution in which most children died, in which poverty and hopelessness overwhelmed many, and in which traumas were piled one on top of another, the fourteen-year-old with limited vision demanded that the well-dressed leading philanthropists of Massachusetts live out their philanthropic ideals.

Sanborn, to his credit, did so. He arranged for Annie to attend the Perkins Institution, the nation's premier educational facility for blind children. Perkins and its founder, Samuel Gridley Howe, were already world famous as educators of deaf-blind Laura Bridgman. The state of Massachusetts would pay Annie Sullivan's tuition.

Annie left Tewksbury on October 7, 1880. According to Henney, a Tewksbury staff member found her two calico dresses—one red and one blue. It was virtually all she carried on the train to South Boston, where she would begin school. All of the women of the ward, young and old, came to wish her farewell. Her friend "Maggie Hogan, the hunchback" carried her small bundle to the carriage. Others were "crippled, two or three were blind, and quite a number were young women about to become mothers."[50]

The residents wished her farewell with lots of advice: "Be a good girl"; "mind your teachers"; "don't tell anyone you came from the poorhouse"; "keep your head up, you're as good as any of 'em." One young woman, perhaps one of the pregnant ones, warned her to not "let any feller fool you about getting married. . . . He won't mean what he says." Another asked her to send tobacco; yet another to write when she learned how. Maggie Hogan squeezed her hand. At the train station she received her final advice from the carriage driver, Tim: "'Don't ever come back to this place,' he said, shoving me into my train seat. 'Do you hear? Forget this, and you'll be all right.'"[51]

The difficulty, of course, was that no human being could forget the Tewksbury Almshouse. The almshouse forged indelible marks on the mind, body, and future relationships of the young girl who spent the formative years between the ages of ten and fourteen there. As an adult, Macy repeatedly tried to make sense of her life at Tewksbury. She tried to draw meaning, tried to salvage a self that wasn't irreparably damaged. This past brought her much shame. When she briefly told her life story in public speeches she always skipped over the almshouse, going directly from her mother's death to Perkins. She would not tell her dear and nearly lifelong friend Helen Keller about life at Tewksbury until the 1920s.[52]

In the scant materials Macy left about her life at Tewksbury, all most likely written when she was in her early sixties, she tended to insist to herself and her dear friends that the almshouse had little lasting effect on her. At one point she wrote, "I often wonder how I escaped contamination in that slum. . . . For some reason sordid things did not stick to me. All the hateful beasts of poverty herded together in that jungle of 'Christian charity' did not harm me, except that they left in my mind a gallery of painful portraits." At another point she insisted that because she was a child of curiosity and a receptive mind, she simply observed, and the trauma easily slid off: "Everything interested me. I was not shocked, grieved, pained or troubled by what happened. Such things happened. People behaved like that—that was all there was about it—that was all the life I knew." The fictional Johannah, she speculated, "must have been a superior nature to be able of her own initiative to get out of a place" such as Tewksbury: "Only a Job like spirit could have resisted condemnation from that horde of outcasts and the sinners in that filthy lodging house."[53]

Indirectly, however, Macy acknowledged that Tewksbury shaped her life and psyche. Referring to the teaching of children, she wrote that "a child brought up in extraordinary circumstances, surrounded by old people, by misery and shameful aspects of existence builds up his own image of a world, often a harsh one." The fictional Johannah developed a harsh view of the world as a "dark drama." The life knowledge she attained "in that strange school was not joyful. It was concerned with a long tragedy of human injustice, failure and misery." As an adult Macy rarely saw life in optimistic and pleasurable terms, but instead defined herself as "but a small incidental figure in a great canvas of human misery"[54]—a worldview that would later frustrate, and sometimes annoy, Helen Keller, with her belief in the great goodness of humanity.

Yet the fictional Johannah, if not the real Annie Sullivan, was still a young girl who clung to, but hid, hopes for a fairytale ending. The fictional child "knew the story of Cinderella, and she never doubted that there was a fairy God-mother somewhere in the wide world who would some day turn her desolation into a kingdom of delight. . . . She had kept her heart proud, and carried her head high in many humiliating situations because of this dream kingdom."[55] Because she found a means of escape—even if random events conspired to make it succeed—life set her apart from others at Tewksbury.

CHAPTER 3

Perkins, 1880–1886: Part One

THE TRAIN FROM Tewksbury to South Boston, from the alms-house to Perkins, may as well have been a train to another universe.

Though the teenage Annie Sullivan frequently chafed at the strictures of the Perkins Institution, the South Boston school and its staff provided her with one of the best educations available to blind students at that time. It provided consistent food, warmth, and security for the child previously denied them, and it provided a space for the fierce, wounded, and stubborn adolescent to safely grow from fourteen to twenty. At times she resented Perkins and all it stood for; at other times she loved it. Regardless of what she felt about the school, however, she was a child alone in the world, and it became her home from her admission on October 7, 1880, until her graduation in June 1886. Even after graduation, for several years she and Helen would move into and out of the Perkins campus, in and out of the sphere of influence of its director, Michael Anagnos. Her name, like that of Helen Keller, remains tied to that of Perkins even today.

Perkins shone as one of Boston's premier educational institutions—the most well-known school for blind students in the United States, and perhaps the world. For almost fifty years its larger-than-life director, Samuel Gridley Howe, had dominated the institution and its reputation. Through perseverance, masterful publicity, and the education of the deaf-blind Laura Bridgman, he had built a venerable institution before he died in 1876. By 1880, when Annie arrived at Perkins, the institution had formally marked its successful transition from the leadership of Howe to that of his son-in-law, Michael Anagnos.

In later years Anne Sullivan Macy and her pupil Helen Keller would make Perkins even more famous.

Howe's successor Anagnos organized Perkins around the belief that the intellectual and social deprivations of blind people were caused by isolation and segregation. If blind people lived lives similar to those who were sighted, if they didn't live and learn only among themselves, then they had the potential of moving fully into society. In 1877 Anagnos changed the second part of Perkins's name from "Massachusetts Asylum for the Blind" to "Massachusetts School for the Blind" to reflect this philosophy. He explained that asylums provided "permanent maintenance of blind persons," and "render[ed] the lives of their inmates aimless and well nigh useless, because they are removed from the necessity of doing something for themselves." Asylums caused blind people to "associate very closely with each other," resulting in a "clannish spirit, and a tendency to morbidness." All in all, "such places are, in short, museums of drones rather than hives of diligent workers, and crush the spirit while they seem to aid the body." Never would asylums result in economically self-sufficient adults.[1]

Anagnos insisted that Perkins, regardless of name, had always been "so conducted as to prevent it from degenerating into an asylum or refuge." "Enlightened experience and true philanthropy" demanded that Perkins live out its only "legitimate" business—which was to educate students and send them out of the institution to make their own way in the world economically, morally, and socially. The "cottage system," in which small groups of students lived in homelike cottages with a "housekeeper" (whose tasks were primarily maternal and disciplinary), formed a base from which to avoid the dangers of asylum living. Through the study of literature, music, and manual skills, and through physical development, "sightless children" could receive the "same kind and degree of instruction as can be had in the best common schools for those who see."[2]

Achieving economic self-sufficiency, however, was never as easy for educated blind adults as Howe and Anagnos made it out to be. Employers did not want them. Throughout the 1870s and 1880s Anagnos received nearly continual letters from graduates, particularly women, who'd been unable to earn a living. When the twenty-year-old Annie Sullivan graduated in 1886, she would face the same problem.

During Sullivan's years at Perkins the educational theorists Johann Pestalozzi and Friedrich Froebel shaped the school's curriculum and pedagogy, as they did that of schools across the United States. These European romanticists emphasized the innate intelligence of children and their play; the importance of the simultaneous development of mind, body, and morals; and the maternal suitability of female teachers. Though Samuel Gridley Howe did not write of them directly, his faith in human perfectibility and in children's natural intelligence grew from the same intellectual framework.

Anagnos twice identified 1880, the year Sullivan began at Perkins, as the beginning of Perkins's efforts to integrate Pestalozzian and Froebelian ideas into the school's curriculum. The institution, he wrote, sought to adopt the "many-sidedness and wisdom" [of their theories] ... physical, intellectual and moral" with "careful adaptation to each individual bent, capacity, and temperament; as well as to the whole idea of perfect womanhood and manhood." Physical training mattered; play and pedagogical flexibility suited student needs; and even blind children could develop into vital citizens. In order to accomplish all that, he reassured institutional supporters that Perkins teachers rejected "mechanical teaching" and "the evil tendency of obliging pupils to commit to memory the words of the textbook [that] has been constantly disapproved and persistently avoided." In fact, he wrote, "all available measures have been taken to increase the vital sap and suppleness of fresh life in the school, and to prevent it from running the risk of becoming petrified."[3]

Throughout the 1880s, Anagnos attempted to implement Froebel's educational theories by raising funds to establish a permanent kindergarten at Perkins. Anagnos insisted, "There is no scheme of training so admirably adapted to the condition, wants, and peculiar requirements of sightless infants as that of Froebel." As he appealed for money he dramatically pledged that kindergarten would "be to little sightless children what the light of the sun and the dew of heaven are to tender plants." By helping him implement Froebel's kindergarten system, donors could help him continue the "marvelous results" that rescued "many of the younger pupils from the very depths of sluggishness and feeble-mindedness."[4] Though the kindergarten wouldn't open until the year of Annie's graduation, Froebel's emphasis on play and student manipulation of physical forms (for example, cubes, squares, and models of animals) increasingly permeated the Perkins curriculum.

Perkins admitted students of "good moral character," ages ten to nineteen, for the substantial fee of three hundred dollars per year. "Indigent blind persons" could seek admission by writing to the Massachusetts governor. The lengthy admissions questionnaire included more questions about potential students' parents and extended family than about the students themselves, reflecting the belief that moral and physical health went hand in hand and that moral and physical well-being were inherited from one's parents. Were the parents subject to "fits" or "scrofula"? Were their senses "perfect"? Were they "temperate"? Were they related by blood? In which country were they born? Were there "known peculiarities" in the extended family?[5] On most counts, Sullivan would have failed these eugenics-based admissions criteria. Her father drank. Her mother died of tuberculosis. Both were poor Irish immigrants. Her brother walked with a marked limp because of a hip problem.

Annie Sullivan was a charity case. Perkins admitted her in October of 1880 only because of Franklin Sanborn, working through the bureaucracy of the State Board of Health, Lunacy, and Charity. Soon afterward Massachusetts reimbursed Perkins for the "necessary clothing" it provided the indigent girl, and later the almshouse contributed $21.09. At least three individuals wrote Anagnos regarding other blind indigent students during the fall Perkins admitted Sullivan. A doctor from Vermont pled the case of a "bright young girl" of Irish heritage, poor but "worthy of an education." A minister from Maine asked Anagnos to take a six-year-old boy, orphaned, "in singular solitude and destitution." The city of Taunton, Massachusetts, asked Anagnos to admit a "very poor" eleven-year-old boy.[6] No remaining correspondence indicates that Anagnos accepted these children.

As an adult reflecting back on her life at Perkins, Macy wrote that she was "like a round peg in a square hole. . . . I was large for my age, and utterly unacquainted with the usages of civilized society. In some ways I was as mature as a woman, in others as undeveloped as a young child." Other Perkins students had their tuition supported by the state, but none had her background. None of the others had fought for their education as she had. And as Macy acknowledged, "The years at Tewksbury had opened mental windows and doors, pushed back concealing curtains, revealed dark depths in the lives of human beings which would have remained closed to a more happily circumstanced child."[7] Tewksbury made her markedly different.

When Annie arrived at Perkins she'd never been in school before. Originally school administrators placed her with the other beginning students, all much younger than her. As she remembered it, because of her size and age the teachers ridiculed her when she made mistakes. When she misspelled simple words, "the class laughed uproariously." According to her chronicle of life at Perkins, the first class she attended was a sewing class. She had never before held a needle—the quintessential signifier of successful femininity. Nor did she know how old she was—or she just wouldn't admit it. And to her teacher's question regarding where she came from, she evaded and replied, "I don't know." Given an instruction, she remembered her response as "I will if I want to, and I won't if I don't."[8] Belligerence became her most frequent mode of relating to teachers.

Quickly, because of her size and age, she was moved to classrooms with older students, whether or not she had done the required work. The perceived insults spurred her on but also "remain[ed] scars in my memory which time has not effaced." Intellectually, she advanced rapidly. Looking backward, Macy credited her intelligence to the "deep, dark soil" of what she called her "Tewksbury experiences." In such soil ideas grew rapidly, "sending out wild shoots that spread and overshadowed the puny thoughts of my school-mates which were more delicately nourished."[9]

She rarely felt at home with other students, particularly in her early years at Perkins. At the base of it she was simply a solitary person, but she also felt profoundly uneasy. Reading served as the best escape. As an adult Macy considered reading "better than the conversation of people." Blindness, however, complicated her wish to find company in books. She failed to develop good Braille skills and never referred to using the raised letter format. Thus she could read on her own only when her eyesight allowed it. "Had I been able to read with my fingers with comfort," she once wrote, "I should perhaps have escaped some of this mental harassment."[10]

Annie characterized herself as "ill at ease with everyone." She lashed out frequently at fellow students. As an adult she blamed herself, reasoning that "if they were not helpful to me, it was because I effectively resisted their good-will." She considered herself "a difficult friend, changeable, disquieting, and unsocial." It surprised her that some of her classmates liked her. Perhaps she erred in her self-characterization. During her frequent bouts with teachers or with Anagnos, other students "almost invariably ... approved my outspoken defiance of rules when I thought them unfair or oppressive."[11]

Anne's relationships with other students and teachers were uneasy and uneven. She resented them fiercely, for they had all that she lacked: "I told myself that I hated them because they were fools, oceans inferior to me intellectually, yet way back in my head I knew they possessed refinement, poise, pleasant speech, graceful limbs—things I would have sold my soul to Satan for."[12] In self-defense she considered them intellectually inferior, petty, and worthy only of disdain, but then resented them if they did not befriend her in the ways she desired.

As an adult, she explained that "after a year of self-assertion, pretence, rebellion and secret mortification, I fled into the tower of my own soul and raised the drawbridge." Her solitude and scorn for others kept them away. In her analysis, "It was many years before I emerged from my self-imposed purdah." Others from her adult life, particularly her future husband, John Macy, would accuse her of never emerging from her "self-imposed purdah."[13] While a student at Perkins, she must have been a difficult person to befriend.

Teachers, more than other students, successfully befriended the young adolescent. Yet, even this was limited. As Macy wrote later, "I did not like my teachers—there were two exceptions—and they did not like me." The two exceptions were Mary C. Moore and Cora A. Newton. They "seemed to understand the battle that was going on within me. They did their best to smooth out difficulties, and open my mind to gentler influences."[14] To the future teacher of Helen Keller, the two illustrated the ability of teachers to transform and make a young adult.

The teacher that emerges most vividly from Macy's memoirs is Mary C. Moore. Miss Moore's apparent understanding of her—"There was little in my mind, I think, which she did not comprehend fully"—was both tantalizingly attractive and off-putting to the struggling adolescent: "Sometimes I had an uncomfortable feeling that she was getting me under her thumb, which made me uneasy and suspicious. The mind was willing and docile, but the spirit carried a chip on its shoulder. I now wonder at her good-will towards me. It might easily have collapsed before a student so retractable as I was." Yet, Macy believed Miss Moore to have "exerted a salutary influence." Perhaps it was true, as the adolescent imagined, that this favorite teacher "did not think I was quite such a dyed-in-the-wool black sheep as others did."[15]

Moore opened up the world of Shakespeare to the adolescent. The one hour a week with Miss Moore and Shakespeare "were Paradise to me," Macy later recalled. She described those hours as "containing all that was stimulating and fine" in her education. They read *The Tempest*, *King Lear*, *As You Like It*, and *Macbeth*. Shakespeare and Miss Moore provided Annie with her first intellectual thrills, with a sense of beauty, of the power of words, of magic, and of the larger world as a place of potential. She wrote, "The impression the plays made upon me was profound. I literally lived them. . . . It was as if my perceptions had gained intensity in the starved, stunted years of my childhood." Though Shakespeare "lit up" her imagination "like a sun," his presentations of life's dilemmas forced self-examination, and Annie didn't always like what she found. "I began to reflect on the real nature of my attitude toward life. A realization of my inadequacy rushed upon me. I was aghast at my own ignorance and dense vanity. Without the elements of education or knowledge of the world outside my little experience I had set myself up as the spokesman of the larger part of humanity."[16]

Moore was a caring and creative teacher. In 1881 the students of her "advanced class in the girls' department," which likely included Annie, initiated a festival celebrating the birth of the New England poet John Greenleaf Whittier (whose works were published in Braille by the Howe Memorial Press). The resulting "charming and much enjoyed evening" included poetry readings and music. Moore had written to Whittier of her students' delight in his work, and she read aloud his letter of response as the highlight of the evening. Sullivan, who called poetry "the noblest and most spiritualizing influence I have known," must have been thrilled by her 1881 evening of Whittier.[17]

While Annie valued several of her teachers, as an adult she remembered her overall experience with teachers at Perkins unfavorably. The world-famous teacher struggled with the "optimism" of her teachers and believed such optimism a problem of female teachers in general. Always she felt different from others, shaped by experiences incomprehensible to any of them. The "kind of optimism" they "constantly" exhorted her to adopt included statements like "If you haven't as many blessings as you think you should have, you should be thankful that you have any" and "If your stomach aches, thank God that you have a stomach to ache in." These, and particularly the dictum "all is well with the world," infuriated her.[18] She felt her teachers naive, limited, and of narrow imagination.

Teacher Cora Newton remembered Annie with mixed feelings, and perceptibly less enthusiasm than Annie had for her. To this teacher, she was "a wholesome, vigorously active, impulsive, self-assertive, generally happy girl, inclined to be impatient and combative toward criticisms or any opinion not in agreement with her own." Newton also remembered Annie's "executive ability and initiative" and fondness for "pretty clothes," as well as her deep interest in literature, composition, and history.[19]

Reading was taken seriously at Perkins. Newton sometimes directed the evening "reading periods," introducing her students to Charles Dickens, Sir Walter Scott, Jane Austen, and George Eliot. Each year the Howe Memorial Press expanded its Braille offerings in literature, history, science, poetry, and theology. As Anagnos explained it to the general public, such works aided students in acquiring "those great truths which relate to the happiness of the human race and the general welfare of mankind." Teachers facilitated the process by avoiding glib

Anne Sullivan, circa 1881. Courtesy of the American Foundation for the Blind, Helen Keller Archives.

memorization requirements and "typical oppressiveness," and instead giving instruction "in a simple and natural way." This way, Anagnos insisted, "the fog of dullness has been shut out from the atmosphere of the school-room by the charm of novelty and the warmth of ever fresh and unfailing interest."[20]

Whether all the students felt that "the fog of dullness" had been removed from the classroom is doubtful; Annie certainly did not. She particularly disliked geometry: "It bored me stiff." At one point, with a blind teacher and blind fellow students, she smuggled books into the classroom and surreptitiously read during class. (This is one example of how her eyesight fluctuated throughout her time at Perkins, likely due to her periodic surgeries. At other points she recorded not being able to read printed materials.) She fought with the teacher; impudently and audaciously retorting that her brain only awoke when she left the room, and that geometry had not helped to train her teacher's mind.[21]

Sullivan also disliked physical training. The American followers of educational theorist Pestalozzi, as well as feminists and progressive social reformers, argued that physical, moral, and intellectual fitness went hand in hand, and thus advocated physical exercise. As Anagnos explained it, physical training put into practice the "doctrine of inter-dependence of body and mind." Physical exercise built "a strong pedestal upon which the statue of their education and professional training [was] to be raised." Physical training particularly mattered at Perkins, Anagnos argued, because blind students were more likely to contend with "consequent inferiority in physical health and stamina." These "physical blemishes and peculiarities" had "corresponding intellectual imperfections." In order to fight those blemishes and imperfections, in 1877 the school built a new "gallery" for girls, where even in bad weather they could "carry on all sorts of exercises, accompanied by any amount of fun and frolic." Separated by sex, all students were required to do four hours per week of calisthenics, gymnastics, and military drills. The result, at least as reported, was "marked improvement." The students' "muscular system is stronger, their carriage more erect, their limbs are firmer, their lips fuller than heretofore, and even the bloom of their cheeks is in many instances flushed with faint vermillion."[22]

Despite rosy cheeks, Anagnos wanted yet more "eagerness and enthusiasm" from students. He didn't get it from the adolescent Annie. She felt herself "too stout to be graceful." She considered herself clumsy, and envied those girls with bodies she believed more attractive. For her, "the fact that I was always put in the back row when the class did team-work aggravated my chagrin."[23] Physical training became one more place where she believed herself set apart from other students at Perkins.

In Anagnos's pedagogical statements, he also stressed the importance of musical and technical training. Besides recording her dislike of her sewing teacher, Sullivan would make little mention of these classes later. Technical training was considered the inherently practical part of preparing students for gendered self-sufficiency. In technical training the female students, "a hive of cheerful workers," learned sewing, knitting, crocheting, cane seating, hammock making, and fancy needlework. A large part of the class involved domestic tasks—mending, polishing silverware, light housecleaning, and basic cooking. After all, as Anagnos reported to the general public, "a woman's sphere of knowledge is incomplete unless it embraces some acquaintance with work of this sort." During several of Annie's years at Perkins the girls learned to make Indian baskets, one year from a native woman hired by the school for this purpose. Rather than basic housekeeping, boys learned hand manufacturing, so that they might "enter into the sphere of real business." Advanced male students learned upholstery and mattress making. Such training was good, Anagnos argued, because it "carries a man forward."[24]

Perkins provided its students with musical training for cultural enrichment as well as, for some of the boys, possible employment (piano tuning). Many students studied piano, organ, violin, clarinet, or voice individually. Students frequently attended concerts and performances in the Greater Boston area with donated tickets (long lists of the events appeared in each annual report), and many performers came to campus. Music's goal in the curriculum was to provide the "sublime," to reveal to students "depths and heights of elevated thought, of profound feeling, of noble aspiration and of lofty imagination."[25]

Anagnos succeeded in his efforts to provide musical exposure. In the last week of January 1881, for example, students attended "concerts of a high order" at least once and sometimes twice a day. On Sunday evening they heard Mozart and Beethoven performed by the Handel and Haydn Society. Monday and Tuesday included three recitals at Tremont Temple and a Tuesday evening performance at Perkins. On Wednesday students attended a performance by a group called Euterpe; Thursday offerings included an afternoon concert by the Harvard symphony and an evening performance at Perkins by a member of the King's Chapel. On Friday students could attend a concert at the New England Conservatory and one at the Apollo Club, and for those who had energy remaining, Saturday evening included a piano recital. Anagnos acknowledged this frenzied schedule wasn't typical but proudly proclaimed, "there is no city in the whole civilized world in which the blind enjoy one-half of the advantages which are so liberally bestowed upon our scholars by the musical organizations of Boston."[26]

Annie left no documentation about her music class (though while at Radcliffe she rented a piano), but remembered fondly many of the musical performances she attended. During W. S. Gilbert and Arthur Sullivan's first trip to the United States, she attended performances of *The Mikado* and later saw *The Pirates of Penzance* and *Iolanthe*. She followed the pair in the newspaper as they traveled the globe. The former almshouse child noted, "crude as my knowledge of music was, I can truthfully say I experienced a new sensation at hearing the Gilbert and Sullivan operas. The effect of the singing was thrilling. I thought I could listen to it forever." She also saw famed beauty and singer Lillian Russell onstage in Gilbert and Sullivan's *Patience* and considered her "the loveliest thing that ever tripped upon a stage."[27]

The medical care, the cultural events, the influence of teachers, the formal and informal education Sullivan received while at Perkins, as well as the passage of time, changed her as she grew from fourteen to twenty years old. Presumably she grew to physical womanhood at this time, imagining herself as a sexual being with adult relationships of all kinds. She likely grew uneasy about her future. Most of the other students had families to help them financially once they graduated; virtually all had family members to provide them emotional support and a physical home. She had none of these and knew she would have to find her own way in the world, financially and emotionally. She would have to develop her own home.

The woman to whom Annie turned for guidance, hugs, and mothering was Sophia C. Hopkins, who came to Perkins in 1883, halfway through Annie's student years. At approximately forty years of age, Hopkins left her home in Brewster, Massachusetts, to become a housemother at Perkins. Her husband, a shipmaster, had died at sea; her only child, Florence, had died at sixteen years of age.[28]

Prior to Hopkins's arrival at Perkins, summer school breaks caused problems for Annie and Anagnos. What should be done with her? Tewksbury clearly was a poor solution. The first summer, the summer of 1881, she went home with fellow student Lily Fletcher, whose parents farmed in Nashua, New Hampshire. As Macy later remembered it, the girl's father was a spiritualist. Every morning at breakfast he reported the names of the women whose spirits had visited him the previous night. Not surprisingly, he and his wife fought. Two of the girl's uncles, one of them married, tried to woo Sullivan. As Henney reported, "Anne spent an extremely harassed and unrestful vacation." The second summer Annie did housework at a rooming house in Boston.[29] Though this seems to have been a much preferred experience, it also emphasized the class differences between her and other students. Others went home; she became a domestic.

Sophia Hopkins, however, provided Annie a home and extended family in Brewster, to which she would return over and over again. Macy remembered her summers in Brewster as glorious times. To the adolescent who so often felt herself abnormal, Brewster became a place in which she lived a life of normality and calm. Hopkins lived in a large house on the shore, built by her carpenter father. Macy remembered it as being filled with blue china from Holland, silver goblets from Portugal, the slippery "black hair-cloth chairs" enjoyed by children everywhere, and books, books, and more books (one of which, *Birdie and His Fairy Friends*, contained the story "The Frost Fairies," and would later cause her immense problems). Neighbors came to chat; she learned to ride horses and to sail; camp meetings and revivals provided entertainment; and everyone ate plenty.[30]

Though Perkins sat relatively close to the coast, Annie had not seen the ocean until she summered at Brewster. She gloried in the rural landscape, markedly different from the inland valleys of Feeding Hills that she had roamed in her life before Tewksbury but similar in their shared natural state. A "sandy, deep-rutted, grass-grown lane" ran from Hopkins's house to the shore—goldenrod, wild asters, purple milkweed, Queen Anne's lace, black-eyed Susans, sea grasses, wild plum bushes, and blackberries accompanied her as she ran barefoot to the dunes. There she learned to swim and to rest: "It was heavenly to dig into this sea-washed sand after our swim, and lie in it for hours, listening to the little white feet of the waves running up and down the beach and the whirr of gull-wings."[31]

Another favorite memory of Macy's from Brewster summers was the annual visit to a revival in nearby Yarmouth. The religious spirit of the event failed to speak to her, but she savored the food, the excitement, the horses, the crowds, and the drama of the exultations and confessions. Each year Annie and Mrs. Hopkins left home at 4 a.m. in a hired buggy that Annie got to drive. Hopkins insisted on "a snail's pace" that tested the teenager's patience immensely. During a worship service one year, Annie broke into uncontrollable giggles at the exuberance of "an old maid of uncertain age, very much excited." A "solemn brother" led her outside and preached to her of her sin, wrestling "mightily with the powers of darkness for my young soul." As Macy later wrote, "I wouldn't miss the revival for worlds."[32]

Hopkins and Brewster also provided Annie with an extended family. Mrs. Hopkins's brother, Frank Crocker, a grocer, accepted her as part of the community. She often shared his day, and treasured those moments: "I was happy as a queen to go with him on his rounds, sitting beside him on the high seat of the rumbling wagon." Crocker also told stories, a skill Annie had grown to value while at Tewksbury. She described him as "a willing historian of the skeletons hidden away in dark closets," who told the family histories of everyone on his route. She described herself as "an insatiable listener."[33] For an adolescent who lacked family and community, these stories became a way to be a part of both.

Another storyteller who captivated Annie was a mysterious hermit who lived in the sand dunes. Having only heard stories of him, and un-sure of their truthfulness, she sought him out. She found him asleep: "His bushy white hair was so long, it joined with his beard, which reached nearly to the ground. His feet were bare and brown; his hands were hanging between his legs. All I could see of his clothing was the ragged half of a pair of blue overalls." She came to call him "Captain Dad" and he called her "daughter." As an adult she remembered him fondly: "We would sit in a sandy nook (he knew every pleasant spot in the sand dunes for miles) and he would tell me stories of his life on the sea, or we would go out in his dory, and while he fished and chewed his cud of tobacco, he would tell me tales of whaling days and the strange doings of men 'who go down to the sea in ships.'"[34]

Mrs. Hopkins helped to create continuity for Annie by returning with her each fall to Perkins. After 1883 Annie always remained in the cottage supervised by Hopkins, but the group of girls who lived with her varied. They included Mabel Brown, a "semi-blind school friend," who at least once took Annie home with her on a weekend; Sadie Sheehan, whom Annie remembered as also having some sight; and Mary Hoisington.[35]

For several years, Sullivan also shared the cottage with the much older Laura Bridgman. In many ways, the fifty-some-year-old Bridg-man embodied the Perkins Institution. For several years in the 1830s Samuel Gridley Howe had traveled New England seeking a deaf-blind student suitable for his grand intellectual and philosophical experi-ment proving the innate humanity of all. Rejecting several, he selected the eight-year-old Bridgman in 1837. Her acquisition and use of the manual alphabet made him—and her—world famous after his 1840 report on his educational success. Reading Charles Dickens's account of meeting Bridgman would lead Helen Keller's mother to Perkins.

By the 1880s, however, Laura was no longer the charming and vir-ginal deaf-blind girl, but an aging woman with a campus reputation for grumpiness and severity who lived at Perkins because she had few other options. Her formal education had ended in 1850. She had be-come, in the words of Anagnos, "that living monument to Dr. Howe's patience and sagacity."[36] Placing her onstage at Perkins events always guaranteed a crowd and large donations, but other than that she had no specific role at the school. Thus, while she represented Perkins in the public imagination, she had an unusual status at the school: neither student nor staff.

Perkins teachers often presented Bridgman as a model for young blind girls. In 1885, while Bridgman likely lived in the same cottage as Annie, Anagnos reported that she spent much of her time helping the female students with their sewing. He considered it "very touching to see her now threading the needle of some one with the tip of her harmless tongue, now helping others to take up dropped stitches, and always eager to be of service to those who need assistance."[37] Bridgman's ability to thread a needle with her tongue was one of her most widely publicized skills. While Keller would eventually be able to do the same, Annie never could. She vehemently disliked her sewing classes.

Bridgman's atypical status may have resonated with Sullivan, who often felt herself abnormal and separate from the other girls. We know little about the relationship between them, except that the two spent many hours conversing by using fingerspelling.[38] Presumably Annie learned her manual alphabet skills from Bridgman. At this time, she had no indication that another deaf-blind individual—Helen Keller— would later provide her with friendship and a purpose in life.

Besides Mrs. Hopkins and teachers Mary Moore and Cora Newton, the two adults who figured most prominently in Sullivan's life at Perkins were Michael Anagnos and Julia Ward Howe, the widow of Samuel Gridley Howe. Anagnos acted as a paternalistic authority figure for many years, thus becoming a prime target for both affection and defiance. Julia Ward Howe seemed only to be annoyed by and to annoy the petulant adolescent.

Michael Anagnos directed Perkins with authority and charisma. Being the son-in-law of Perkins's founder conferred legitimacy on the lawyer and journalist. Howe had met Anagnos while the Howe family visited Athens in 1867. In their varying ways, Howe, his wife, Julia, and daughter, Julia Romana, all grew fond of the Greek patriot and citizen. Howe invited Anagnos to be trained as his successor at Perkins. And with the impeccable logic of a daughter who knew her place, Julia Romana married him in 1870. Michael Anagnos would play a pivotal and contentious role in Sullivan's life for many years.

Annie's first recorded memory of Anagnos involved confrontation. It was Exhibition Day, apparently Annie's first, in which the masterful publicity man and fundraiser welcomed the public, particularly wealthy donors, to tour Perkins. Students held special exercises, dressed in their best, and did all they could to impress the giving public. As a student with some eyesight, it was Annie's task to bring the plants from each cottage and arrange them around the exhibition room as attractively as possible. Energized, the fourteen-year-old helped herself to the powder and rouge of her housemother, Mrs. Hopkins. Running to the exhibition hall, she of course ran into Anagnos and his tour group. In front of the tour group, and presumably in hearing range of numerous students, he ordered Annie to wash off the makeup. To the young adolescent, who had only been at Perkins for approximately two weeks, and who already believed herself inferior and ugly, the rebuke was devastating. As she wrote almost forty years later, "Wash it off! The sink! And before strangers! The words burned into my flesh like hot irons. I ran, seething with rage, to my room. I did not return to the hall, nor did I go to the sink. It was my tears that washed away all the traces of my first effort to beautify myself."[39]

Annie and Anagnos battled once again over a theft from a school locker. Teachers initiated an investigation in which they questioned each girl, demanding that the girls not speak to one another until the court adjourned. Annie, of course, resisted—telling the girls they reminded her of "a nest of blind mice." Tattled on for her comment, she responded only with belligerence, refusing to answer questions and challenging the right of the teachers to "treat us like thieves without any evidence." Anagnos unexpectedly supported her stance and disbanded the court. Accompanying her outside, he seized her arm, telling her he suspected her of being the thief and that he was going to search her. As Macy later narrated the event, "Before I could give voice to my wrath, he laughed in his loud way and said, 'What would you have done, Miss Spitfire, if I had searched you?'" Annie replied that she would have scratched his eyes out. Putting his arm around her "caressingly," Anagnos replied, "'You know what happens to undesirable cats.'"[40]

According to Macy's narrative written decades later, the lesson she took from this exchange was that she "liked men better than women, and I have never changed my mind since."[41] The relationship of the adolescent Annie to the adult male Anagnos set the pattern for her later relationship with him once she became an adult and the teacher of Helen Keller. While Anagnos's personality is hard to discern, in their relationship both individuals were playful, contentious, and slightly flirtatious, and each brought the other to anger frequently.

While Anagnos directed Perkins, his mother-in-law continued to be a major presence on campus—and a focal point for Annie's frustrations. Samuel Gridley Howe had died in January of 1876. At that time his widow, Julia Ward Howe, left the family home at Perkins and traveled for almost two years. She returned in July 1879, more than a year before Annie arrived, with a firmly established national reputation as a poet, feminist, and suffragist. At Perkins she used her commanding presence to uphold the memory of dead husband. In the midst of these years, sometime during the 1885–1886 school year, her daughter and Anagnos's wife, Julia Romana, died. Of Julia Romana Anagnos, we know virtually nothing. Nor is there much evidence about the relationship between Anagnos and the imposing Julia Ward Howe. Howe, however, was a fierce and powerful woman. No one pushed around the author of "The Battle Hymn of the Republic."

The adolescent student Annie never behaved as graciously, appreciatively, or deferentially as Julia Ward Howe desired and expected. Once, Howe read the *Iliad* to the girls of Sullivan's class. Rather than being honored by her presence and the literary enrichment she was bestowing on them, the girls resented the loss of their Saturday afternoon and plotted against her: when one of them dropped her thimble (all brought their sewing as they were supposed to), all would yawn. Of course, Annie was the only one with the nerve to act so disrespectfully. Howe ignored her, Annie yawned again, and Howe kicked the girls out with a good scolding. Sullivan, however, seemed never to have been intimidated by a scolding, and simply succeeded in getting her way.[42]

Another time Annie resisted more contentiously and publicly. In anticipation of a Harvard performance of *Oedipus Rex*, Howe read the play aloud to the older girls. Gathering afterward in Anagnos's drawing room, with Annie already belligerent because she "refused to be interested in anything Mrs. Howe extolled," Howe led the girls in a discussion of life after graduation. Annie declared she wanted to be an evangelist, despite the fact that she had long since terminated any formal relationship with Christianity. As Macy wrote about the exchange later, "After a deliberate pause she [Howe] answered, 'I am afraid you sacrifice modesty to your ambition, young woman.' Angered, I flashed back, 'Self effacement is not your brightest virtue, is it, Madame Howe?' "[43] Few would have responded to the aristocratic and renowned woman as Sullivan did. Despite the consequences, she often refused to retreat from the more powerful, to defer to anyone from whom she perceived arrogance or disdain.

Despite the vast quantity of archival materials Howe left behind, she left no remembrances of Annie Sullivan Macy. To the world-famous Julia Ward Howe, Annie may have been just one of the many Perkins students. Howe may have remembered her only as an upstart and ill-behaved adolescent. Howe, however, did not die until 1910. By then Macy had already made a significant name for herself, one that would grow larger and come to equal if not pass that of Julia Ward Howe on the international scene. It is unlikely that Howe did not remember the cheeky and ill-mannered adolescent Annie. Following a controversy that arose several years after Annie had left the school, many of those closely affiliated with Perkins resented Sullivan fiercely, and believed her to have deeply insulted the reputation and memory of Samuel Gridley Howe. It's more likely that Julia Ward Howe simply and imperiously chose to ignore her existence.

Howe left few remembrances even of Perkins itself. Her biographers all state that she had little interest in the education of blind children. Her marriage was not the happiest, and she constantly struggled for independence from Samuel Gridley Howe. At the beginning of her marriage she'd had to compete for attention with her husband's star deaf-blind student Laura Bridgman. Throughout her marriage, she sought constantly to be not "simply the wife of a great hero and reformer but a woman with a reputation of her own."[44] The fiercely proud woman had no desire to define her life by Perkins, or by her relationship to its star students.

Similarly, Macy held no fond memories of the older woman. To her, the afternoons in which Howe held audiences with the older Perkins girls were onerous and boring—not a privilege. And Annie didn't like condescension. As Macy remembered Howe later, "Mrs. Julia Ward Howe had the air of one who confers a favor by acknowledging one's existence. She liked to create an impression by appearing to fall asleep while one was speaking to her."[45]

Despite this, Macy's later remembrances of the older woman contained begrudging respect. The two women shared similarities in character—pride, a fierce will, a sharp tongue, and intelligence. Macy acknowledged, "A Julia Ward makes her own rules of conduct, and really it required a great social personage to put it in practice constantly." Macy envied such skill and presumption, despite herself: "I could think of it and put it in practice occasionally when a bore has taxed my endurance to the dozing-point, but I have not sufficient egotism to carry it off nonchalantly."[46] When the adult Annie wrote these words she was approximately the same age that Howe had been when the two women first encountered one another at Perkins.

CHAPTER 4

Perkins, 1880–1886: Part Two

IMAGINING THE mental and emotional state of Annie Sullivan during her years at Perkins is almost impossible. She had stepped from the crowded, chaotic, and disreputable adult world of the almshouse to a highly structured sphere. Her food, her clothing, her bed—all of it changed overnight. The abrupt transformation of her world must have been astounding, both appreciated and disconcerting. Annie's years as a Perkins student were intellectually and emotionally tumultuous but profoundly transformative. She tried to remake herself, leaving Tewksbury behind.

One moonlit Boston winter night Annie got permission from her teachers to "model in snow" on the campus grounds. Her teacher Cora Newton remembered that "Three of us teachers remained in the schoolroom over looking the quadrangle to guard her from possible intruders, while she modeled a graceful, full-sized figure clothed in bow-neck, short-sleeve, long train evening gown; the hair arranged in heavy coils high on the head, and a big curl over the shoulder!"[1]

The image of Annie in the moonlight, solitary and creatively expressive, wistful but not miserable, made a strong impression on Newton. She knew her student well enough to sense that the transitory snow maiden embodied Annie's hopes for her future adult life, as well as her unmet desire for fine clothes, beauty, and glamour.

The material that remains about this period is again from Macy's final decade, as she struggled to make sense of her life. At that point, she came to terms with life at Perkins by understanding herself as having had an "inferiority complex."

> I had desired intensely to go to school. I was ambitious to speak like educated people. I wanted to wear clothes like the fashion-plates Jimmie and I had pasted up on the walls of the death-house. Above all, I wanted to forget that I had spent six years of my childhood [sic] in an almshouse. And yet when I was put in the way of achieving these things, something within me fought against them. My mind had unconsciously absorbed [the] alms-house point of view. My thoughts were dyed in its dark colors. A psychoanalyst would say I had developed an "inferiority complex." Perhaps I had. It is a rather easy way of explaining a difficult mental phenomenon.[2]

At another point she explained her Perkins life by saying, "I was not a normal girl. The experiences which had moulded me were not normal." Over and over she emphasized her otherness, her abnormality, her difference from those around her. As she saw it, "All my experiences unfitted me for living a normal life."[3] This feeling followed her for much, if not all, of her adult life.

Sullivan's classmates remembered her with varied impressions. Lenna Swinerton remembered her arriving "unkempt, and badly clothed . . . [with] strong prejudices and [a] narrow point of view." Sullivan's political commentaries rankled her, for "Annie was always a radical Democrat, with which point of view I had no sympathy." In the end Swinerton characterized her as a person who had "much to overcome personally, and yet, with her eager mind and natural vivacity, soon became an excellent student and a companionable comrade." Lydia Hayes, by 1927 the New Jersey Commissioner for the Blind, remembered Annie as an older student who helped her comprehend Greek history lessons. Even then the future teacher's pedagogical creativity revealed itself. The girls acted out the difficult lesson, one taking the character of Aristides and the other Pericles.[4] Perhaps relationships with younger girls, not as a friend but as a guide, came easier.

Religion also separated Sullivan from other students and teachers at Perkins, as she sought to unify her intellectual life and her spiritual identity. At Tewksbury the child baptized Catholic at the Springfield cathedral "shook off the authority of the Church" by refusing to attend confession. At Perkins, Anagnos expected that the Irish-Catholic girl attend morning mass and evening vespers. She did so for what she remembered as two years. Her "religious inclinations weakened," however, as her "knowledge of history and the sciences increased." Then, she related, "when I no longer accepted the idea of God sitting somewhere in His heavens dictating laws and meting out punishments for all manner of actions, whether the offender had any choice in the matter or not, I served notice on the good Father who presided at the gate of Heaven that I would not attend mass again." Once again, she and Anagnos tangled. To "avoid unnecessary complications," Anagnos sought compromise. He asked only that she remain at mass until the end of the school year. She had the more difficult task. As she later characterized it, "I swallowed my impetuosity, and continued to exchange meaningless amenities with the Roman Church three months after I had renounced it."[5] Giving in, even compromise, was not her strong suit.

Though Sullivan rejected Catholicism, she embraced her identity as an Irish American during her years at Perkins. The limited positive memories she had of her parents, particularly her father, centered on the endless stories of Ireland—the land, the famine, the people, the fairies and ghosts. The women of Tewksbury had shared similar stories with her. They read the Irish American journal *The Pilot*, praised Irish dissident Charles Stewart Parnell, and fed her "on the persecutions of Catholics by Protestants."[6] So embedded were these stories in Annie's mind that she initially rejected her history lessons on the Spanish Inquisition, believing them exaggerated by continued anti-Catholic sentiment. Catholicism remained linked enough with her Irish identity that she could defend it. Being Irish also gave her an obligation to champion the downtrodden. Throughout her life she remained stubbornly resistant to authority, often no matter what the cause, price, or likely outcome.

Besides religion, there were physical differences from the other students as well. Perkins, of course, was a school for blind children, so the children there were supposed to need no medical care for their eyes. By the time Annie arrived at Perkins she already had endured five surgeries: two while at Tewksbury, one at the Sisters of Charity hospital in Lowell, and two at the Boston city infirmary during her brief foray away from Tewksbury. The presumed purpose of these undoubtedly painful surgeries had been to improve her eyesight by scraping away the scar tissue that developed on the inside of her eyelid from the infection and inflammation of trachoma.

When Sullivan arrived at Perkins, the staff assumed that nothing could be done to improve her eyesight. Most likely she experienced eye pain or at least discomfort due to her trachoma; if so, the staff presumably also assumed that little could be done about that. The only further medical care she received came at the instigation of a near stranger. During Annie's summer employment as a domestic at a Boston boardinghouse, a resident arranged for her to meet a Dr. Bradford, who performed two surgeries on Sullivan at the Massachusetts Eye and Ear Infirmary that gave her enough sight, at least initially, to read printed materials. When Dr. Bradford performed these surgeries is not clear: one source indicates that Annie spent three months at the infirmary and returned to Perkins seeing; another source indicates her two operations were twelve months apart.[7] This cycle of surgeries, of varying levels of sight, and of pain continued for the rest of Annie's life. Neither consistently blind nor sighted, she existed in a nebulous state between the two.

Perhaps the greatest indication of Sullivan's claim to a new and emerging self, built on but separate from her past experiences, was her adoption of a new name while at Perkins. Other girls at Perkins, like Sullivan's future student Helen Adams Keller, used three names in formal circumstances. It signified refinement, sophistication, and a lineage of note. Sometime during these years the orphaned Annie, without an extended family to claim her, read of Mansfield Hall, an Irish baronial site. It must have seemed a perfect fit—noble, Irish, and literary sounding. She became Annie Mansfield Sullivan, in one move, setting aside one past and claiming another. It did not remake everything, but it helped.

Somehow, sometime during her first years at Perkins, Sullivan received news from Tewksbury of the death of Maggie, painted in the stories of the fictional Johannah as a redeeming maternal figure, protective of and vigilant toward the almshouse orphan. Did someone from Tewksbury—another patient, an employee—care enough to notify her of Maggie's death via a letter? Had someone kept track of her whereabouts? Did she unexpectedly run into someone from Tewksbury while at a public event or on a walk? All we know from the adult Macy is that she heard of the death in "some roundabout way." As an older woman, she wrote, "The news awakened slumbering memories, but my life was too crowded with the present to dwell much on the past."[8] She did all she could to forget.

After almost three years at Perkins, the seventeen-year-old Annie may have felt she had successfully left her Tewksbury past behind. She was slowly and carefully building a new self as she grew into young adulthood. She was beginning to feel less different. From March until August of 1883, however, her life at Tewksbury appeared before her almost daily, splashed across the front pages of Boston's newspapers. Tewksbury became a household name, shouted on the streets by the newspaper boys and tantalizingly associated with the horrendous, the unsavory, and the sensational. Now she could not hide from her markedly different past.

Benjamin Butler, against whom so many accusations of various types were leveled during this period, can be blamed. Back in 1877, during Sullivan's short respite from Tewksbury, the Lowell Sisters of Charity, characterizing him as a friend to the poor, had pointed out the house of the nationally known Irish American to their young charge. They praised him for his advocacy of the ten-hour workday (rather than twelve or fourteen) and his steadfast resistance against language and literacy requirements for voting. Annie likely had read of him frequently in *The Pilot*, which she read both at Tewksbury and at Perkins. According to Henney, he was "her first hero, a shining knight in armour."[9]

To much of the nation, however, he was something else. As a Civil War major, Butler developed a controversial reputation as the Union "Beast" of New Orleans and a supporter of black military regiments. In the decades after the war he endorsed female suffrage, measures punishing former Confederate leaders and veterans, and social welfare programs for the poor of Massachusetts. In 1882 he became the Democratic governor of Massachusetts, after unsuccessfully running four previous times on three different tickets (twice as a Republican, once as a Democrat, and once as an independent). As governor he shocked the staid New Englanders of Massachusetts by appointing both an African American and an Irish Catholic to judicial positions.

Butler reentered Sullivan's life when he instigated an investigation of Tewksbury's finances and its treatment of residents. In his inaugural message as governor, Butler accused the previous administration of mismanaging public institutions—hospitals, asylums, and almshouses—and specifically cited Tewksbury. Pushed forward by Republican members, the state legislature initiated a formal investigation. For months, everyone involved battled it out almost daily on the front pages of the newspapers, and the lurid details made for easy embellishment.

The sensationalism began immediately. The very first hearing in late March included allegations of the pickling and skinning of bodies—complete with tanning of the skin—and their unauthorized sale to Harvard medical students in the dead of night. The scandalous details of the first day drew such a crowd that on the second day the hearings were moved permanently to a bigger room. Even this room was "crowded to stifling, and many men were compelled to stand." As one paper reported, the room held "about as interested an audience as it ever contained." A handful of women attended; their presence was unusual enough for reporters to take note. The hearings became the summer entertainment of 1883. As one newspaper reporter wrote, "The sun may shine or the rain may pour, but the Tewksbury investigation goes on forever."[10]

As the hearings continued over the summer months the allegations expanded. Former Tewksbury employees and residents frequently accused Superintendent Thomas J. Marsh and his family of allowing, and sometimes directing, the theft of residents' clothing and valuables. A night watchman accused Mrs. Marsh, a matron of the institution, of pilfering clothing from the trunks of incoming female residents, particularly silk dresses and shawls, for her own use as well as for sale.

Others charged that Superintendent Marsh allowed food intended for residents to be sold or consumed by his own family, and routinely had residents perform family household labor.[11]

The descriptions of daily life at Tewksbury given in the hearings provided titillating and horrid details for newspaper readers. Mary Bowen, an employee in the women's ward during Annie's years at Tewksbury, described the rats as "so thick I have seen them run across my lap when I was eating." Just as the fictional Johannah and her brother Jimmie chased rats through the steam pipe, so did she. She testified that "there was [sic] steam pipes with large holes in between the pipes, where the rats used to go; and they used to close the door nights because the rats would come out . . . and annoy the patients, and get up on the beds and annoy them." Bowen recalled the ever-present rats consuming the dead and the dying. She and other patients had tried to drive the rats away from a dying woman, too weak from consumption to even cry out when the rats attacked her feet and toes.[12]

Being a favorite of the matron, Bowen testified, meant getting first access to the bath water. Bathing occurred two days a week in the female ward, with half the women bathing on each day. All shared the same bath water and a limited number of towels, regardless of vermin, head lice, or open sores.[13] Such conditions were ideal for spreading trachoma—as well as other bacteria.

Many of the hearings focused on Tewksbury's "lie-in" ward, where Annie had spent so much of her time listening to the stories of pregnant and forsaken women. Mrs. Charlotte A. Thomas, in charge of the ward during Annie's years at Tewksbury, testified that many healthy women died due to one doctor who routinely gave them too much medicine. Her printed testimony included the names of specific women who had died in the ward. One wonders if those names meant anything to Annie. Did they bring up memories of friendship? Did she have stories of seduction, love, or assault to attach to the names? Annie had remembered the frequent deaths of the babies born to the women of the lying-in ward. Several who testified in the summer of 1883 attributed many of those deaths to the morphine fed to babies to keep them quiet and manageable.[14]

Over and over again, the hearings included testimony referencing

Tewksbury's dead house and the vandalism of bodies. To most readers, this was simply one more sordid detail, one more example of the depths to which money-hungry Superintendent Marsh would stoop. For others, it served as an opportunity to mock prestigious Harvard, its doctors, and its medical students, who reportedly received the bodies for dissection.

To Annie, however, the dead house and reference to the bodies of dead residents represented a most painful aspect of Tewksbury—the death of her brother Jimmie. She had placed lilacs and geraniums on his gravesite. She must have wondered whether his body had been among those removed and used for medical research, the gravesite dug up in the middle of the night by asylum employees attempting to make a profit.

Not surprisingly, such drama drew a crowd. Newspapers described "eager listeners" who howled, laughed, and booed as Butler and the various lawyers and witnesses attempted to woo public opinion. Most days 250–300 spectators crowded the room: it was "packed almost to suffocation. Not only were all the seats taken, but the aisles were occupied as well, and all available space near the doorway was packed full with interested spectators. Footholds on settee-arms were at a premium." Court officials saved some seats for legislators and a few for lawyers and journalists. At least twice lines developed early in the morning as the general public attempted to secure good seats. The audience included the rich, the poor, men and women. It even included a mysterious "lady in deep mourning, who has sat in the front row of spectators' seats at every session since the investigation was commenced."[15]

Annie followed the Tewksbury hearings closely in the newspapers and, at least once, among the audience. The Perkins teachers who read the daily news had omitted the stories of the scandal, but she ferreted them out. She stole newspapers and covertly had one of the girls with more sight read her the stories of the hearings. At some point between May and August of 1883 she sought the permission of Anagnos to attend the controversial hearings. He forbade it. No doubt, it was not the sort of thing he and other teachers encouraged or desired to list in the yearly compilation of extracurricular activities.

Annie, of course, disobeyed. She and Perkins classmate Sadie Shee-han claimed an appointment at the City Hospital for Annie's eyes but instead went to the State House. Anagnos learned of their adventure and expelled Annie. Sympathetic teachers pled her case, and Anagnos relented. As Henney described it, "probably because they felt sorry for her. There was nowhere to expel her to, out of the Tewksbury Institu-tion, and no one could calmly have endured the thought of her going back there."[16]

The 1883 Tewksbury hearings, however, forced these years to the forefront. As a seventeen-year-old, excelling in school and making friends despite herself, Annie was markedly different from the ado-lescent who had left Tewksbury. Her education and advancing age had expanded her cognitive abilities tremendously; the relative calm of Perkins, its food, safety, and comfortable beds, provided her with security. Students, teachers, and Michael Anagnos provided commu-nity. Decades later she wrote, "I was not conscious of the horror of it all until an investigation made me aware of it. When the newspaper accounts of the Institution were read aloud, my mind quickly perceived that things were pretty terrible, and I began to observe and think about my environment."[17]

Sullivan's growing and tumultuous emotions manifested themselves in fierce loyalty to Benjamin Butler, another sign of her difference from others at Perkins: "I believed every one in the Institution hated him. Therefore I made him the idol of my imagination." He was not a popu-lar man at Perkins or throughout much of Boston. She remembered teachers "read[ing] scathing editorials from the 'Boston Transcript' to us in which my hero was denounced as a demi-god [sic] who was trail-ing in the dust the fair name of Massachusetts." Prior to and after Butler's gubernatorial years the sitting governor always spoke at Per-kins commencements—but not during Butler's years. Even Harvard, which routinely gave the governor an honorary degree, refused to so acknowledge Butler.[18]

In the notes Macy made for her never completed autobiography she recalled one evening when, during the reading of these scathing edito-rials, the young Annie erupted with frustration. Butler did not bring shame on Massachusetts, she insisted aloud. The state, the supposed cradle of liberty, was instead "the cradle where Liberty was rocked to sleep!" Rather than a scolding, her teacher Cora Newton asked for an explanation. Fighting back tears and shocking the other girls with her admission, Annie cried out,

> I don't know the names of histories that tell the truth yet; but I do know nobody here knows the truth about Tewksbury. You don't know Gen. Butler. It isn't he that is a disgrace to Mass., it's the State itself because it knows that T[ewksbury] is a terrible place, and pretends that it is a nice institution! I have lived there. . . . I know all about it, and every word Gen. Butler says about it is true. People like to hear lies better than the truth. They would rather be ignorant about Tewksbury and all the poor people who stay there than have Mass[achusetts] blamed. That's why I said Liberty is asleep.[19]

The seventeen-year-old sat down, "trembling violently." In her memory, the silence dragged on. It terrified her. She had exposed herself and all she had previously tried to hide. At the same time, the competitive young intellectual experienced "a feeling of happiness" that she had "remembered to get in that last shot about Liberty asleep." She later lost her admiration for Benjamin Butler, but "his way of attacking the evils upon which the mighty sit so complacently" would stir her forever.[20]

The Tewksbury hearings reinforced Sullivan's separation from others at Perkins. Their differing political views and life backgrounds seemed too wide a chasm to bridge. After her dramatic classroom exposure about Perkins and Butler, she even rejected her beloved teacher Cora Newton. Newton responded to Annie's outburst not with a scolding but with an invitation to talk. "I do really want to know the truth," the teacher said. Her student, who would not tell anyone else about life at Tewksbury until she was in her sixties, instead went to her room and "coddled" her wrath.[21]

Tewksbury had taught Sullivan great disdain for the powerful. As she finished her last years at Perkins, and solidified her early intellectual analyses, the highly publicized hearings and the anti-Butler campaigns reminded her even more deeply of that disdain. She questioned the authority of her teachers, questioned the stories and lessons taught to her about history, and questioned the values of those around her. All, it seemed to her, were frauds: "The men 'nice people' admired rose on the bleeding backs of slaves, black and white, to power and wealth and education."[22]

As an adult reflecting back on her life at Perkins, Macy indicated that during this time, despite the echoes of her past, she slowly settled into an adulthood she could live with: "gradually I began to accept things as they were, and rebel less and less. The realization came to me that I could not alter anything but myself. I must accept the conventional order of society if I was to succeed in anything. I must bend to the inevitable, and govern my life by experience, not by 'might-have-beens.'" The brutal rules of life taught to her at Tewksbury didn't fit the world as she now experienced it; nor, however, did (what she characterized as) the overly cheerful platitudes taught to her at Perkins. She had to develop her own understanding of the world. Sometimes, she wrote, she "tried very hard to look at things through their spectacles," but the life experiences of others varied dramatically from her own.[23]

Time, combined with "a mind capable of growth and discrimination," aided Sullivan in her growth to adulthood. "Many of the false ideas I had hugged to my breast," she wrote decades later, "fell away like dead leaves, and truer ones came to take their place. The light of knowledge spread slowly, putting darkness to flight. Little by little abstract notions grew into concrete things. Love, understanding and sympathy began to take the place of bitterness and ignorance."[24]

How much of this transformation Sullivan credited to Perkins, and how much to time and her own capabilities, is unclear. Undoubtedly, however, she knew that she owed much to the institution.

Impressively, the child who had started Perkins far behind other students academically graduated as valedictorian of the class of 1886. June 1, 1886, was her day. Commencement exercises at the Perkins Institution and Massachusetts School for the Blind served as both a graduation ceremony and an ideal public relations event. For Sullivan, it served as a thrilling day of personal accomplishment and a sobering reminder that she had nowhere to go next.

Her housemother, Sophia Hopkins, graciously provided beautiful clothing—perhaps not unlike that worn by Annie's snow maiden, but modeled on the graduation dress of Frances Folsom, who had just married President Cleveland in what the girls considered the most romantic and glamorous event possible. She'd never had pretty things before—"the plainest, coarsest cotton garments were all that the money provided by the state would purchase"—and years later Macy remembered the clothing in detail from undergarment to outer sash.

The layers started with "dainty underclothes": first, a one-piece combination of "drawers and chemise," then a "short underskirt with its plain edge of hand-embroidery." The "outside petticoat with its deep Hamburg ruffle" topped the undergarments, all of which had matching scalloped edges. Her white muslin dress, her first white dress, had elbow-length sleeves, three ruffles, and Valencia lace. Mrs. Hopkins lent her the pink sash that her own deceased daughter had worn at her high school graduation. Furthermore, Hopkins gave Annie white slippers. The very thought of these left her uncharacteristically speechless: to Macy, "they were the delight of my heart, even more than the white dress with its three ruffles." To top it all off, Hopkins piled the young woman's hair on her head and made ringlets at her temples, "like Mrs. Cleveland's."[25]

As it did every year during this period, Perkins's commencement took place at Boston's historic Tremont Temple. Each year Perkins offered free tickets to the public, with the best seats saved for financial benefactors and the prominent. The year before, thousands reportedly were turned away from the event. The demand for tickets in 1886 must have thrilled Anagnos. As he reported later, "To the disappointment of multitudes of applicants, every available space for standing, as well as sitting, was secured many days before the festival." In many ways commencement operated similarly to the Exhibition Days begun by Howe and continued by Anagnos. The purpose of the day was not only to celebrate graduates, but to display to the giving public the seemingly miraculous things that blind children could do if given an education. Anagnos must have been even more pleased by the fact that "the assemblage was composed of people of the highest social standing."[26] Pity and awe were to motivate the opening of pocketbooks.

On the platform at the front of the room sat graduates, pupils, teachers, the trustees of the institution, and other dignitaries. The newly elected Massachusetts governor, George Robinson, sat alongside Julia Ward Howe, embodying the link to Perkins's founder Dr. Samuel Gridley Howe. The almost fifty-seven-year-old Laura Bridgman, who could still draw a crowd as the world's most famous deaf-blind figure, featured prominently in the ceremony.[27]

The program included music performed by Perkins students, an opening address by the governor, a recitation that used a sewing machine to explain the laws of mechanics, gymnastics drills, and various other exhibitions of student skills. A "peculiarly interesting feature," according to the *Boston Home Journal*, was that performed by the kindergarteners and entitled "Early Boston in Clay." The audience watched while the youngest students used clay to create "designs suggestive of incidents in the history of Boston," accompanied by an appeal for funds for the new kindergarten. Considering the sculptors were kindergarteners, "suggestive" is probably the key word. Historical "incidents" deemed worthy of sculpting included clay windmills, lighthouses, ships, and pens, as well as a beacon from Beacon Hill.[28]

The valedictory address of Annie Mansfield Sullivan and the awarding of diplomas completed the program. Later she remembered being terrified: "I listened to the speeches and the music as one in a dream. Then my time came, I heard the Governor speak my name, I rose trembling in every limb."[29]

In some ways, Annie's valedictory address is typical. She thanked teachers as well as the visiting dignitaries. She exhorted her seven fellow graduates to improve the world. She mentioned God. The address is sober, restrained, and sometimes borders on the boring. She included a respectful reference to the recent death of Julia Romana Howe Anagnos.

Yet, in other ways, the short address reflects Annie's intense and resolute efforts to create a self that she liked and could live with. She began by reminding her fellow graduates of the challenge that stood before them: "Today we are standing face to face with the great problem of life." To deal with that problem successfully, each individual must "obey the great law of our being"—perhaps she would have liked to add that one should obey one's own being regardless of how annoying, stubborn, or belligerent others thought one to be. The twenty-year-old, who had faced almost nothing but problems in life, insisted that change and self-improvement were not only possible but important: "We also have the power of controlling the course of our lives. We can educate ourselves; we can, by thought and perseverance, develop all the powers and capacities entrusted to us, and build for ourselves true and noble characters." The orphaned and abandoned child insisted that a drunken father, the almshouse, and poverty did not define her. Instead she claimed difficult experiences as ennobling. "It is by battling with the circumstances, temptations and failures of the world," she maintained, "that the individual reaches his highest possibilities."[30]

As she reached the moment of adulthood at graduation, her future yet very precarious, Sullivan insisted to herself and to others that her past did not taint her. She had the capacity for "true and noble character." Her purpose, like that of all others, was "to grow, to expand, to progress."[31]

It is interesting that in the midst of this celebration of education for blind children, Sullivan did not mention blindness or blind people. In the Perkins annual report, admittedly designed for its benefactors, Anagnos emphasized her blindness and that of other students. He described her "high thoughts" as exemplary of students "whose early-darkened childhood had brightened into happy, hopeful youth under the fostering care of the school."[32] To him, she was not simply a valedictorian, but a poor blind child transformed into a valedictorian by Perkins.

Local newspapers gave Sullivan positive reviews. The *Boston Home Journal* praised her address for its "felicity of thought and grace of expression." The *Christian Register*'s description went further. In paternalistic fashion it started by noting that the entire event solicited "surprise," "sadness," and "sympathy" for the blind children from the spectators. Though its description of her address only included "a tithe of what we could," the paper described it as having "an altogether earnest, sincere, thoughtful spirit, full of wise suggestions, and spoken in tones that vibrated with true feeling and with genuine refinement."[33]

Annie left Tremont Temple with more ambivalent feelings. Afterward she returned to her room and reluctantly removed her "white splendor." She brushed the dust off her white slippers, wrapped them in tissue paper, and returned them to their box.[34]

Her concerns were realistic and numerous. Her education had not given her all she wanted. Indeed, the whetting of her intellectual appetite by six years of schooling seemed a cruel joke. "I knew better now than I had six years ago," she wrote much later, "how abysmal my ignorance was. I was heavy with discontent, with pent-up anger against what seemed to me a cruel fate." Her "desire to read everything amount[ed] to a passion," but her eyes failed to cooperate and her fingers refused to move fast enough. "How was I," she thought, "handicapped as I was both physically and mentally, to satisfy my insatiable appetite for literature?"[35]

More pragmatically, how was she going to feed her appetite literally? The possibility of returning to Tewksbury terrified her. Perkins had long insisted publicly that one of its primary purposes was to prepare "the youth of both sexes to free themselves from the incubus of dependence." The institution's annual reports constantly stressed the ways by which the school curriculum successfully prepared its students, male and female, for economic and personal self-sufficiency. Annie, however, knew it was not this easy. So, presumably, did Michael Anagnos. It was not unusual for him to receive letters from former graduates, mostly females, seeking financial and employment assistance. Just two weeks prior to the 1886 graduation he had received an appeal on behalf of former student Ella Shaw. She sought suggestions for ways to support herself, hinting he provide a job for her at Perkins. Her father had mortgaged and lost the piano by which she had made a living, and the income from crocheting caps and making bead baskets was insufficient. No evidence remains that Anagnos assisted Shaw.[36]

Sullivan's prospects were equally limited. Discrimination left few employment opportunities for women in the 1880s, even fewer for blind women. She thought her "partial blindness" an "insurmountable obstacle" to a profession. Some of her teachers suggested attending a normal school (a teacher's college) and Anagnos promised funds if she desired to do so. This had no appeal; in fact, it "repelled" the future famous teacher. Observing her own teachers left Anne believing teaching to be "a life of self-abnegation," "uninteresting, and the results very far from being commensurate with the effort." She also believed, surely accurately, that her visual disability made a position at a school for sighted children near impossible. Another teacher suggested she serve as an attendant to children, an idea she dismissed quickly. She half considered selling books door to door until another student who had done so previously persuaded her of its difficulties. Anagnos dreamed of inaugurating a postgraduate program at Perkins, but this possibility was nowhere near reality.[37] Perkins was opening a kindergarten school in the fall, but Anagnos made no move to hire Sullivan as a teacher for that program.

Other students had homes to return to and familial resources to draw on. Female college graduates of the era often struggled with what Jane Addams called "the family claim." Addams, for example, struggled with adult siblings who assumed she would live in their homes and provide the household assistance expected of a maiden aunt. Though such expectations frequently could and did frustrate women such as Addams, they provided a financial safety net unavailable to Sullivan. No evidence indicates that she tried to find or even considered contacting extended family members in this period.

Perhaps Annie dreamed of marriage. Occasionally blind women employed at Perkins left to be married, and the institution celebrated these occurrences. Anagnos approved, but only as long as, in his words, there was not "a marked hereditary tendency to any physical infirmity." If one's blindness was hereditary, "intermarriage between two persons so predisposed" was "invariably wrong, very wrong."[38] Annie, however, considered herself outside of this category. She loved beautiful things and stories of romance, and dared to hope about her future despite what must have seemed like overwhelming obstacles. Marriage may have been an improbability, but likely a highly appealing one.

Following graduation Annie accompanied her housemother, Sophia Hopkins, to Brewster, Massachusetts, just as she had done the previous three summers. Evidence indicates that neither she, Hopkins, nor Michael Anagnos knew what she would do in the fall.

She surely stood, as she had proclaimed in her valedictorian address, "face to face with the great problem of life."[39]

CHAPTER 5

Becoming Teacher, 1887

FOR SULLIVAN, the summer of 1886 began with uncertainty and waiting. The proud Perkins graduate had little to claim as her own. What would happen to her? How would she support herself? Would she have to live her life as an eternal ward—of Perkins, of Sophia Hopkins, of Michael Anagnos, or even worse, of Tewksbury? Summering in Brewster, Massachusetts, with Hopkins, previously idyllic, must have felt intolerable and endless.

Near the end of August, Michael Anagnos wrote to her with a way out. "My dear Annie," he said, "please read the enclosed letters carefully, and let me know at your earliest convenience whether you would be disposed to consider favorably an offer of a position in the family of Mr. Keller as governess of his little deaf-mute and blind daughter." He knew little about the Alabama man's "standing and respectability," but assured her that such information could be attained easily.[1]

Once Helen Keller became famous, with Annie Sullivan on her way to doing the same, Anagnos wrote in the Perkins annual report that when he was contacted by Arthur Keller his thoughts had "almost instinctively turned towards Miss Annie M. Sullivan." He had recommended her "most highly and without any reservation."[2] Perhaps this is so, but Anagnos also had little taste for putting her out on the street. He must have seen this employment opportunity as a welcome relief for him and an opportunity for her.

Near the end of her life, Macy remembered her own reluctance. "When Mr. Anagnos read me Captain Keller's letter, and asked if I thought I could teach his little girl, I was very sure that I couldn't. I told him I was not trained for that sort of teaching, or indeed for anything." She struggled to imagine herself as capable: "I did not think I was serious minded enough to make a success of it." She knew her own teachers "laughed in their sleeve at the idea of Annie Sullivan undertaking any child's education."[3]

Anagnos, however, was persuasive, and Annie, of course, was desperate. With a plan and a purpose, Sullivan and Mrs. Hopkins returned to Perkins. Hopkins resumed her position as housemother, with Annie taking up once again her bed in Hopkins's cottage.

After multiple exchanges of letters in numerous directions, Captain Keller agreed to hire Sullivan. In turn, despite earlier discussions in which she scorned caring for children as a means to make a living, Sullivan agreed to the governess position and began to prepare for the tasks ahead of her. By January 1887 the two men involved had ironed out the details. The father of Annie's future pupil assured Anagnos that she would be treated "as one of our immediate family." He would pay her twenty-five dollars per month, a significant salary. Decades later Macy wrote, "It seemed like a chapter out of a romantic and impossible tale."[4]

At Perkins, Sullivan, other students, the faculty, and the staff lived surrounded by the legend of Samuel Gridley Howe. Though he had been dead for more than a decade, his reputation as the educator who unleashed the mind of deaf-blind Laura Bridgman lived on in the names of buildings and the school press, in the history taught to students, and in the formidable presence of his widow, Julia Ward Howe. Even more so, the front-row prominence of Bridgman at nearly every Perkins commencement and fundraiser reminded everyone of Howe's accomplishments.

Making her way to the Perkins library, Sullivan read Howe's reports on the education of the world's most famous deaf-blind person, Laura Bridgman—or, at least, years later she claimed to have done so.[5] To the twenty-year-old Sullivan, studying the education of the young Bridgman must have seemed strange. Almost fifty years later, the older woman living alongside her in the cottage of Mrs. Hopkins, considered grumpy and stern by most of the younger Perkins students, bore little resemblance to the young girl described by Howe. Sullivan left no evidence that she discussed her future task with Bridgman, though we know the two communicated over the years by using the manual alphabet. In this period Bridgman lived at Perkins approximately ten months out of the year, so presumably she shared the Hopkins cottage during the months Sullivan spent preparing. Did knowing Bridgman reassure Sullivan of the potential for success, or make the task appear more formidable? Whatever else knowing Bridgman did, it ensured that Sullivan knew how to use the manual alphabet proficiently.

No evidence indicates that Anagnos or any of the teachers at Perkins assisted Sullivan in her preparations or took her under their wing intellectually. She received no pedagogical training other than whatever time she spent with Howe's reports on Bridgman. On the advice of an *Atlantic Monthly* article, she read a basic psychology text and books on child psychology. Years later she wrote, "I cannot say they helped me much, except that they supplied me with the special vocabulary of my profession." Her sharp tongue, not her pedagogical skills, concerned others the most. No one wanted her to be forced to return to Perkins because of bad behavior. Friends warned her that she should "hold my peace while south, that any reference to conditions before or during the Civil War would cause my instant dismissal."[6]

Sullivan's final preparation was medical. Just a few days before she left, she once again entered a hospital for eye surgery—probably her eighth surgery in approximately ten years. Her right eye was "a little crossed," and she was "very anxious to have it straightened before going south."[7] Later on she couldn't remember why she had not had the operation sooner.

With her right eye still painful, on what must have been a cold February day, Mrs. Hopkins, Michael Anagnos, and Miss Marrett (a Perkins teacher) accompanied Sullivan from Perkins to the street corner, the horsecar, and, finally, the train station. There, she wrote much later, she "began to feel really nervous and shaky for the first time." She had never before left Massachusetts, never been on a train alone, and she was traveling to the unknowns of Alabama and the Keller household.

Her friends provided what help they could. Hopkins expressed her maternal affections in a sack lunch. Anagnos made arrangements for a friend of his to meet her at the Washington, D.C., station to help her transfer trains smoothly. They accompanied her on board, barraged her with instructions on train decorum, and left her in the hands of the porter and conductor. She said goodbye with a "very full" heart.[8]

Since we know the happy ending of Anne Sullivan Macy's journey as Helen Keller's teacher, it's easy to forget that she knew of no such guaranteed result. Despair, panic, tears, and desperation dominate the memories that were left of her first trip south. With an inflamed and painful right eye, with feet that by the second day were too swollen to fit into her new and only pair of shoes, the state of her body matched that of her spirit. Train travel, restaurants, and the other novel experiences of the trip gave her little joy.

During this first experiment in independence one thing after another went wrong. She started the trip seated next to a "fidgety, fussy, and inquisitive" elderly woman who promptly lost both their tickets and drew much attention to the pair, only to find the tickets much later safely secured under her false hair. Boston, Philadelphia, Baltimore, and then Washington, D.C., flew by her window. There she missed her connection and learned she would have to spend the night in a hotel. "I thought I would choke," she wrote much later, "my heart was beating so fast. I actually felt dizzy, my mind was a blank." Anagnos's friend, whom she felt considered her a great burden, accompanied her to the hotel only after she begged. With considerable time remaining in the day, he walked her around the White House and Treasury Building. The heat of the day and her tight new shoes, however, left her miserable and they returned to the hotel. "Never had I been so physically uncomfortable and mentally harassed," she remembered.[9]

The hotel felt like an "awful prison cell." Tears exacerbated the soreness and swelling of her right eye; "pain and anxiety made my dreams a continual nightmare." In the morning her watch stopped and only her felt slippers fit over her now swollen feet. In search of the time, she left her room but then couldn't find her way back or remember its number. She barely caught the train that took her from Washington to Lynchburg, Roanoke, Chattanooga, Knoxville, and finally, Tuscumbia. En route a porter kindly brought her ice and towels to ease the pain and swelling of her eye. Later she wrote, "By the time the train stopped in Tuscumbia, the ache in my heart was sharper than that in my flaming eye. Gathering my things together, I longed intensely for my friends back there in Boston. Perkins had never seemed home to me until that moment."[10]

Over the coming years Sullivan wrote most eagerly and with the least restrictions to Hopkins, weekly for at least the first year. When she went through the pile of letters several years later, their quantity surprised her: "[I] wondered how I had any time left for teaching."[11] The majority of these letters, unfortunately, were later destroyed by the leaking attic roof of the home she had shared with her husband, John Macy.

The transformation of Sullivan's letters into a "pottage of yellowish pulp," letters written to the older woman she depended on for maternal care and advice, left her much saddened. They told the story not only of her education of Helen Keller, but also of the beginning of her own slow recognition of herself as a more confident, less volatile, less forlorn young woman. As she reflected on them years later, "Probably, those letters contained the most intimate story that has ever appeared about a young teacher in the heart of a southern family, and the nearest thing to an honest confession of a change of attitude towards many questions that ever happened to me. They told simply, without striving for effect, the story of how an ignorant, opinionated young woman proceeded with her work of teaching a handicapped little girl in unfamiliar and disturbing surroundings, and how her own mind developed as she went along."[12]

Sullivan found the Tuscumbia, Alabama, of 1887 "unfamiliar and disturbing surroundings." Though it was rural and agricultural like Feeding Hills, the social structure and weather bore little resemblance to the countryside of her early years. And life on the margins of culturally sophisticated, reformist, Brahmin Boston bore little resemblance to Alabama's Jim Crow world.[13]

As Sullivan rode from urban Massachusetts to the rural south of Alabama, the train ride itself served as her introduction to southern culture and attitudes toward race. From the capital onward, her train carriage was racially segregated. If any African American woman—such as the Perkins valedictorian two years prior to her, whom she undoubtedly knew—had ridden with her, they would have been forced to move from the "ladies' coach" to the second-class smoker car at the Washington station. Only three years before Annie's ride, African American journalist Ida B. Wells had sued in response to train segregation.

The Keller family that the twenty-year-old Sullivan came to serve embraced an esteemed southern heritage. Helen's father, Arthur H. Keller, had served as a Confederate captain under his mother's second cousin, Robert E. Lee. Captain Keller formerly edited the *North Alabamian* and in 1887 served as U.S. marshal for the northern district of Alabama. Through him, the young Helen claimed Alexander Spotswood, Alabama's first colonial governor, as her great-great-grandfather. The family of Helen's mother, Kate Adams Keller, came originally from Boston but had long lived in Memphis. Helen's maternal grandfather served as a brigadier general for the Confederacy. Through her mother, Helen claimed ancestors in the Everett family (Rev. Edward Everett Hale later played a role in Helen's life).[14]

Captain Arthur Keller considered his family part of the deserving upper-class white elite, though they likely had less than he desired or believed they were entitled to. When Sullivan arrived, the family lived on the homestead Arthur Keller's father had built and named Ivy Green decades earlier due to the "beautiful English ivy" covering trees and fences.[15] Like many other southern landholding, and formerly slaveholding, whites, however, they had lost much of their wealth between 1860 and 1887. The daily physical labor demanded to sustain the household, even when aided by formerly enslaved people and their families, had surprised and exhausted Kate Keller.

At the time of Annie's arrival in 1887 the household consisted of Captain Keller, fifty-one, and his twenty-nine-year-old second wife, Kate. His sons, eighteen-year-old James, only two years younger than Annie, and thirteen-year-old Simpson, remained from his first marriage. Evaline, his unmarried older sister, lived in the household also, helping her brother's family with the housekeeping. Based on the birth dates of Simpson and Helen, Kate married Arthur sometime between

1874, when she would have been sixteen, and 1879, when she would have been twenty-one. Helen, the first child of Arthur and Kate Keller, was born in 1880. Kate gave birth to her second child, Mildred, only four months prior to Anne's arrival.[16]

Helen had become blind and deaf due to an illness at the age of nineteen months. Her parents didn't know what to do with their child. Family members, friends, and neighbors encouraged them to institutionalize her. Talladega, only 170 miles away, hosted both the Alabama School for the Deaf (founded in 1858) and the Alabama School for the Blind (founded in 1867). While technically separated, the schools had at one point shared a campus and were only blocks apart. Keller would not have been the first deaf-blind student, for another had enrolled as early as 1867 (what became of this student educationally is not clear). Neither school admitted African Americans.[17] Apparently neither parent considered sending Helen to either of these schools, which had few resources and plummeting reputations. Like other southern social welfare institutions, both floundered in the years after the Civil War.

As a parent Kate Keller had hopes for her daughter's life and resisted sending her child away from home, though like many Americans at the time she doubted that a deaf-blind child could be taught. In the mid-1880s the literate and well-educated Mrs. Keller read Charles Dickens's *American Notes* (1842) and in it his reference to Samuel Gridley Howe and Laura Bridgman. Mrs. Keller reasoned that if Bridgman had learned such communication, so might her daughter Helen.

As Keller later told the story, and as it has entered our popular culture, Kate Keller's first efforts ended after learning that Howe had died in 1876, but the mother of the young deaf-blind girl persisted. She and her husband tried again, contacting Baltimore oculist Dr. Chisholm. He encouraged them to contact Alexander Graham Bell. Arthur Keller traveled by train first to Baltimore, then to Washington, D.C., with his sister Evaline and a six-year-old and apparently very unruly Helen to consult with Bell personally.[18]

Southerners often looked at educational institutions for deaf and blind children with suspicion because of the link between educational reformers and abolitionism. At Perkins, through Samuel Gridley Howe and Franklin B. Sanborn, the linkage was clear and direct. Despite this,

Arthur and Kate Keller were not alone as they turned to northern educational institutions. Southern whites with resources tended to send deaf or blind children to schools in the North. Northern educational institutions had stronger reputations, greater fiscal resources, enhanced international ties, and more highly educated teachers than did those in the South. When Arthur Keller wrote to Michael Anagnos in search of a governess, he thus allowed his concern for his daughter to trump any hesitancy he had about northern educational institutions.

Neither the Keller household nor the Tuscumbia community had ever encountered anyone like twenty-one-year-old Annie Sullivan. When Kate Keller waited at the segregated train station for her arrival on March 3, 1887, possibly along with stepson James and her husband (sources vary), she was joined by a crowd eager to see "the Yankee girl who was going to teach the Keller child." Sullivan must have appeared less than impressive with her felt slippers and inflamed right eye, dirty and exhausted after several days of traveling. Four days later she told Mrs. Hopkins that "the journey was very long and very tiresome, and when I got here, I was the most forlorn and heartsick girl that had ever been seen in these parts." Mrs. Keller later told Annie that she had been "shocked" and "much troubled" when she saw the eye of the young woman who was supposed to care for her daughter. It was not an auspicious beginning.[19]

When Sullivan entered the gardens of Ivy Green she did so with a northern identity as fierce as the Keller family's southern one. She had grown up idolizing several sworn enemies of slavery and the Confederacy. Both Franklin B. Sanborn, who as General State Inspector of Charities in Massachusetts had enabled her escape from the Tewksbury Almshouse, and Samuel Gridley Howe, the founder of the Perkins Institution, had conspired against slavery as part of John's Brown's Secret Six. In the almshouse and at Perkins she had pored over *The Pilot*, drawn to its coverage of abolitionist and orator Wendell Phillips. And it would have horrified Captain Keller if he ever found out that Sullivan admired Benjamin Butler—the infamous (at least in Alabama) Union "Beast" of New Orleans, supporter of black military regiments in the Civil War and punisher of the Confederacy—because of his rigorous investigation of Tewksbury. Though, as historian Nina

Silber notes, many northerners increasingly "overlooked the history of American slavery" by the 1880s, Sullivan did not do so. All in all, as she later put it, she "did not like the idea of going south to live in a family that had probably been slave-holders."[20]

By the time of Helen Keller's birth in 1880, white Alabamians had brutally silenced the discussions of racial equality and freedom formulated by African Americans during and immediately after the Civil War. As Sullivan arrived in March of 1887, white Alabamians were creating and perpetuating Lost Cause mythology via memoirs, memorials, parades, the glorification of veterans such as Arthur Keller, and a widely celebrated statewide public tour by Jefferson Davis. In the words of historian David Blight, it was the "diehard era" of the Lost Cause, in which Civil War remembrance became "a lucrative industry."[21]

As she left the train station, however, Annie Mansfield Sullivan had more immediate concerns than the post–Civil War development of Lost Cause mythology. Her student awaited her.

Many years later in a public lecture, Macy stated, "I shall not try to tell you of the first months with Helen—what nostalgia, what moods, what doubt, what nights of despair and gathering storms of failure that vanished suddenly with a new word learned by my little pupil, hopes and hidden fears."[22] In published and unpublished form and in public lectures, and during nearly all the remaining periods of her life, however, she left behind more materials on her first years with Helen Keller than on any other phase of her life.

Assessing this material is difficult, most particularly that about Helen. Sullivan's writings on her education of Keller were nearly all produced after her success had become clear—but also contested. At Anagnos's insistence, and with his editing and annotation, she first chronicled her education of Helen for publication by Perkins. In 1901 she and her husband, John Macy, edited and expanded her letters to Sophia Hopkins in a collection meant to accompany the 1903 publication of Keller's *The Story of My Life* and further explain the educational process Sullivan used with her student. In later decades, in response to monetary and professional demands, she produced repeated stories of Helen's early education, some as responses to attacks on her validity as a teacher. Others she produced as various individuals tried to wrest Helen from her life. In literary form, these materials are all markedly similar. Focusing on her initial year with Helen, they describe mounting difficulties, heightened frustration, and fears of failure, followed by joyous and nearly instantaneous success. The overall story left behind is that of the dramatic and stunningly successful education of Helen Keller. The narrative of Annie Sullivan is harder to discern.

Following her intense eagerness to meet six-year-old Helen, Sullivan's first impressions were stark and contradictory. The child standing waiting in the doorway both appalled and attracted her. Helen rushed at the visitor's body and handbag, groping them in search for candy. The Keller family attempted to exercise virtually no control over the willful, impatient, and frequently violent child and gave her free rein to disrupt the household in whatever ways she desired. She rejected Sullivan's attempts to woo her with caresses, tender care, or a doll, and responded peacefully only to cake. Physical coercion seemed the only way to contain her.

Sullivan's initial descriptions of Helen's physical appearance, and the importance she placed upon it, reflect contemporary notions about the appearance of people with disabilities. She expected to see "a pale, delicate child" (perhaps, she admitted, due to Howe's descriptions of Laura Bridgman). She wrote to Mrs. Hopkins that she did not mind "the tumbled hair, the soiled pinafore, the shoes tied with white strings." In fact, she felt much relieved about Helen's appearance, "for if she [Helen] had been deformed, or had acquired any of those nervous habits that so often accompany blindness, and which make an assemblage of blind people such a pitiful sight, how much harder it would have been for me!" Instead, Helen's physical appearance and strength encouraged Sullivan to believe that a correspondingly strong intellect existed. "There's nothing pale or delicate about Helen," she wrote. "She is large, strong, and ruddy, and as unrestrained in her movements as a young colt." Furthermore, "her body is well formed and vigorous, and Mrs. Keller says she has not been ill a day since the illness that deprived her of her sight and hearing. She has a fine head and it is set on her shoulders just right."[23]

Sullivan had limited vision, an inflamed right eye, and still needed to recover fully from her eighth surgery. Her emphasis on bodily presentation is defensive and unflattering, and indicates an inability or refusal to integrate her own disability into her sense of self.

The first week presented difficulties beyond Sullivan's imagining, but the battle of wills emerging between her and Helen (and Helen's parents), and her anxiety over her own future, energized Sullivan. She knew how to be disobedient, belligerent, and stubborn. She knew how to resist and infuriate teachers. Helen's behavior thus made sense to her. Though she packed her bags to leave at least once, was frequently in tears, and suffered pain from her eye at least all the way through May, she embraced her task. Over and over she referred to the "two essential things" she sought to teach Helen: "obedience and love." Sullivan quickly surmised that "it was useless to try to teach her language or anything else until she learned to obey me." She came to believe that "obedience is the gateway through which knowledge, yes, and love, too, enter the mind of the child." Obedience and love were what she had most resisted giving to her own teachers, but were what she most wanted, in fact desperately desired, from Helen.[24]

The two engaged in lengthy, drawn-out physical duels of will. Almost immediately they battled over Helen's "appalling" table manners. The Keller family was accustomed to letting Helen cruise the dining room table, using her unwashed hands to scoop whatever food she desired off of their own plates or directly out of the serving dishes. Sullivan insisted on good table manners. In the ensuing "battle royal" the Keller family evacuated and Sullivan locked the door behind them. Left alone with this new and mysterious household member, Helen lay on the floor, kicking, screaming, and attempting to pull Sullivan's chair out from under her. Repeatedly Helen pinched, and Annie slapped. She physically forced the six-year-old to the chair, "compelling her" to use the spoon. Helen complied temporarily but another "tussle" ensued over folding the napkin. The two battled for hours before Annie released Helen to the warm sunshine and she fell on her own bed exhausted.[25]

Sullivan relied on force. "She wouldn't yield a point without contesting it to the bitter end," she lamented to Hopkins. "To get her to do the simplest thing, such as combing her hair or washing her hands or buttoning her boots, it was necessary to use force, and, of course, a distressing scene followed."[26]

Keller's parents didn't agree on the necessity of force, but they certainly agreed that the resulting physical scenes were distressing. Sullivan considered Helen's family a significant problem. They "have always allowed her to do exactly as she pleased," she complained to Hopkins. "She has tyrannized over everybody ... and like all tyrants she holds tenaciously to her divine right to do as she pleases." Arthur Keller disliked seeing his daughter cry and "naturally felt inclined to interfere" with Sullivan's efforts to gain obedience. This further frustrated Sullivan, never having been one to "give in for the sake of peace."[27]

Within the first week after her March 3 arrival Sullivan came to believe that her only hope for success lay in separating Helen from her family. She first approached Mrs. Keller, arguing that the child needed to "learn to depend on and obey" her before she could make "any headway." Kate Keller agreed to discuss it with her husband. The couple acquiesced, and Captain Keller suggested the use of the family's garden house. It lay only a quarter mile away from Ivy Green but was unfamiliar enough to Helen that she would not be able to find her way home. Her parents could visit every day, surreptitiously viewing their child through the window. A servant could bring meals from the house and tend to the fire. Sullivan felt the garden house was "a genuine bit of paradise." She wrote to Mrs. Hopkins that it included "one large room with a great fireplace, a spacious bay-window, and a small room where our servant, a little negro boy, sleeps." A vine-covered "piazza" spread across the front of the house and a garden lay beyond.[28]

Even in paradise, however, Helen "kicked and screamed herself into a sort of stupor," calming down only for supper. Bedtime resulted in another "terrific tussle" lasting "nearly two hours." "I never saw such strength and endurance in a child," Sullivan wrote Mrs. Hopkins. "But fortunately for us both, I am a little stronger, and quite as obstinate when I set out." A letter from Michael Anagnos assured her that she was doing the right thing. "Strive by every possible means to conquer and control her," he directed. He called their move to the garden house "a movement in the right direction."[29]

Within only a few days Sullivan reported that "my experiment is working out finely." A week later she wrote, "My heart is singing for joy this morning. . . . The wild little creature of two weeks ago has been transformed into a gentle child." Helen could now crochet, string beads quietly, and occasionally let her teacher kiss her, though "she does not return my caresses." By this point, a little more than two weeks after Sullivan's arrival, Helen efficiently fingerspelled several nouns, but Sullivan felt "she has no idea yet that everything has a name." She insisted, however, that "the great step—the step that counts—has been taken. The little savage has learned her first lesson in obedience, and finds the yoke easy."[30]

When Helen and Sullivan returned to Ivy Green on March 27 at the insistence of Mr. and Mrs. Keller, she didn't expect "any serious trouble with Helen in the future." She resolutely wrote to Mrs. Hopkins that "I don't intend that the lessons she has learned at the cost of so much pain and trouble shall be unlearned. I shall stand between her and the over-indulgence of her parents. I have told Captain and Mrs. Keller that they must not interfere with me in any way." The six-year-old, of course, had other plans and tested everyone at the first meal by refusing to use her napkin. Captain Keller stood in the way of Sullivan's discipline, but she succeeded in scolding Helen later.[31]

Pedagogically, Sullivan departed quickly from her original strategy. She had assumed that she would easily "win the love and confidence" of Helen, but in less than a week learned that "I was cut off from all the usual approaches to the child's heart." She accepted the uselessness of her preparations philosophically, with seemingly little stress, and wrote to Mrs. Hopkins that all she could do was "rely on something within us, some innate capacity for knowing and doing." She then used a simple daily routine: playing in the garden, needlework, gymnastics, an hour of learning new words, visits with the farm animals, calls on extended family members when the weather was fine, bedtime preparations, and bed. Sullivan, the self-proclaimed admirer of abolitionists, refused a nurse to attend to Helen's dressing needs, telling Mrs. Keller that "I concluded I'd rather be her nurse than look after a stupid, lazy negress."[32]

"Besides," she admitted to Mrs. Hopkins, most truthfully of all, "I like to have Helen depend on me for everything."[33]

At this point Sullivan still relied on a specific lesson time to teach Helen new words but was beginning to be flexible. By April 3 she reported that Helen "knew" twenty-five nouns and four verbs. She spelled the names of things constantly into Helen's hand and was finding it "easier to teach her things at odd moments than at set times." Helen, however, had not yet made the link between the fingerspelling and communication: "She has no idea as yet what the spelling means." She still failed to realize that every thing and every action had a name, much less the more complex realization that emotions had names or that these words could be strung together to form sentences. She had quickly memorized the fingerspelling for specific objects, but used it only as Sullivan requested. The words still had little meaning.[34]

On April 5 Helen made what Sullivan called "the second great step in her education." For weeks the child had failed to differentiate between the nouns "mug" and "milk," and confused both with the verb "drink." That morning Sullivan taught her the word "water" and realized that it might help resolve the confusion. She took Helen to the pump house and had the child place hold her mug under the spout. While the cold water poured into the mug Sullivan spelled "w-a-t-e-r" into the girl's free hand. "She dropped the mug and stood as one transfixed," Sullivan wrote to Mrs. Hopkins that evening. "A new light came into her face. She spelled 'water' several times." And immediately the child asked the name of "nearly every object she touched," including "Teacher." Within hours she had learned thirty new vocabulary words.[35]

That day Annie claimed a new name: "Teacher." By using it as a name and not simply a descriptive noun, the child Helen allowed Annie to assert herself as a professional and make herself anew.

Sullivan quickly reported the success both to Mrs. Hopkins and to Michael Anagnos. Anagnos urged her to keep "an exact account" of everything "she learns and does every day, without any remarks or comments. Every word she learns should be preserved in chronological order." He directed her to develop "a biographical sketch of Helen." Though he didn't mention Samuel Gridley Howe by name, his instructions coincided almost exactly with Howe's reports on Laura Bridgman's education.[36]

It was Mrs. Hopkins to whom Sullivan expressed her truest emotions. "Last night when I got in bed," she wrote gratefully, "she [Helen] stole into my arms of her own accord and kissed me for the first time, and I thought my heart would burst, so full was it of joy."[37]

Helen's intellectual and emotional transformation led Sullivan to similarly dramatic pedagogical transformations. Within days she asked herself, "How does a normal child learn language?" and rejected the established lesson times and conventional curriculum encouraged by Anagnos and Howe. For weeks, embedded in the female world of socializing and children, she had observed Helen's fifteen-month-old cousin. Like most children of that age, the toddler understood words, sentences, and questions far beyond those that she could speak. Sullivan thus resolved to "talk into her [Helen's] hand as we talk into the baby's ears," using complete sentences rather than word-by-word vocabulary memorization as Howe had. She would assume that Helen had "the normal child's capacity of assimilation and imitation," and simply "wait for results."[38]

The results came exponentially. Helen quickly learned adjectives, adverbs, verbs, location indicators (for example, *in, on*), question words, and pronouns, and began to use simple sentences and idioms. In early June she surprised Sullivan by pretending to write a letter on the Braille slate, emulating her teacher. She expressed an intense desire to share with others what had been taught her, including the manual alphabet. She first learned counting, then basic mathematics, and went on to multiplication. Sullivan taught her to print "square-hand letters" (a form of printing in which all letters are based on the shape of a square), to read words printed with raised letters, and then to read Braille, a skill at which Sullivan never excelled. Once Sullivan had been there a year, she and Helen's Aunt Evaline tried to compile a complete listing of Helen's vocabulary. They got as far as "P" and quit at nine hundred words.[39]

Evidence in letters to Sophia Hopkins indicates that Sullivan also corresponded with Lilian Fletcher, who taught Edith Thomas, a deaf-blind girl at Perkins who was only one year older than Helen. In October, while Helen gobbled up sentences and vocabulary, Fletcher wrote that Edith had only a few nouns but would soon start learning verbs. Fletcher's strategy, emulating that of Howe, was to teach Edith one word at a time. Sullivan privately reveled in her comparative success. To Hopkins, she expressed a competitive pride in her accomplishments: "Poor Lillie—or should I rather say, poor Edith! I didn't suppose that a more incompetent girl could be found to undertake the education of an unfortunate child than myself; but I think Lillie has me beaten by a head at least."[40]

Sullivan also found herself teaching the unexpected, in a parental role. In the fall, as new calves, new puppies, and then a new baby appeared in the extended family, the seven-year-old Helen asked questions about reproduction. "It's a great mistake, I think, to put children off with falsehoods and nonsense," Annie wrote Hopkins. "If it was natural for Helen to ask such questions, it was my duty to answer them." She took Helen and her botany book up into the tree they often used for reading, "and I told her in simple words the story of plant-life." They discussed the seeds she had planted in the spring, and Sullivan explained that "all life comes from an egg." She reassured Hopkins that "the function of sex I passed over as lightly as possible," but that she had tried to teach Helen that "love is the great continuer of life."[41]

Sullivan, whose education in sexuality and reproduction primarily occurred at Tewksbury, perhaps had inadequate or mistaken knowledge of sex. Perhaps she felt herself to know far too much for a woman of her desired social standing. Regardless, the remaining letters to Hopkins and her discussion of this event include no indication that she included an explanation of reproduction, or asked permission of Helen's parents to do so. Increasingly she took responsibility, without hesitation, for all aspects of Helen's education and well-being.

Even in the partial materials remaining from this period, Sullivan's increased assuredness and sense of self emerge. She had no doubts about her decision to discard the existing curriculum and Howe's teaching strategies. In fact, she wrote as early as May of 1887 that, "I am beginning to suspect all elaborate and special systems of education." In June she told Mrs. Hopkins in confidence that "something within me tells me that I shall succeed beyond my dreams." Though she knew it "high improbable" and "absurd," she wondered if "Helen's education would surpass in interest and wonder Dr. Howe's achievement." Her own abilities and self-confidence as a teacher awed and amazed her: "I had no idea a short time ago how to go to work; I was feeling about in the dark; but somehow I know now, and I know that I know ... [that] when difficulties arise ... I know how to meet them. ... It is wonderful."[42]

Helen, the same age as Jimmie when he died, satiated the desires of the twenty-year-old for love, physical contact, connection, and family in ways that Mrs. Hopkins could not, and in ways that Michael Anagnos certainly did not. Sullivan freely expressed her affections for Hopkins. "Have I not all my life been lonely?" she wrote. "Until I knew you, I never loved anyone, except my little brother." Yet, Helen provided something new. For the first time in her life, she felt lucky: "There must have been one lucky star in the heavens at my birth, and I am just beginning to feel its beneficent influence." Helen threw herself and her affections at Sullivan in the unrestrained way that only a child could, and Sullivan clung to that affection. "I feel in every heartbeat that I belong to Helen, and it awes me when I think of it—this giving of one's self that another may live. God help me make the gift worth while! It is a privilege to love and minister to such a rare spirit. It is not in the nature of man to love so entirely and dependently as Helen. She does not merely absorb what I give, she returns my love with interest, so that every touch and act seems a caress."[43]

As she started the new year of 1888, Sullivan freely acknowledged the transformation occurring within her and Helen's responsibility for that transformation. "It is a great thing to feel that you are of some use in the world, that you are necessary to somebody. Helen's dependence on me for almost everything makes me strong and glad."[44]

Increasingly confident, Sullivan simultaneously struggled. Some letters indicate she struggled emotionally. After six months she had expressed enough dissatisfaction to Anagnos that he wrote her a pep talk. "Look steadily at the polar star of your work," he wrote. "Do not allow yourself to be troubled by petty annoyances, or to remember them and harbor ill feelings even temporarily against anyone, however ignorant or indiscreet he or she may be." Even after being in Tuscumbia a year, as Helen's education was celebrated nearly across the globe, she admitted to Mrs. Hopkins that she struggled with "that feeling of restlessness that takes possession of me sometimes. It overflows my soul like a tide, and there is no escape from it. It is more torturing than any physical pain I have endured." She placed her hope for happiness in Helen: "I pray constantly that my love for this beautiful child may grow so large and satisfying that there will be no room in my heart for uneasiness and discontent." As an older woman reflecting back on her life, she acknowledged that her first year in Tuscumbia often included "periods of mental distress and oppression." She admitted that "sometimes they were frightful." She blamed her youth and isolation: "I was young, and there was no one near whom I could trust to lead me through the labyrinth of change and disillusionment. Outwardly I was aggressive and opinionated, but within I was timid and uncertain."[45]

Sullivan's descriptions of her life in Tuscumbia focused almost exclusively either on Helen or on the characteristics that made the region both southern and disagreeable (in her opinion). Her criticisms ranged widely, including the "untidy, shiftless manner of keeping house," "the shabbiness of the grounds and out-houses," and the muddy state of country roads. "Finding it very difficult not to air my righteous indignation," she ignored the advice of her friends and argued the Civil War vigorously with Keller family members, particularly Captain Keller's brother Frank. After one bitter argument with "Uncle Frank"—in which "all the torrents of my wrath broke restraint, and I opened fire, and I did not cease until I had my say out to the last bitter word"—she temporarily packed her carpetbag to leave.[46] Reflecting on her first year, she wrote to Mrs. Hopkins, "The arrogance of these southern people is most exasperating to a northerner. To hear them talk, you would think they had won every battle in the Civil War, and that the Yankees were little better than targets for them to shoot at." She reassured Mrs. Hopkins, however, that her "quick temper and saucy tongue" had been curtailed. In perhaps an exaggeration, she said that though there was often "murder and treason and arson in my heart . . . they haven't gotten out, thanks to the sharpness of my teeth which have often stood guard over my tongue."[47]

Yet, Sullivan grew to find Tuscumbia agreeable. Years later she could acknowledge that "I found life in the South pleasant when I stopped discussing the Civil War with Uncle Frank." She remained busy and entertained, yet calmer. As she wrote years later, "There was more lei-

sure, more sociability, more enjoyment of the little pleasures of existence, less strenuousness and emphasis on culture, less desperate effort
to stem the tide of life that can never be stemmed."[48]

By Sullivan's first fall in Tuscumbia, it was becoming clear that she
and Helen could become public figures. Anagnos asked her to prepare
"a brief account" that included "Helen's history and education, giving
her age, the cause of her blindness and deafness, her temperament, her
natural aptitude, the steps taken and methods employed in her training, and what has already been accomplished." As Howe had published
his reports on Laura Bridgman, Anagnos wished to publish accounts
of Helen Keller in the forthcoming Perkins annual report. He urged
his former student to do this for her own sake as well as "for the credit
of your alma mater." In subsequent letters he requested photographs
and copies of letters Helen had written. Captain Keller agreed, telling
Sullivan that it was her "duty to give others the benefit of my experiences." She did so but told Mrs. Hopkins, "I do not know myself how
it happened, except that I got tired of saying 'no.'"[49]

CHAPTER 6

Tuscumbia, 1888–1891

IN JANUARY 1888 the Perkins annual report arrived in Tuscumbia. For months Sullivan had labored over her own report to Anagnos. The entire household had been involved in acquiring photographs and Helen's letters. Captain and Mrs. Keller, Sullivan, and other household members must have eagerly descended, though perhaps with some trepidation, on the publication they knew would be featuring Helen.

In a thirty-five-page section entitled "Helen Keller,—A Second Laura Bridgman," Michael Anagnos spared no grandiosity. No deaf blind student, Anagnos proudly proclaimed, could match Helen Keller. "It is no hyperbole," he hyperbolized, "to say that she is a phenomenon." Her letters, reproduced in the report, proved "their tiny author is a most extraordinary little individual . . . a mental prodigy, an intellectual phenomenon." In fact, he claimed, "her achievements are little short of a miracle." She even, he asserted, "excels her prototype"—Laura Bridgman.[1]

Anagnos made sure that the readers knew of Helen's direct link to Samuel Gridley Howe, Perkins, and himself. "The discovery of ways and means for rescuing persons afflicted with combined blindness and deafness from the dread dungeon of deathlike darkness and stillness" was, he insisted, a grand achievement. And the world owed it all to Samuel Gridley Howe. As an "apostle of liberation," with "no precedent to follow, no indices to be guided by," Howe had "entered upon the task of piercing a trackless forest." His victory, "like a column of holy fire, blazed upon the pathway and indicated the course to be traversed by his successors." Just as "after the glorious discovery of Christopher Columbus the Atlantic ocean became a common thoroughfare," so now were Howe's pedagogical methods adopted as the "standard" across the globe.[2]

Anagnos told of Captain Keller's letter to Perkins, and his subsequent preparation of Sullivan. The Perkins valedictorian, he claimed, "studied Laura Bridgman's case thoroughly," "perused voluminous books on mental development," and took her inspiration from Howe. She "read the reports of Dr. Howe with assiduous care, mastered his methods and processes in their minutest details, and drank copiously of his noble spirit." Only after she was thus prepared had he recommended her "most highly and without any reservation" to the Keller family.[3]

He acknowledged that Sullivan deserved some credit. Getting her age wrong, he gave a much abbreviated and edited version of her life story. From a "very inauspicious" childhood "of a most distressing character," she arrived at Perkins in 1880 with a "painfully meager" educational background. Yet, "the furnace of hardships through which she passed was not without beneficent results," as she rose to "overcome obstacles." She was, he boasted proudly, "a worthy successor" to Howe and "an honor to the graduates of this institution."[4]

The morning after the report arrived, Sullivan wrote to Mrs. Hopkins. She appreciated the "kind things" Anagnos had said but complained that "his extravagant way of saying them rubs me the wrong way." The motives he ascribed to her particularly frustrated her. "You know, and he knows, and I know," she grumbled, "that my motive in coming here was not in any sense philanthropic. How ridiculous it is to say I had drunk so copiously of the noble spirit of Dr. Howe that I was fired with the desire to rescue from darkness and obscurity the little Alabamian!" She had needed a job and had "seized upon the first opportunity" available.[5]

Sullivan's letter to Anagnos differed radically. In the years ahead she would become less circumspect in her letters to him, but at this point she still needed his support. "My dear Mr. Anagnos," she wrote solemnly, "I have read the Report with great pleasure, especially the page devoted to my self." She went on, "I hardly know how to describe the satisfaction I felt at being thus spoken of by you." It left her, she said, "with the desire to deserve" the words of praise. She appealed to him to visit Tuscumbia. In return, Anagnos assured her of his deep interest in her and her work. "I love you and take as much pride in you," he assured her, "as if you were my own daughter."[6]

What Arthur, Kate, and Helen Keller initially thought of the report and its immediate consequences is not known. Arthur Keller enjoyed the letters he received from individuals of prestige. Perkins arranged to have the report's section on Helen reprinted in pamphlet form, and several magazines published articles on Helen.[7] Helen's parents must have been pleased with the report and its subsequent publicity, for they echoed Sullivan's request and offered a formal invitation for Anagnos to visit Ivy Green. Their daughter, who once had caused worry and shame, now generated pride and acclaim.

In March 1888 Michael Anagnos finally met the young Helen Keller, whom he had done his best to connect to Perkins and to make famous. It also was the first opportunity for Captain and Mrs. Keller to meet the man to whom they later often would relinquish their daughter. And for Anagnos, it was the first opportunity to see Annie Sullivan as an adult woman, a teacher, and an independent figure. The visit must have gone well. From a return stopover in Louisville, he expressed his pride to Sullivan. "I take as much interest in you and in the success of your work as if you were my own daughter," he reiterated. "In fact," he expanded, "I consider you as such." He encouraged her to write him "and talk to me freely whenever you feel like doing so." The next day he said the same: "Pray write to me when you can . . . and do not hesitate to let me know if you have any troubles."[8]

As Helen's fame increased, and as Anagnos, on behalf of Perkins and Howe, took responsibility for her successful education, the relationship between Sullivan and Anagnos became both stronger and more complex. While Annie was a student at Perkins, the pair had enjoyed each other despite, or perhaps because of, their often contentious relationship. Their verbal combat and tests of will were playful, while at the same time each fought to win. The older man, widowed and childless, now took great pride in Sullivan and gave her significant financial assistance. He also began to see her as an independent person, and a woman to whom other men were drawn. In practical terms, he must have known that she also held the key to his continued access to Helen and Helen's story. Sullivan often bristled at (presumably) unintentional slights, or what she interpreted as slights, in his letters, and the two danced sometimes awkwardly, sometimes smoothly, sometimes contentiously, through their correspondence.

Sullivan responded to Anagnos's requests for greater intimacy with her own similar requests, and addressed him more familiarly in conversation than she had before. Upon his return to Boston she urged him not to work too hard: "do try to be a little careful, like a good man." She had a favor to ask of him, "something to please me very much." Just as he wanted her to write freely, she asked that he do the same. "I would like so very much to be a 'grown-up' daughter to you. Will you let me? Please do not be offended with me asking so much." She reminded him of her growing reputation with a "funny" story of a journalist who had shown up at Ivy Green with a request to interview her. Captain Keller "refused to allow him to see me," but she expected "another visitation any hour." Sullivan's response "delighted" Anagnos. "I shall count it as a great pleasure," he told her, "to consider you as my daughter, and to be of help and service to you."[9]

Over the next weeks Anagnos wrote Sullivan with instructions regarding both her and Helen. Annie had had "one of those nervous attacks caused by using my eyes too constantly," and had told Mrs. Hopkins but not him. Hopkins told Anagnos, who resented being excluded and cautioned Annie about her health. She responded to the advice with slightly less circumspection than she had the Perkins annual report. "I do not mind the 'little lecture' the least bit," she wrote. "This does not mean that I shall not endeavor to do as you advise in all things in regards to my dear little pupil . . . [but] please remember that 'commands' are quite unnecessary. I dislike them from those I love." She qualified her discontent by adding, "but I will gladly do anything you wish me to."[10]

In the midst of this correspondence Sullivan received a copy of a *Boston Herald* article about Helen. She complained to Mrs. Hopkins about the "stupid article" and blamed Anagnos for furnishing the materials. "The facts have a Greek magnitude which would be rather startling if one didn't guess the source." She thought it "amusing" to read the article's version of her preparations for her task. "Perhaps I am ungrateful," she said, "but I can't get up a great deal of enthusiasm for the wretched, farcical education with which my alma mater furnished [me and] equipped me for life's battle." She found the "little red dictionary" Hopkins gave her "far more useful than all the Physics and Geometry and Physiology they crammed me with."[11]

The contrast between Sullivan's letters to Anagnos and those to Hopkins is sometimes stark. Perhaps she still felt economically dependent on him, still scared for her future, and hesitated to voice displeasure. Frequently, however, she had the upper hand. She often ignored his directives, yet convinced him that she was doing what he desired. Whether annoyed or pleased with him, she manipulated him in order to receive repeated statements of affection and approval. She frequently used him to get what she wanted with the Kellers. Throughout the late 1880s and 1890s the older widower expressed increasing emotional reliance on the young woman, drawing her into his household management details and health concerns.

That spring Sullivan and her student continued to draw increasing attention. In April 1888 the ministers of the Alabama Presbytery met in Tuscumbia and Captain Keller showed off his daughter to those in attendance. The same week Sullivan received her first invitation to give a public lecture, at the Normal School in Florence, Alabama. Being recognized as a pedagogical expert thrilled her, but she belittled it to Anagnos: "Did you ever hear of anything so ridiculous?" In May, some of the household visited a medical convention in Cincinnati. They met medical and political dignitaries, and "wherever [Helen] went she was the centre of interest." The family distributed "the extracts from the report that Mr. Anagnos sent," and "could have disposed of a thousand" if they had them.[12]

Sullivan used these opportunities to communicate her growing reputation, her womanly availability, and her humor to Anagnos. Of the ministers she wrote, "[T]hirty such stupid and homely men I have never met before. If they had only been moderately good looking one might excuse the length, logic and nonsense of their fire and brimstone sermons. But being as ugly as it was possible for them to be one felt like saying very disagreeable things about them." She toyed with him by expressing a desire to offer her educational services to the Duke of Norfolk, who had a blind son.[13]

Anagnos replied as Sullivan wanted him to. The year before he had playfully teased her about a doctor in Tuscumbia whom he believed wished to court her. Now he instructed her to tell Captain Keller that it was "positively dangerous to invite good looking men to dinner or inside his premises," for "masculine beauty and the medical profession are the two weakest points with the teacher of his child." He went on to coyly tell her that Captain Keller should instead "invite as many plain and stupid clergymen as he can afford to feed." He told her that the invitation from the Florence Normal School was "a natural one," and encouraged her to accept it. He counseled her, with "the deliberate advice of one who believes in you implicitly," that her work was "with Helen and not the sons of dukes and princes."[14]

In late May 1888, Sullivan, Helen, and Mrs. Keller left Tuscumbia to visit Perkins and Anagnos. Sullivan had longed for the visit. As early as January of that year she had begged Anagnos to "induce" Helen's parents to let them spend several months in Boston each year. Once the decision had been made she repeatedly told Anagnos, "You can not imagine how anxious I am to come home." Even as she celebrated Helen's April success with the Alabama Presbytery she wrote to Mrs. Hopkins, "I wonder if the days seem as interminable to you as they do to me. We talk and plan and dream of nothing but Boston, Boston, Boston." As the visit came closer, however, Sullivan began to worry about whether or not Bostonians would be "disappointed" in the much celebrated Helen Keller.[15]

Sullivan need not have worried. The trip began with a successful Washington, D.C., visit to Alexander Graham Bell. Since first meeting the Keller family in 1887 he had followed Helen closely and expressed much pleasure in the results of her education. Sullivan, Helen, and Kate Keller then visited President Cleveland in the White House. Helen reported, "Mr. Cleveland was very glad to see me."[16] Only two years earlier Sullivan had followed Cleveland's wedding in the newspa-

pers and envied the beauty of his bride Frances Folsom, who had been
his ward. At that time the much older and recently widowed Anagnos
had told her how much she, his ward, reminded him of the beautiful
Folsom. The visit, and its dramatic reminder of the changes in her
life, must have both thrilled and amazed her. It may have caused her,
perhaps not for the first time, to wonder about her relationship with
Michael Anagnos.

Then they arrived in Boston. Almost two years to the day after her
1886 graduation, Sullivan entered as a returning heroine, a hometown
girl made good who had put Perkins in the pedagogical spotlight once
again. Helen instantly became the institutional darling. For months
she'd been corresponding with students and immediately "entered with
delight into their occupations." For the first time, she experienced a
place where "almost every one she met understood her language." The
two also figured prominently at graduation. Though no one was gradu-
ating that year, announcements advertised the event with proclama-
tions that both Laura Bridgman (celebrating fifty years at Perkins) and
Helen Keller would be present. The "second Laura Bridgman, Helen
Keller" exhibited her use of the manual alphabet. Despite Bridgman's
anniversary, at the close of the event "many lingered to greet little
Helen, to watch her animated face and gestures, and, perchance, to
receive a word or two from her nimble fingers."[17]

Soon after graduation Kate Keller returned to the anonymity of
Tuscumbia. For the first time, Sullivan had sole responsibility for
Helen, and for the first time, Helen left her mother for a long period.
The two stayed at Perkins for approximately six weeks, spent July and
August in Brewster with Mrs. Hopkins, and then returned to Perkins
until mid-October.

These months filled quickly with lessons, new experiences, and socializing with the Perkins community as well as the elite of Boston. At
Perkins Sullivan had access to Boston as well as the library of Braille
books, embossed books, and embossed maps. Over the summer she
began to teach Helen French. At Brewster they both enjoyed the sea.
Helen soon lost all fear, thriving in the waves and unexpected saltiness
of the water. Sullivan took Helen to meet her beloved hermit friend
who lived in the sand dunes, but he had died since her visit two years

before. Her letters to Anagnos no longer remain, but some of his responses do. They reflect her moodiness and his desires to assuage it. Sometimes he thanked her for letters "full of spirit and [truly] representative of yourself in your better moods"; at other times he expressed regret that she was "discontented and disposed to take a gloomy view of your inability to reach the heights of absolute bliss."[18]

Sullivan presumably savored the time with Mrs. Hopkins, whom she had not seen in two years. Her last visit to Brewster had been in the discouraging months immediately following her Perkins graduation. She now had a radically different life. Only four months before, she had expressed her thanks to the older woman from her current vantage point of young adulthood: "I thank you from the bottom of my heart for the mother-love you gave me when I was a lonely, troublesome school girl, whose thoughtlessness must have caused you no end of anxiety. It is a blessed thing to know that there is some one who rejoices with us when we are glad." At one point in the summer the three went to visit the gravesite of Hopkins's only child, Florence. Helen effortlessly read the name inscribed on the tombstone. Upon returning to the house she quickly understood the toys and books to have once belonged to Florence.[19]

That summer Anagnos still communicated easily with Sullivan. He responded to an attack of hers cheerfully, saying he appreciated her "friendly criticisms and suggestions."[20] In the fall the teacher and student returned to Tuscumbia for the 1888–1889 school year, with Sullivan periodically sending discontented letters to Anagnos. The 1888 election kept her entertained, but the possibility of a Republican victory threatened Captain Keller financially due to the probable loss of his appointment as federal marshal. (This did in fact occur.) In November she complained about being "shut up, caged so to speak, in this horrid little town." She later reported that "Our lives here go on in an even monotony. Today is exactly like yesterday and tomorrow will be just like today unless God in his wisdom sees fit to send us an earthquake or a tornado." An unnamed suitor, speculated about by Mrs. Keller, might have kept things interesting, but Sullivan reported, flirtatiously and manipulatively, to Anagnos that Mrs. Keller's "hopes and fears about the Major were groundless. . . . I am doomed to be an old maid."[21]

In late December she picked a fight with Anagnos. "May heaven pour its richest blessings upon your obstinate head!" he responded affectionately. "This is the cordial wish of me who loves you dearly and thinks of you more often than written words can tell." In the one-sided correspondence that remains from this period, Anagnos continued his efforts to placate her throughout January of 1889. Eye pain caused her to be temporarily confined to her room. "I beg of you, darling," he counseled, likely ineffectively, "to make the best of everything. . . . Keep your rebellious heart under strict control. Do not allow yourself either to show temper or say a sharp word."[22]

Anagnos, at this point, had his own problems. He was exhausted and had health concerns. Soon after Sullivan and Helen had left Perkins to return to Tuscumbia in the fall he wrote, "I feel very lonesome without you. I hope that you will continue to think of your poor old grandfather as much as you ever did." He began preparations for a three-month leave of absence in Europe. While he attempted to appease Sullivan with soothing responses to her problems, she in turn scolded him.[23] She laid into him about the 1888 Perkins annual report after it appeared early in 1889. He had hoped for her approval. One-fourth of the 280-page volume, he reported to her as it went to press in December, "is wholly devoted to Helen's case."[24] The resulting report spared no detail.

In his statement in the new report, Anagnos praised Sullivan but in no uncertain terms once again laid the bulk of the glory for Helen's education in the lap of the dead Samuel Gridley Howe. He introduced Sullivan to readers by reminding them that she had no "ground for serious apprehension of failure on her part." All she had to do to educate Helen was follow the "course . . . clearly and definitely indicated by the finger of the illustrious liberator of Laura Bridgman. His glorious achievement stood before her like a peerless beacon, illuminating her pathway, urging her onward, and filling her heart with hope and encouragement." Using this beacon, "following the simplest and most direct methods of Dr. Howe," Sullivan naturally met with "speedy and grand success." The "stupendous feat was accomplished instanta-neously, as by the touch of a magic wand."[25]

Sullivan's responses spared no sarcasm, the opening volley in what would become a long war over who deserved the credit for Helen's education: Howe or Sullivan. She began by thanking Anagnos for "the efforts you have made to benefit me." However, she quickly gave a hint of her forthcoming wrath by qualifying her words of thanks. "I cannot doubt that you have my interest at heart," she said. Still, she wished that "there had been less publicity about the matter of Hel-en's education" for the "notoriety is invariably accompanied by various annoyances."[26]

Then began the serious sarcasm. If information on her education of Helen was of only "the slightest assistance to the busy educators" she would "gladly" share her experiences. However, she reminded Anagnos, repeating his own words back to him, "you say in your report, that there are no uncertain problems to solve, no untried experiments to make, no new processes to invent, and no trackless forest to traverse." If that the case, "is it not the height of presumption to ask teachers and philosophers to read seventy pages of matter on a subject which was exhausted some forty years ago by the 'illustrious liberator of Laura Bridgman'?" She certainly deserved, she wrote, no "special congratula-tion for following a course which *was clearly* and definitely *indicated* by another" [underlined in original]. "Forgive me also when I tell you," she went on firmly, "that if you do believe what your words seem to indicate that I do not share your opinions."[27]

Anagnos spent February and March defending himself to his for-mer pupil. Immediately upon receiving her first letter he responded, "Dearest Anna, you spoke so sarcastically in one of your letters about my remarks on your sketch of Helen, that I do not like to refer to it again." He went on at length, however, trying to assure her that "noth-ing is farther from my mind than the thought of flattering you." He insisted, "my words neither belittle your work nor detract anything from its real value." Her response "deeply grieved" him. In early March he wrote to her that if she read "carefully," she would see that he re-ferred only to the "means and methods" used to educated deaf-blind people, not the "education" itself. "Now," he went on, "is there the slightest doubt that Mr. Howe, and he alone, established this royal road and that his successors follow in his path step by step?" He tried sarcasm, but was never as good as Sullivan: "Has it ever occurred to you to convey information to Helen's mind through her toes, or the back of her head or her nose?" Certainly not, he insisted; but just as Christopher Columbus had set the path across the Atlantic so did Howe set the path for educating deaf-blind children.[28]

A week later he again sought to smooth things over and tried his own hand at manipulation. He reassured Sullivan that "the little discussion which we have had was one of those pressing events which leaves no unfavorable traces behind them." It had, he promised, not "the slightest effect on my love and feelings toward you." His extremely short letter included the fact that he had been confined to his room for several days "with severe pain," and was "still suffering and unable to write a long letter."[29] One wonders if she felt guilty.

While Anagnos went to Europe to repair his health, Sullivan traveled to Boston in June to receive medical care for her eyes. What medical procedure was performed is unclear, but she had been experiencing problems with her eyes for months. Doctors likely scraped her eyes once more to remove the scar tissue of trachoma. Keller later documented that during this time Sullivan could read only by placing books very close to her face, and had to move her head from side to side. With the help of Anagnos, and the approval of Captain Keller, she arranged for a Perkins teacher to serve as "Helen's companion" during her absence.[30]

Whether or not Sullivan returned to Tuscumbia in the fall is unclear, but she and Helen spent the winter of 1889–1890 in Boston—this time without Anagnos in residence. He sent frequent letters detailing how he had told everyone abroad about Helen, including the Queen of Greece. Although Helen's story had attracted immense attention to Perkins, she and her teacher shared a nebulous status at the school. She was not an official student, and Sullivan was neither student nor employee. Anagnos, who possibly held the most sway with Sullivan, could do little from Europe to smooth her relations with others at the school.

Though almost no primary source documentation from this period remains, Sullivan later characterized the winter as contentious. The dynamics of power were shifting and she was uncertain about which way they would go. Helen, as one of the most glorified celebrities and media darlings of the Boston Brahmins, received frequent invitations to prestigious parties. Sullivan often felt herself treated like a servant, called on only as a tool for audiences to use in communicating with Helen. According to Henney, Sullivan once "snatched Helen away" and stomped out of a party. Another time the invitation included Helen's name but not hers. Sullivan refused to attend, which meant Helen did not go. To Boston's elite and wealthy philanthropists accustomed to deference, Sullivan's insolence served as proof of her inappropriateness as a guide for the miracle child.[31]

In the midst of this, Helen began voice articulation lessons. Both she and Sullivan knew of Alexander Graham Bell's advocacy of oralism for the deaf, but never had anyone taught articulation to a deaf-blind person. In March 1890 they heard of a deaf-blind Norwegian girl, Ragnhild Kaata, who had learned to speak. At Helen's insistence, Sullivan sought the help of Sarah Fuller, principal of Boston's Horace Mann School for the Deaf. Helen and Sullivan tried to claim the results of her eleven lessons as a success, but the results frustrated both of them. Helen wanted to speak, and Sullivan, though she never acknowledged it, must have known that if it had worked she could claim success where Howe had not. Helen began to articulate, but her voice nearly always required interpretation by Sullivan or someone accustomed to hearing her.[32]

In the spring of 1890, Sullivan's reputation for insolence expanded. The *Boston Journal* published an interview in which she explained her and Helen's status at Perkins as follows: "I have the whole charge of her, and my salary is paid by her father." This explanation essentially agreed with earlier statements by Anagnos, but to a board of trustees already angered by her lack of deference toward philanthropists and defensive about Perkins's reputation, this threw gasoline on the fire. The events forced Sullivan to write a letter of apology to the Perkins board, which included her earlier hero, Franklin B. Sanborn. "It was farthest from my mind," she pled, "to speak lightly of my obligations to my school; and I beg that though you blame me for indiscretion, you will not blame me for ingratitude." Rejecting her apology, the trustees rescinded plans for Helen to speak at commencement ceremonies in order that the school not claim credit for her education.[33]

In July, after returning to Tuscumbia, Sullivan finally admitted the long series of mishaps to Anagnos with multiple apologies. Though he was still in Europe, his influence mattered. She began with the articulation. Not only had it ended without the results she desired, but Anagnos had learned of it from someone else. She admitted, "You certainly had a right to expect that you would be kept informed of Helen's doings, and you should have been mad were it not." She halfheartedly insisted that she had sent a letter that he must not have gotten, but confusingly went on, "But I have not the heart to enter into details which are so unpleasant again."[34]

With little explanation, she briefly went into the matter of her battle with the Perkins trustees. She enclosed the letter of apology, and said, "it explains itself." Presumably Anagnos had heard of the winter's clashes and the eventual confrontation from other sources. She only added, "You cannot regret more than I do your absence from home this year."[35]

Sullivan's final apologetic explanation concerned Helen's religious education. Samuel Gridley Howe had believed that an educated human soul, thirsting to discern the world, eventually would discover the existence of a transcendent spiritual being on its own. He thus attempted to eliminate all discussions of God, all exposure to religion, from Laura Bridgman's life. This part of his grand experiment failed miserably, for he could not isolate her in such a way. Anagnos wanted to bring Howe's experiment to fruition, encouraging Sullivan to isolate Helen from discussions of religion. The teacher made an effort, but the people around Helen, the literature and history they read, their discussions of creation and science, prompted question after question from the inquisitive child. By early 1890 Sullivan had found Helen's questions too much to handle and sought the assistance of the Reverend Phillips Brooks, the rector at Trinity Church, an Episcopalian preacher at Harvard, and a major Boston religious figure. Sullivan apparently asked neither Anagnos, nor Arthur and Kate Keller, about this decision. She tried to appease Anagnos: "It was impossible to keep the knowledge from her any longer. She had met with so many references to religious things in books that the curiosity was awakened. What could I do but satisfy her thirst for this new knowledge in as broad and Christian a way as I could? I went to Mr. Brooks for advice and I found him very willing to help both Helen and myself."[36]

From the spring of 1890 until November 1891, almost a year and a half, Helen and Sullivan stayed in Tuscumbia. Though Anagnos repeatedly requested that Sullivan submit a "full, authentic account" of Helen's education, and promised she would receive "all the credit" for her work, she wrote nothing. Very little about Helen or Sullivan appeared in the 1889 and 1890 Perkins annual reports. At one point she blamed her eyes, but as she received no medical treatment during this time this explanation may have been only a means of evasion.[37]

Sullivan continued to settle into the Keller household and its life in Tuscumbia. Though the monotony she had complained about earlier may have continued, and though she tried to find a way for herself and Helen to leave for Boston as the school year started in 1891, Tuscumbia offered much easier social terrain than Boston. Years later she characterized Tuscumbia as "a very pretty place in some ways." Its one street held "stores and many nice houses" and the magnolia trees were "very beautiful." Yet, "there was nothing else to speak of in Tuscumbia." She and Helen often took long walks, visiting the area's water spring or the "poor cabins" of the region's African American population. "The negroes were very kind to us," she remembered, "and gave us fruit and berries and sometimes fried chicken."[38]

Captain Keller she considered a "good-natured man, fond of fishing and hunting, a good shot, an agreeable companion" and "one of the best story-tellers" she had ever heard. He was liked, she believed, "for his neighborliness and geniality." He was "hospitable rather than intellectual," and "thought everything southern desirable, noble and eternal." Though she considered his "ideas and abilities" to be "ordinary," the family must have enjoyed verbal repartee. During a household argument over Tolstoy's *My Religion*, his wife once compared his logic to "playing leap-frog blindfold[ed]."[39]

Sullivan left much lengthier reminiscences about Kate Keller, but perhaps only because the two spent significantly more time together.

Not only were both female, but Arthur Keller died in 1896 and Mrs. Keller spent a significant amount of time with Helen and Sullivan before her own death in 1921. Years later Annie described Kate Keller as "a very tall, beautifully formed woman." Though she was "reticent" and "aloof," Sullivan admired her "delicate poise" and admitted that she "awkwardly tried to imitate" this woman who was only seven years her senior. She admired the older woman's "intellectual side" and remembered that a "discussion with Mrs. Keller was a test of one's metal [sic]." Helen's mother read widely, and loved to discuss books. She shared Carlyle, Thomas Hardy, and the poems of Byron with Sullivan. She loved politics, was "an ardent woman suffragist," and had "to an unusual degree the gift of swift rejoinder and vivid phrase."[40]

In addition to pursuing her intellectual interests, Kate Keller worked tremendously hard. In 1888 Sullivan had explained Mrs. Keller's failure to write to Anagnos by saying that "her failure to write is due to the same cause which keeps her house looking as though a hurricane had past [sic] over it, around it and through it. She is careless about everything and yet she is good hearted and sincere." Years later, having managed a household of her own, Sullivan was more forgiving. "In time," she wrote, "I came to have great admiration for southern women. It seemed to me that the burdens of life were carried by them." Kate Keller helped to raise vegetables, fruit, pigs, turkeys, chickens, and lambs. The young bride produced her own butter, lard, bacon, and hams; processed her own pickles, tomatoes, chili sauces, and jellies; was known for her homemade preserves and dried fruits; maintained a beautiful flower garden, featuring roses; sewed for her children; managed her children and stepchildren; and supervised the household servants. In addition she was "a wonderful cook." Sullivan, who had never learned to cook, later wrote that "whatever skill I had in the culinary art I learned from Mrs. Keller."[41]

During the summer of 1891 Sullivan tried to arrange for her and her pupil to return to Perkins for the school year. For financial reasons, Captain Keller said no. Sullivan appealed to Anagnos for help and he responded as she desired. He offered to fund Helen's travel, necessary clothing, railway fares, and other extra expenses so she and Sullivan might spend the school year at Perkins. Captain Keller vetoed the idea.

At the same time, Sullivan finally agreed to resume her contributions to the Perkins annual report. Anagnos warned her in advance that she would be "vexed" by what he had included about Helen's religious education.[42]

Sullivan replied with firmness that "of course" it was his "privilege" to write whatever he wanted, but warned that she claimed "the same right." Making a veiled threat, she reminded him that she trusted him "not to omit from my report anything which explains my position on the matter." Asserting her authority she wrote, "as the responsibility rests wholly with me, I do not wish it to be misunderstood."[43]

She assuaged her sharp response with the inclusion of "a little story Helen wrote" for his birthday—"The Frost King." It was, she thought, "pretty and original." The story delighted him. He thanked her, saying that despite the lengthy and already finished annual report, he "must make room in it for the Frost King." He called the story "a most marvelous production." He assured her and Helen that "there is no man, woman or child in the state of Alabama who can write such a story."[44]

Whatever tensions existed between Sullivan and Anagnos quickly disappeared in mid-November 1891 in the face of more immediate concerns. One of Helen's dogs, a mastiff named Lioness, given her by admirer and philanthropist William Wade of Pennsylvania, bit Sullivan on the hand. The household feared rabies. Either Sullivan or one of the Kellers quickly contacted Anagnos, revealing whom everyone believed most responsible for Annie, and gave him the power to decide what to do. "Pray go at once to the Pasteur Institute," he directed her, "and arrange to remain there for treatment as long as it may be necessary." He could not meet her in New York but would request that a friend of his tend to her needs. "If you are in need of money," he went on, "write to me at once and I will send it to you."[45] Once again, Anagnos stepped in with direction, support, and financial resources.

Though rabies (hydrophobia) killed only several dozen people each year in the United States, it held a prominent place in the American imagination in the 1880s and early 1890s. Rabies always killed, and because of its lengthy incubation period, fears of a horrid and painful death could last for weeks after a wound had healed. Press reportage of rabies cases, and possible rabies cases, saturated popular culture, including "fascinatingly gruesome details." Louis Pasteur's successful 1885 production of an inoculation initially met with little press coverage. The dry news of a French laboratory's discovery hardly could compete with dramatic stories of vicious dogs. After a stray dog bit six New Jersey children, however, and the press provided minute-by-minute coverage of their travels from Newark to France and back again, the Pasteur treatment drew much attention.[46] Everyone knew of it—from blind girls in Boston to rural farmers in Alabama.

Thus, when the mastiff bit Sullivan, it is no surprise that Anagnos sent her directly to the New York Pasteur Institute that had opened the previous year. Neither Boston nor Alabama had serum to treat a potential case of rabies. Sullivan, accompanied by a Tuscumbia doctor, traveled to New York. Helen, without a teacher in Tuscumbia, went to Perkins for an indefinite period.

From New York, Annie's letters to Anagnos must have expressed frequent concern about money and the "trouble" she caused, for he constantly expressed reassurance: "Pray do not have the least anxiety about the future. Be Capt. Keller's circumstances what they may, Helen and you will not be allowed to suffer."[47] Rabies treatment might have been unpleasant, but New York held French food and the glamour of a backstage meeting with famed actress Sarah Bernhardt. And it was not Tuscumbia. Once healthy, Sullivan joined Helen in Boston.

They would have been better off in Tuscumbia. The extravagant praise of the Perkins annual report of 1891 was about to appear. The report and its contents would unintentionally disrupt everything.

Just as he had done in the 1888 annual report, Anagnos began the 1891 report with Samuel Gridley Howe. He undoubtedly knew he would incur Sullivan's wrath. In great detail, he told of Helen's physical well-being, her daily activities, her visits while in Boston, and of the famous people she had met. Her oral lessons, he exaggerated wildly, had been "a complete triumph." He reprinted many of her letters, essays, and "The Frost King," her fictional tribute to his birthday, in its entirety. "If there be a pupil in any of the private or public grammar schools of

New England who can write an original story like this, without assistance from anyone," he proudly proclaimed, "he or she certainly is a rare phenomenon."[48]

Though Helen's glories took up 257 of the report's pages, Anagnos reassured the readers that "we beg leave to repeat the assertion and renew the assurance that the facts embodied in it have been scrupulously verified and are entirely free from error and exaggeration. . . . If they appear miraculous . . . let it be remembered that the little girl herself *is a marvel.*"[49] Anagnos would regret his words.

CHAPTER 7

The Battle for Helen, Round 1, 1891–1894

SULLIVAN, HELEN, the Keller parents, and Michael Anagnos must have begun 1892 in a glorious mood. The immediate needs of Annie's medical crisis had eased the tensions in her relationship with Anagnos. After leaving the Pasteur Institute in December 1891, she had traveled from New York to Boston to meet Helen, intending to spend the rest of the school year at Perkins. She may have felt satisfaction that despite Arthur Keller's earlier refusal to allow her and his daughter to spend the school year at Perkins, the threat of rabies had made it happen. And even if Helen's parents had some lingering reluctance about their daughter being in Boston for the rest of the school year, they must have been relieved to know of Annie's good health.

On top of it all, though Sullivan frequently voiced annoyance at Anagnos's publicity efforts, his unflinching and unhesitating veneration of Keller and (to a lesser extent) Sullivan in the 1891 Perkins annual report had spread the fame of Helen Keller, Annie Mansfield Sullivan, and Perkins around the globe. He even reprinted "The Frost King" in *The Mentor*, the Perkins alumni magazine.

Then everything came to a screeching halt. On January 30 Anagnos received a letter from Job Williams, principal of the American School for the Deaf in Hartford, Connecticut. Williams told Anagnos of allegations that Helen had not authored "The Frost King." The saga began when the *Goodson Gazette*, the weekly newspaper of the Virginia Institution for the Deaf and Dumb and Blind, reprinted "The Frost King" in its January 9 edition. A reader noticed the story's strong resemblance to "The Frost Fairies," a short story written by Margaret T. Canby. On January 16 the *Goodson Gazette* compared the stories directly. Though Perkins received the *Gazette*, obviously no one read it. Another two weeks went by before Anagnos or anyone at Perkins heard the news. By that point the information must have run rampant through deaf and blind educational circles.

The letter brought chaos to Perkins. Anagnos confronted his former student and valedictorian Annie Sullivan. Sullivan confronted her student, Helen Keller. Virtually all the staff members then assisted in turning the institution upside down in a futile effort to find the damaging copy of "The Frost Fairies."

Sullivan left little information about the day. Helen, in a diary excerpt reprinted for the public in 1903, chronicled the confrontation with misery: "This morning I took a bath, and when teacher came upstairs to comb my hair she told me some very sad news which made me unhappy all day. Some one wrote to Mr. Anagnos that the story which I sent him as a birthday gift, and which I wrote myself, was not my story at all." Her teacher shared her sorrow. "It made us feel so bad," she wrote, "to think that people thought we had been untrue and wicked. My heart was full of tears, for I love the beautiful truth with my whole heart and mind." The eleven-year-old knew that Anagnos was "much troubled." "It grieves me," she went on, "to think that I have been the cause of his unhappiness, but of course I did not mean to do it."[1]

Alexander Graham Bell stepped in as Sullivan's defender. How he learned of the allegations is not clear—perhaps through deaf education networks, perhaps he or one of his staff read the *Gazette*, or perhaps Sullivan requested his assistance. He asked Mrs. Annie C. Pratt to meet with Sullivan and Anagnos about the matter. Pratt, whom Sullivan and Helen later referred to as Aunt Polly, had worked in the Volta Bureau (an information center for deaf people directed by Bell) for many years. In early 1892 her tasks included preparing an edition of the bureau's publication, *The Souvenir*, that featured Sullivan's educational methods. She socialized frequently with Bell's wife, Mabel, and his children. Bell trusted Pratt. He hoped she would discover that

Helen had written the story while Sullivan was receiving treatment at the Pasteur Institute, the teacher and student far away from one another.[2]

Pratt prepared by arranging an "interview" with Sullivan and Anagnos for February 1. She visited the Massachusetts State House to get a copy of the 1891 annual report with its printing of "The Frost King." To her dismay she learned that the report had already been distributed to every Massachusetts state legislator and approximately fifty additional individuals.[3]

Arriving only forty-eight hours after the Perkins community learned of the plagiarism allegations, Pratt found "poor Miss Sullivan and dear little Helen greatly distressed and exceedingly unhappy." All were in tears. Sullivan and Fanny Marrett, the Perkins teacher who had accompanied Annie to the train station as she first departed for Tuscumbia, were trying to wrest information from Helen about the story. Pratt persuaded the two adults to leave Helen alone until everyone calmed down, and they sent the young girl out to play.[4]

Pratt took Annie's side, emphasizing her "nervous strain," "very great trouble," "over-burdened heart," "suffering," "severe mental strain," and "over-burdened thoughts." As Pratt told the story to Bell, Anagnos had interrogated Annie in a "tone and manner that evinced such irritation and annoyance, throwing the burden of responsibility for this mistake upon her." She told Bell that she had given Annie his support: "the assurance I knew you could expect me to furnish her, that of your earnest support, sympathy, counsel and defence [sic]." And out of her own "womanly sympathy," she had done her part by providing Annie with "what she very much needed, motherly love."[5]

Pratt shared with Bell the frustration that Annie felt about Anagnos, and agreed with it. She quoted her as saying that Anagnos always made such a fuss over Helen's "remarkable genius" that "no one would think of doubting the originality of anything she might do or say." Anagnos, Sullivan complained to Pratt, "drags everything I write or say of Helen into print." The former star student didn't like it, but explained that she was "under great obligations to Mr. Anagnos, and could not well oppose him in anything." Once begun, the publicity was difficult to stop. "There seemed to be no place to stop, as the public had become interested, and we were a telling card for the Inst[itution]." Sullivan blamed Anagnos: "About *this* I do not see how I am to blame any more as much as he is. . . . He has always printed things about Helen and myself without consulting us." Pratt supported Sullivan and advised Bell to go forward with the edition of the *Souvenir* praising her educational methods.[6]

Either because she took it upon herself or because Anagnos assigned her to do it, Sullivan had the onerous task of sharing the news with Arthur and Kate Keller. Unfortunately the letter Sullivan wrote, with her initial version of the events, no longer remains. The two men involved—Keller and Anagnos—sidestepped Sullivan. Rather than writing back to her, Arthur Keller immediately responded to Anagnos. "I am greatly mortified and grieved," he wrote, "to learn . . . that Helen should ever have been allowed to send you anything not original." He reassured Anagnos, somewhat falsely, that the inability of his household members to communicate with Helen meant that no one there could have shared the story with her. He asked for a copy of "The Frost Fairies" and requested that Anagnos share their innocence with the author Margaret Canby. It was, he concluded, "a very disagreeable matter."[7]

Newspapers from other educational institutions for deaf and blind students continued to criticize the affair. Berating an eleven-year-old deaf-blind girl, however, got to be too much for almost anyone to take. On January 30 the West Virginia Institution for the Education of the Deaf and Dumb and Blind, in its newspaper the *W. V. Tablet*, criticized Keller's unnamed "instructors who are supposed to include, in their teaching, morals." In early February the *Goodson Gazette*, the source of the original charges, reassured readers that its publishers did not "blame little Helen Keller for this attempted fraud, far from it. She is not to blame. She has done merely what she was told to do." "The blame for the fraud," it went on, "rests not upon her, but upon whoever knowingly attempted to pass off the Frost King as her composition and there the blame will lie."[8] Who could that be but Annie Sullivan?

From the perspective of Anagnos and those who identified with Perkins, the controversy threatened the credibility of the institution and the reputation of the dead Samuel Gridley Howe. Julia Ward

Howe must have been furious. From the perspective of Sullivan, the controversy threatened the successful adult future she had forged out of virtually nothing, and she feared the loss of her relationship with Helen.

The now sullied teacher and student remained at Perkins. A decade later Helen wrote that in this period she "tried not to be unhappy" in order to please Anagnos. Trying not to be unhappy, however, didn't work. Less than three weeks later, the night before a long-planned celebration of George Washington's February 22 birthday, everything fell apart again. Fanny Marrett, who weeks earlier had sat with Sullivan and Keller when Annie Pratt visited Perkins, initiated a conversation about "The Frost King" with Helen at the request of Anagnos. Marrett received what she believed to be a confession of the guilt of both Helen and Sullivan. Despite Helen's "most emphatic" insistence that Marrett was mistaken, the teacher told Anagnos and the interrogations began again. As Helen understood the event, "Mr. Anagnos, who loved me tenderly, thinking that he had been deceived, turned a deaf ear to the pleadings of love and innocence."[9]

At this point Anagnos initiated a more formal investigation. Sullivan and her young student left Perkins for the refuge of Sophia Hopkins's Brewster home. At some point Annie shared the recent events with Hopkins, but whatever letters they exchanged don't remain and are not quoted in the voluminous discussions of the affair. At some point in the search for "The Frost Fairies," they concluded that Hopkins had read the book to Helen during the summer of 1888. The book, however, couldn't be found.[10] Years later, after Keller and Sullivan published their version of the event in the 1903 edition of *The Story of My Life*, an unnamed defender of Perkins made much of the fact that no one explained how this conclusion was reached, particularly when neither Helen nor Hopkins remembered the reading of the story, and when the book was never discovered.

In early 1892, however, Anagnos accepted the explanation and wrote a brief public apology that was inserted into each remaining copy of the 1891 annual report. He had conducted "careful inquiry," he wrote, and determined that Hopkins had read the book to Helen while Sullivan was away briefly. Neither Helen nor Hopkins, he said, remembered the event. "No one," Anagnos concluded his apology, "can regret the mistake more than I."[11]

In early March Anagnos continued to investigate, issuing a written list of questions to both Marrett and Sullivan. From Brewster, Annie replied with fury and indignation: "I know of no good reason why I should answer the questions," she wrote on March 6, likely echoing her belligerence in response to his earlier interrogations of her while she was a student at Perkins—about skipping school to attend the Tewksbury hearings or wearing makeup, or about her sassiness with Julia Ward Howe. She responded, however, to his three questions. One, she acknowledged that she could not say "positively" whether or not Helen differentiated between "original composition and reproduction." Two, she had explained the meaning of plagiarism to Helen the night before. And three, Helen's own diary could give him a better idea of the child's feelings on the matter than she could.[12]

Succinctly, Sullivan used the letter to twice snub Anagnos. Indicating to him that he was no longer the preeminent authority on the education of Helen Keller, she explained that she would be "very happy to furnish" a "copy" of Helen's diary entry for January 30 but implied that Alexander Graham Bell, via Mrs. Pratt, held the original. She indicated that she would say no more about it; however, later she spoke much more about the incident, and would for years to come.[13]

Events surrounding "The Frost King" pushed the now nearly twenty-six-year-old Sullivan to distance herself from Anagnos, the most prominent male figure in her life from the time she was fourteen years of age. Since he had first publicized Helen's education, Anagnos had made it clear that he considered her pedagogy to be merely derivative of the great Samuel Gridley Howe. He considered her a woman who simply, but competently, followed the directions of the male originator. By allowing Helen to be involved in this scandal, regardless of where the fault lay, Sullivan had betrayed Anagnos, Perkins, and the great man Howe. Now he had less reason to trust her and more reason to protect Perkins. The almshouse orphan kindly let into the fold had turned into a snake.

Alexander Graham Bell, however, had neither institutional nor personal allegiance to Howe. Nor had Bell known Sullivan as a destitute, mouthy, and unpolished adolescent. His only prior involvement had been to direct Helen's parents toward Perkins, an institution he now believed to be doing a disservice to both Sullivan and Helen. Ultimately, unlike Anagnos, Bell believed Annie Sullivan to be a brilliant pedagogical innovator.

Bell believed Sullivan's methods could solve what he considered a primary weakness in the education of deaf people: a deficit in the knowledge and comprehension of idiomatic English. Sullivan taught language to Helen by speaking, via the manual alphabet, to the deaf-blind child as she would have to any seeing and hearing child—in full sentences and phrases—even before her student understood them. She read the same books to Helen that she would have read to any seeing and hearing child of the same age. Helen thus learned idiomatic English. By using Sullivan's methods, Bell believed, teachers of deaf children could more successfully teach complex literacy.

Bell, Annie Pratt, and Bell's colleague John Hitz swung into action. As far as Bell was concerned, "Helen and her teacher seem to have been treated in a most unjust and outrageous manner by Mr. Anagnos—who seems to have failed to grasp the importance of the Frost King incident—and seems to suspect either Miss Sullivan or her dear little pupil—of an untruth." He intended to be "of much assistance to Miss Sullivan." His wife, Mabel, approved, encouraging him and characterizing him as "a perfect Knight errant going about to succor distressed damsels."[14]

At some point in March, as part of his formal investigation, Anagnos called together an "investigation committee," in essence a jury, to hear and decide the truth. It was a scene of high drama. Eleven-year-old Helen experienced it as a trial of her own truthfulness. Sullivan knew it to be more: a trial not only of Helen's truthfulness, but of her capacity to generate original thought, and of Sullivan's legitimacy as a teacher. Was Sullivan a fraud? Had she manipulated Helen to lie? Had she misled everyone about the capabilities of her student? Did she not come from the almshouse? The outcome could have removed Sullivan from all future employment with Perkins, with blind students, and with Keller—and from respectability as well.

In her 1903 autobiography *The Story of My Life* Helen described the trial as a traumatic event. There was, she wrote, "something hostile and menacing in the very atmosphere." As Sullivan remained outside, someone else ushered her to her place before a jury of "teachers and officers of the Institution," individuals unidentified to her. As an adult she considered the "court of investigation" to be unfair: "I was questioned and cross-examined with what seemed to me a determination on the part of my judges to force me to acknowledge that I remembered having 'The Frost Fairies' read to me." Afterward, alone in her bed, "I wept as I hope few children have wept. I felt so cold, I imagined I should die before morning, and the thought comforted me. I think if this sorrow had come to me when I was older, it would have broken my spirit beyond repairing."[15]

Anagnos's version of the court, offered to John Macy as he helped Keller prepare her 1903 book, differed dramatically. Anagnos considered the calling of the committee his duty. It included four sighted and four blind people, the majority "distinctly friendly to Helen." Throughout the event, at his insistence, "every precaution was taken to prevent any misapprehension or error," partly by providing interpreters (to fingerspell for Helen) who were "teachers of Helen, good and most faithful friends of hers and women whose sense of justice and honor was unquestionable." And though "Helen's replies to some of the questions were of a damaging nature," the results were inconclusive. Half the committee believed "Helen had been put up to telling an untruth," presumably by her teacher, and half considered the facts "not sufficient to justify that conclusion." Thus, the two possible results were Annie's guilt or insufficient evidence. Anagnos sided with insufficient evidence, "and thus the matter was left, not proven."[16]

Arthur and Kate Keller must have written to Helen and her teacher in this period, but the letters don't remain. Nor do letters remain from Sullivan or Helen to the Keller family. Sophia Hopkins wrote to Keller's parents at least once, though the contents of her letter remain unknown. Kate Keller had given birth to Phillips Brooks Keller in the summer of 1891 and likely couldn't have left Tuscumbia, no matter how badly she might have wanted to be near her daughter. Two letters sent by Arthur Keller to Anagnos signify that the two men considered themselves to be in charge and that the two exchanged more letters than those that remain. In late March, presumably after the Perkins trial, the Keller patriarch wrote with a gentle request that Helen and her teacher return home to Tuscumbia soon. He left the decision, however, to Anagnos. Perhaps Hopkins had suggested that Helen and Annie needed to leave Perkins. Perhaps Keller's father was motivated by his wife's yearnings for her daughter, as his letter stated.[17]

In late April Arthur Keller thanked Anagnos for his kind treatment of Helen but spoke firmly of "Miss Annie and Helen" returning to Tuscumbia. The weather, he insisted vaguely, required it, and he used the expertise of their physician to substantiate his point. The two should leave Boston in mid-May. In previous years the pair had waited until after commencement in late May to leave Perkins. They left in the middle of May but first stopped for several weeks at the Hulton, Pennsylvania, home of philanthropist William Wade. Wade had been involved in Helen's life since at least 1889. While in Hulton the famous teacher and student acted as fundraisers for Perkins. Anagnos approved and reminded Sullivan that "Mr. Wade is one of Helen's truest and best friends, and I am exceedingly glad that you were able to make him a good visit."[18]

From Hulton, Sullivan wrote to Anagnos with much the same intimate, slightly bossy tone that she had used prior to the tumultuous preceding months. She tried to play Anagnos and Bell off each other, telling Anagnos that he should "try to help me out like a good father" by helping her avoid the meeting of the American Association to Promote the Teaching of Speech to the Deaf, to which Bell had invited her. Though Bell waited in the wings, it was in her best interest to repair the relationship. "I do with all my heart wish that we were to live nearer," she wrote, "but it is no use wishing you will come South as soon as you can. Will you not? And in the meantime you will write to me."[19]

Annie and Helen arrived in Tuscumbia exhausted, dispirited, and discouraged. Their time at Perkins had been anything but pleasurable. They "suffered dreadfully," as Annie reported to Wade, on the railroad trip from Pennsylvania to Tuscumbia due to the heat. Rather than a refuge, they found the Keller household to be in turmoil. Kate Keller was "in miserable health," baby Phillips had whooping cough, and everyone feared that oldest brother James had typhoid. The "frightfully hot" weather took its toll, and Captain Keller's finances were strained, perhaps even more so than Annie realized. The first letter she wrote to Anagnos after their return hints of a welcome descent into immobility, which may have been a great relief after the constant striving of the last months. "I have absolutely no composure of soul for writing. . . . The indolence which has taken possession of me is positively transcendental," she wrote. "I am utterly powerless to shake it off."[20]

Customarily the Keller household escaped the hottest months of the summer at their "summer cottage" on a wooded mountain called Fern Quarry, fourteen miles from Tuscumbia. In her 1903 autobiography *The Story of My Life* Helen described it idyllically. Three "frolicsome little streams," "leaping here and tumbling there," ran through a fern-filled meadow containing the small cottage. The cottage itself, "beautifully situated on the top of the mountain among oaks and pines," was "a sort of rough camp," but comfortable and surrounded by "a wide piazza, where the mountain winds blew, sweet with all wood-scents." The children gathered nuts, fruits, and flowers and would "ramble in the woods, and allow ourselves to get lost amid the trees and vines." Visiting men played cards and attempted to out-tell tall tales of "their wonderful feats with fowl, fish and quadruped." As the "wily hunters" performed their manly task of securing meat, the women prepared the barbecue—the white folks, that is: "Around the fire squatted negroes, driving away the flies with long branches."[21]

Keller conveniently glossed over the summer of 1892. Or perhaps the twelve-year-old simply experienced the summer differently from her exhausted and downcast twenty-six-year-old teacher.

In early August Anagnos sent a brief letter to Annie: "What has become of you?" Apparently she had not written since the end of June. He tried to tease her into their previously relaxed relationship, but even these words held the possibility of resentment, of anger about her possible ties with Alexander Graham Bell. "Are you so busy with your correspondence with distinguished persons," he toyed, "that you cannot find time to write a few words to those of your friends who belong to the ranks of ordinary mortals?"[22]

Annie responded with a lengthy letter, but with a litany of complaints and her own passive-aggressiveness. The summer heat and rain had spread illness, ruined crops, and made "respiration difficult and existence intolerable." Helen, her brothers James and Phillips, and her sister Mildred all became sick; even Helen's new dog, Elmer, acquired "the mange . . . this most disagreeable of dog diseases." Once baby Phillips, the sickest of all, was well enough to be moved the household packed for Fern Quarry. Rather than rest and repose, however, the move to the country brought the opposite; as Sullivan wrote, "[the] trials were just beginning." Sullivan blamed Arthur Keller. During the previous two months the family had lived on $35 of Helen's earnings from the sale of a brief article and a $35 loan Annie made to Captain Keller. Sullivan believed everything else to be mortgaged and the Captain to be "heavily in debt." He had not paid her a salary in years. The household help that previously had made their summers at Fern Quarry easy did not appear when unpaid. With Phillips still recovering and fretful, Annie and Mrs. Keller carried water a quarter mile uphill and fetched milk from a mile away. Arthur Keller had "hastened back to Tuscumbia," and left "us two lone women here in the woods, without . . . protection." "Did you ever hear of a greater outrage?" she lamented with sarcasm. "We lived this way for nearly two weeks—until the election was over and the head of the family found time to bestow a thought upon his beloved family." Relations between the Kellers strained the mountain retreat. They were not "in a honeymoon state of mind as regards each other," Annie confided, and when Arthur Keller infrequently visited, "the rest of us [found] the woods pleasanter than the house."[23]

Sullivan insisted to Anagnos that such conditions harmed Helen, perhaps with the intent of pushing him to find another place for the two of them. "Already the shadow of trouble has fallen upon her sensitive heart," the teacher claimed, and the child's diary entries "would distress you inexpressibly." (In the previous paragraph, however, she had claimed that "Phillips and Helen have been daily growing strength in this lovely mountain retreat.") "If they would only give me Helen," she prodded, "I am sure I could find a way of making her life brighter than it will ever be here."[24] Sullivan likely knew that the chances of Anagnos acting on her behalf were slight, but that it was far more likely he would act on what he believed to be Helen's behalf. She must have known that their welcome at Perkins was wearing thin, or had been worn out entirely.

Yet, Sullivan did not give up her attempts to hold on to the man over whom she previously had held such great sway. She seemingly took his jibes about "distinguished correspondents" at face value and blandly assured him that she wrote little to Alexander Graham Bell or his colleague John Hitz—but teased him with the fact that they wrote to her far more than she wrote them. She made clear her between-the-lines threat that other men, more distinguished than Anagnos, desired her attention.

She then ended the lengthy letter with gusto, skillfully keeping her strongest and most womanly swipe at Anagnos until the end of this round in their lengthy contest of wills. "I only wish I were near you, dear," she began. Though "a woman is constantly getting warned against following in the impulses of her heart," she would follow hers. "I have flung my understanding to the dogs, and think, do, say and feel first exactly as nature prompts me." With this promising caveat, she went on: though he would not approve of her forthrightness, "nevertheless, it is time, and I wish to be near you because I love you and I am happier near you than anywhere else in the world." She then quickly retreated, sent the affections of Helen and young Mildred, and closed the letter.[25]

Was Annie in love with Michael Anagnos? It's unlikely, but the letter hints at marriage. She had grown accustomed to depending upon his goodwill, however she might get it, to secure her position at Perkins and her consequent economic security. At Perkins, where she frequently felt out of place, and felt the hostility of female students and teachers, she easily wooed and manipulated the older and childless widower. At this time of emotional insecurity, worried about her future, seeing her position at Perkins deteriorate, it was easy to once again lean toward him for security.

How Anagnos received such a letter is unclear. His next known remaining letter is from December, almost four months later. Sullivan's letter from late November stayed away from such emotional outpourings and personal appeals but concluded, "I wish you would write to

me sometimes. Are you going to say anything about Helen in the report? *Do* write to me." In mid-December she pushed harder: "Write to
me what you think . . . that is, if you are ever going to write me again."
When he finally responded nearly a week later, he pled busyness as an
excuse.[26]

Over the fall of 1892, the continued fallout from the Frost King
events slowly eroded the flirtatious—sometimes father–daughter,
sometimes courtship—relationship reflected in the language used by
Sullivan and Anagnos. Annie tried her best to reel him back in, to placate him, but the older man valued his reputation, and that of Perkins,
far more than he valued his continued relationship with the attractive
but complicated young woman. By Anagnos's calculation, Sullivan received the blame for the Frost King debacle so that Perkins would not.
Anagnos prized Helen for what she did for Perkins, and assumed that
he and Perkins could retain their hold over Helen while slowly chilling
their relationship with her teacher.

Sullivan and Alexander Graham Bell had other plans, which met
with resistance from Anagnos. While Anagnos worked to diminish
Sullivan's ties to Helen, Bell worked to elevate her professional stature.
In the midst of the scandal, the man whom Mabel Bell had called "a
perfect Knight errant going about to succor distressed damsels," or-
chestrated a first behind-the-scenes and then quite public campaign
to secure Sullivan's pedagogical reputation and draw her, and Helen,
into the deaf educational community. Bell hoped that Sullivan's pedagogical methods could enhance deaf education, and that oralist experts
from the deaf education community could enhance Keller's articulation skills. Any stature gained by Bell, or by deaf education, thanks to
Keller and Sullivan would have benefited him and the oralist cause.
Throughout March (the month of the Frost King trial) and April,
both men attempted to initiate meetings, but it's unclear whether the
two actually met to discuss the events. Once in mid-March Bell tried
to include the principals of the Northampton and Boston schools for
the deaf in the conversation.[27] In mid-April false rumors circulated,
apparently initiated by Sullivan, that Helen was to go to the Clarke
Institution at Northampton for instruction—a leading oralist school
favored by Bell, who hoped for such a possibility. Near the end of April

Helen took lessons of some sort from Bell, presumably in oral articulation, but the extent of it is unclear. It's clear, however, that Anagnos felt confident enough in his hold on Helen that he made appointments for her elsewhere during her lesson times with Bell.[28]

Bell continued to wage both a private and public campaign. He invited Sullivan and Helen to the family birthday party of his daughter Elsie, drawing them into his personal sphere. As president of the American Association to Promote the Teaching of Speech to the Deaf (AAPTSD), he formally invited Sullivan and her student to attend the association's upcoming meeting in Lake George, New York, and sent an equally formal letter regarding the invitation to Arthur Keller, whom he assured that all expenses would be paid by AAPTSD. Only reluctantly taking no for an answer, he went on to use the pages of the *Silent Educator* to argue publicly that Sullivan's "discovery" was of "enormous importance to teachers of the deaf." Rather than a fraud, she was a pedagogical innovator. The "fortunate discovery" of the language similarity between Keller's "Frost King" and Margaret Canby's "The Frost Fairies" only proved that Helen's language acquisition depended on Sullivan's brilliant use of literature.[29]

Bell may have had the best interests of Sullivan and Helen at heart, but he also hoped to use them in his growing campaign to transform deaf education and hold back the emerging Deaf culture by eliminating signed language and replacing it with oral speech. He, along with others such as Sarah Fuller, principal of Horace Mann School and Keller's earlier articulation teacher, and Caroline Yale of the Clarke School, had formed the AAPTSD only two years earlier. The irony, of course, is that Keller never developed strong articulation skills, and because educators relied increasingly on oralism the literacy rates of deaf people plummeted in the coming decades.

Though Annie had reassured Anagnos in August that she "did not trouble about writing" to John Hitz and wrote rarely to Bell, she did write at least one intimate letter to the much older Hitz, the man she called *mon père*, as her correspondence with Anagnos grew increasingly businesslike. In November she wrote to Hitz, "It would be strange indeed if I could forget you. I have had few friends in my life so deserving [as he] of my grateful remembrance." She vaguely referred to "other trials, misunderstandings which I cannot explain here, which made my summer peculiarly unpleasant"—perhaps her growing conflict with Anagnos, perhaps tensions within the Keller family. She wished she could have "a long talk" with him and expressed regret for not corresponding with Mrs. Pratt. Though she wrote of Helen's continued pain over the Frost King episode, she did not refer to her own pain over the events.[30]

In December Annie's frustration and anger at her lack of control over Helen's reputation bubbled over once again, this time directed at Anagnos and the Perkins community. Reports had circulated in deaf as well as general circulation newspapers that Helen was a "wreck," "broken down mentally and physically," "given over to melancholy," and "dwelling constantly on the thought of death." The reports infuriated her. In her correspondence with John Hitz, who had sent the clippings, she had characterized Helen as "pale and listless," "so unlike her own bright self that a great anxiety took possession of my heart."[31] However, she insisted to Anagnos that she had written about Helen's condition only to him and to Sophia Hopkins. She blamed Anagnos for the press reports. More specifically, she blamed him for sharing her private letters with teachers at Perkins: "I believe all these reports and exaggerations originated at the Institution. Helen's old enemies were the originators and malice was the motive." Just as she had blamed and continued to blame nameless but jealous women at Perkins for hysterically amplifying and overdramatizing events around the plagiarism accusations, so she blamed them for these reports. Anagnos replied quickly, insisting that the leaks had not come from him. He blamed Sophia Hopkins but assured Annie he would see to it that "the whole matter is set right." His advice was to avoid confiding in women. "Love women with all your heart and soul," he wrote, "but do not tell them what you do not want other people to know." That same week Helen confided to John Hitz that her teacher's eyes "have been hurting her so she could not write to any one."[32]

With Anagnos, Annie continued to move back and forth between sharp anger and coy statements of affection. Blithely and perhaps willfully ignoring the growing division between them, she wrote, "You have ever been kind and forbearing with me, and I cannot believe that any force of circumstances, or inconsideration on my part will ever make any difference with you." Her language continued to ride the slippery line between romance and simple fondness. "There is only one thing I would write to you, which were not better unwritten, and that would be once and once again, Mon Cher Amie; I often think of you and have the same affection for you that I have ever had."[33]

She continued with a litany of complaints about life in Tuscumbia. Though Helen had received $100 for a "sketch" to be published in *The Youth's Companion*, a Christmas present of $50 from William Wade, and sugar company stock from donor John Spaulding, Arthur Keller had taken it all. And in Sullivan's opinion, he had rudely dismissed Helen's generous ideas about spending the money: a public library for Tuscumbia and Christmas presents for servants. Despite her anger at Helen's father, she asked Anagnos to help him find a job: "If he does not get an appointment of some sort I do not see what is to become of us." Arthur Keller also sought a substantial loan from Spaulding, and Sullivan sought Anagnos's influence in encouraging Spaulding to agree to it.[34]

As Anagnos prepared the Perkins annual report that winter, he must have wrestled with what to write about Helen. The 1891 report that included "The Frost King" had caused nothing but trouble. Should he ignore the events? Pretend Keller never existed? Go on as if all had been resolved happily? At his request Annie had written something for the report, and he'd returned it heavily edited. She ignored at least two requests to send it back. In late January she responded with belligerence, perhaps not unlike what she had demonstrated toward him while she was his student. She apologized for not returning the notes, but insisted that he had not asked for them often enough. And because Helen's *Youth's Companion* piece was so lovely, she'd simply burned her notes (not quite a logical leap). Later in life she would burn much more of her diaries and letters. Now she simply told him that she was "truly glad when these particular notes disappeared never to be seen again." A synopsis of 1892 would only pain and embarrass her.[35]

From Sullivan's perspective, perhaps the only good thing to come from that winter was the second election of Grover Cleveland. The defeat of Democrat Cleveland in 1888 had meant the loss of Captain

Keller's federal position. Annie and the whole Keller family hoped that Cleveland's return to the presidency in 1892 meant the return of a steady paycheck. In celebration, and perhaps hoping that his famous daughter would secure him an audience with Cleveland in order to further his employment opportunities, Captain Keller planned for himself, Sullivan, and Helen to attend the March 1893 inaugural.

Whether by design or accident, the trip planned for only a week resulted in a sojourn of many months away from Tuscumbia for Helen and Sullivan. They didn't get in to see Cleveland, though Helen sent an inscribed copy of the 1892 Volta Bureau *Souvenir* featuring her to the First Lady. Sullivan was likely disappointed at losing the opportunity to meet the First Lady, Frances Folsom Cleveland, whose charm and clothing she had admired since her student years at Perkins. In Boston Anagnos did not provide the reception Annie desired. The day after her arrival at Perkins she turned to John Hitz with her disappointment: "Mr. Anagnos's reception of me has not been cordial. I do not mean that he has been rude or anything of that kind; but he has made me understand his displeasure in many ways." Annie hurt her arm somehow, leaving her and Helen with sufficient reason to stay north while Arthur Keller returned home (but accidentally left his shoes at Perkins).[36]

Visiting Perkins made it clear that relations between Annie and Anagnos, between Annie and the teachers at Perkins, were not going to heal easily. She increasingly turned toward Bell and those affiliated with him, John Hitz and Annie Pratt, for emotional support and professional standing. Bell eagerly connected further with the teacher and student. When the Keller party traveled through Washington for the inaugural, Bell had made it clear to Arthur Keller that he wanted Helen and Sullivan to visit the deaf schools in both Northampton, Massachusetts, and Pennsylvania. The frosty reception at Perkins, at least as Annie perceived it, increased her receptivity to his overtures. Not long after their March 1893 arrival in Boston, Sullivan and Helen abruptly left Perkins—not to return for almost a year and a half. As Helen wrote to her mother, she, her teacher, and Pratt "very unexpectedly decided to take a journey with dear Dr. Bell." They visited Rochester's School for the Deaf and later Niagara Falls. For at least part of the time, when not in Chelsea with Pratt, the pair enjoyed the hospitality of Beacon Street's Lucy Derby (later Fuller), "receiving and returning calls with some of our best Boston families," as Pratt described it.[37] Annie undoubtedly tried to repair the damage done by the Frost King trial and Anagnos's disapproval, courting support among the elite where she could.

In April Bell tried once again to invite them to the upcoming meeting of the AAPTSD, this time in Chicago near the World's Fair, with all expenses paid.[38] Bell met with Annie and Helen many times, in Boston and Washington, and once spoke with Annie about teaching a deaf girl living in the capital. At least once she helped him court philanthropists interested in his organization and the cause of oralism. Mabel Bell cautioned her husband not to pressure the pair too hard: "We have been working Helen for all she is worth for our benefit and not hers. I hope that she will get some good out of it all. At the same time I have no doubt she enjoys it, it is Miss Sullivan upon whom the burden and fatigue really comes."[39]

During 1893 and 1894 the pair increasingly became publicly identified with Bell rather than Anagnos. At a widely publicized spring 1893 meeting of Washington, D.C., intellectuals Bell used a poem Helen had written about Niagara Falls to illustrate the brilliance of both teacher and student. Likewise, the immense publicity accorded Helen's visit to the World's Fair in July 1893 and the consistent mention of Bell's presence there with them reinforced the public link between the three. As Sullivan and Helen moved across the country, Bell, either directly or more often through John Hitz, remained updated on their whereabouts and doings. They spent most of the summer, fall, and winter of 1893 (except for Chicago in July and a brief Tuscumbia visit in September) at the quiet and luxurious countryside estate of William Wade, Robinswood. February through June 1894 they spent in Tuscumbia. At Robinswood Sullivan relied extensively, for the first time, on someone other than herself for Helen's education. With Wade's financial largesse, Mr. Irons, a local Episcopal minister, tutored Helen in Latin and helped with arithmetic and poetry.[40]

Sullivan left little evidence about her state of mind during this period. Money remained a constant source of stress. Should she stay with

Helen? Was Helen's education complete? Should she seek other, more financially lucrative and stable employment? Would she ever marry, though at nearly thirty already of an age to be considered an old maid? Was there any hope of a personal or professional future with Anagnos? Could she rely on Bell and a career in deaf education? Her eyes continued to cause her pain. Would the pain increase or her eyesight diminish? The future must have seemed frightening and uncertain.

Though she cared for Bell, and he for her, their relationship never had the emotional charge and flirtation, the coy manipulation, that she and Anagnos had shared. The inventor's focus never went beyond professional matters. His wife was very much alive (the two had a strong relationship) and his children active and present. Biographers recognize that Bell's children sometimes grew jealous of Helen, but the same suggestion has never been made regarding Annie.[41]

John Hitz, on the other hand, became an emotional anchor for Annie until his death in 1908. This relationship too differed sharply from that between Sullivan and Anagnos. Nearly always she referred to Hitz as *mon cher père*. His role in the relationship was that of a wise and caring father or grandfather. All who knew Hitz characterized him as kind, and his long, flowing gray beard contributed to the perception of him as a wise man. In June 1893 Sullivan wrote to him with what was perhaps a veiled reference to her troubles with Anagnos. With almost palpable relief, she wrote, "I intuitively know that you will never misunderstand or mistake whatever I may do or say."[42]

That winter Annie wrote what likely became her last two letters to Michael Anagnos (though she saw him briefly in the summer of 1894 and Helen continued to write for several years). When Helen's letter describing the World's Fair and a poem entitled "Autumn" were about to be published, she could not help but brag. She used the compositions to argue once again for Helen's intellectual capacity and originality, and to protest the plagiarism allegations. "I am not prepared to say that these ideas are *original* in the sense that nobody has ever had similar thoughts," she acknowledged. "But it seems to me that a thought may be original, though it had been uttered a thousand times. The memory, imagination, and associations of the mind through which it has passed give it their hue, and individualize it by a new arrangement of its elements." Helen's composition, she argued, "breathes of the essence of *truth* and is filled with the sweetness of happier spheres." Implicit in all of this was the insistence that she, as a teacher, as a person, was not an unprincipled fraud. She *was* a good teacher. At that point she said nothing of their relationship, but couldn't resist picking up the theme again in February. She toyed with him, asking, "do you deserve that we should send any letters, any sympathy, any love, anything, thru dear, provoking, incomprehensible me?" "I think not," she responded, "but if everyone had his just desserts, which of us should escape whipping?"[43]

As Annie reformulated her relationships and contemplated her own future, she, Bell, Hitz, Pratt, and philanthropic donors interested in Helen began in early 1894 to discuss the future of the emerging adolescent. Bell and those around him believed Helen was ready for a college preparatory school, ready to compete directly with sighted and hearing students. In April philanthropists George O. Goodhue and John Spaulding began discussing the creation of a group that would ensure long-term funding for Helen's future and wrote to Sullivan about the effort. They hoped and planned to enlist the assistance of Bell, Hitz, William Wade, Sophia Hopkins, Annie Pratt, and Lucy Derby. Goodhue consulted with Anagnos, who offered his opinion that a "higher kindergarten school" would be appropriate.[44]

Hitz and Bell debated the matter thoroughly, always believing college—and not a "higher kindergarten school"—the appropriate goal for Helen. Hitz warned that any arrangement smacking of charity would be "very distasteful" to Sullivan and Kate Keller (interestingly, his letter did not refer to Arthur Keller) and strongly discouraged the "subscription affair" presented by Goodhue. He suggested that a "voluntary offer from two or at most three of Helen's friends" would be more appropriate. Hitz, unlike others, recognized that though a college preparatory course would be best, it would "be actually exacting double duty on the part of Miss Sullivan—pupil and assistant tutor." He believed her, however, "both capable and willing—to learn and teach at the same time." The longer he knew her, he told Bell, "the more I realize her exceptional character, her genius for teaching."[45]

In July Sullivan and Helen once again attended the AAPTSD meeting at the invitation of Bell. This time, however, Sullivan agreed to give a public address. As Anagnos diminished her and her pedagogical legitimacy, Bell praised her and her expertise. His wife, Mabel, kindly offered to provide an appropriate wardrobe for her and Helen. Annie, who still loved beautiful clothing, accepted.[46]

Sullivan's address illustrated her growing conception of herself as an intelligent and capable pedagogical theorist and teacher. At the same time, perhaps reflecting her still contradictory sense of self—vacillating between the confident professional and the insecure charity case— extreme last-minute nervousness led her to insist that Bell read her address.[47] Never before had she spoken to a large crowd of educational professionals, with herself positioned as the expert.

The content of the address, "The Instruction of Helen Keller," included nothing startlingly new. Its tone, however, is mature and professional and lacks the hyperbole used by Anagnos in other sketches of Helen's education. It is relatively sophisticated theoretically and reflects great thought. The narratives in the Perkins reports had emphasized what a miraculous and exceptional marvel Helen was, while contradictorily declaring that because Sullivan followed the brilliant path laid out by Samuel Gridley Howe her results were inevitable. Sullivan's narrative at the AAPTSD meeting acknowledged Helen's personal and intellectual singularity, but presented her as a child with the curiosity and interests of a child. In Sullivan's theorization, the pedagogical methods she used with Helen had simply and logically followed the natural learning patterns of children.[48]

Sullivan began with a subtle dig at Anagnos. Complaining that "one can scarcely take up a newspaper or magazine without finding a more or less exaggerated account of her [Helen's] so-called 'marvelous accomplishments,'" she asked the audience to set aside their "pre-conceived notions and theories regarding this case." She hoped to convince them that Helen was not a "'phenomenal child,' 'an intellectual prodigy,' or an 'extraordinary genius,' but simply a very bright and lovely child."[49]

Language and knowledge, Sullivan claimed, "are indissolubly connected." Thus, she "*never taught language for the PURPOSE of teaching it;* but invariably used language as a medium for the communication of *thought;* thus the learning of language was *coincident* with the acquisition of knowledge." Rather than drill Helen with vocabulary, as Howe had done with Bridgman (though she left this unstated), she brought Helen into contact with "the living language itself"—in continual conversation and description of the world, just as "I should have talked to her with my mouth had she been a hearing child."[50]

Sullivan revealed an extraordinarily positive perspective on human nature. "I believe," said the woman who had grown up with so much ugliness, "every child has hidden away somewhere in its being noble qualities and capacities which may be quickened and developed if we go about it in the right way." Nature, she insisted, provided this to children. "The child who loves and appreciates the wonders of the outdoor world will never have room in his heart for the mean and low."[51]

Again extremely positive, she emphasized the vital role of books in Helen's intellectual development and acquisition of "idiomatic English," the phrase so often used by Bell. Perhaps she reflected internally on the books read to her while at Tewksbury and their essential role in her well-being. Even when children could not comprehend everything, she argued, they "invariably manifest the greatest delight in the lofty poetic language." Books provided "delight," and "intellectual enrichment and enlargement." Helen "drank in language," which then "fitted itself naturally and easily into her conversation and composition." Without explicit mention, she reinforced Bell's earlier argument that Helen's "Frost King" story simply proved that in the best education, literature, "the great works of the imagination," became part of the reader, "as they were once of the very substance of the men who wrote them." By reading, by immersing oneself in "the beautiful thoughts and ideals of the great poets," one could embody those ideals.[52] Herself an avid reader, she likely hoped that *she* embodied those ideals.

Reflecting the context in which she spoke, the last section of Sullivan's address focused on Helen's acquisition of oral speech. Here Sullivan's uncertainty came through the most. She knew very little about this and made no claims to do so. The section is the least theoretical of the address. Those around her believed in oral speech acquisition by deaf people as a possibility and as an ideal pedagogical method. They also considered themselves the leading authorities and advocates of oralism. Sullivan explained that the drive to speak came from Helen, and "feeling my own utter incompetence to teach her," she had turned to leading oralist educator, Sarah Fuller. She insisted that "Helen's success has been more complete and inspiring than any of her friends dreamed or expected," but acknowledged that Helen did not "speak naturally."[53]

How the audience received the address is unclear. Sullivan never claimed herself an expert on the education of deaf students, and educators of deaf students never embraced her—with the notable exception of Bell. Nor did she ever express an interest or choose to involve herself in the oralism debates. The report on the AAPTSD meeting in the *Silent Worker*, a leading deaf newspaper, mentioned Helen's appearance but never mentioned Sullivan or her address.[54] Bell, however, liked the address enough to reprint it in the 1899 Volta Bureau *Souvenir*, which devoted an entire issue to Keller upon her acceptance to Radcliffe.

In March of 1892, as Annie had sat tensely, likely back in her own cottage room at Perkins, and waited for Helen to return from the plagiarism trial, she had undoubtedly feared the loss of her teaching position. And that was just the beginning. Over the next year, despite her best efforts to resist, she had felt herself slowly dethroned at Perkins—no longer the star pupil, no longer the valedictorian returning victorious, no longer the spoiled favorite of Michael Anagnos.

The most life-changing impact of Sullivan's presence at the July 1894 AAPTSD meeting was the discussion of Helen's continued education. Bell insisted college preparatory work was the best path. He and others pretended that Arthur Keller would make the final decision, but even Helen's father deferred to Sullivan on this decision. Not Anagnos, not Arthur Keller, not Alexander Graham Bell, nor Helen, but Sullivan would make the future decisions on Helen's education. Though the debate over whether or not she deserved credit for the education of Helen Keller would surface repeatedly over the next years, and though Anagnos and others affiliated with Perkins would refute much of the credit she later received, she had emerged whole.

CHAPTER 8

The Battle for Helen, Round 2, 1894–1900

IN THE MONTH after Sullivan's attendance at the July 1894 meeting of the American Association to Promote the Teaching of Speech to the Deaf, she chose New York's Wright-Humason School for the Deaf as the lucky facility for the fourteen-year-old Helen Keller. Nearly everyone had offered their opinions on the matter, except, apparently, Michael Anagnos, whose opinion she had not sought.

Alexander Graham Bell strongly advised a college preparatory path and assured Arthur Keller that "Helen's friends" would assist with finances. He suggested that Helen's father consider Burnham's Classical School, the preparatory school related to the prestigious Smith College. He felt it to be "one of the best young ladies' schools in the country,—and it's [sic] proximity to the Clarke Institution [a leading school for the deaf] would be of special advantage." The preparatory schools linked to Vassar, Wellesley, or Radcliffe would also do. Bell argued against an oral school for deaf students. Whether at a deaf or blind school Helen would still require an interpreter, he pointed out, so they might as well "send her to whatever may be the best private school for hearing and seeing young ladies."[1]

Bell specifically argued against the Wright-Humason School, scheduled to open that fall. Getting Dr. Thomas Humason's name wrong, he wrote, "Messrs Wright and Henderson are anxious to have Helen go to their school in New York." While he considered Humason and John D. Wright capable educators, he doubted they could do much for Helen. Securing Helen Keller as a student would help the fledgling school establish its reputation, but he felt she would do more for them than they for her.[2]

Others had differing opinions. "Fashionable lady friends" in Boston wanted Sullivan and Helen there, as did John Spaulding. Mount Vernon Seminary in Washington, D.C. (now part of George Washington University), attended by Bell's daughters, also became a possibility. Sullivan explained to Annie Pratt the undesirability of these options: too many "fashionable entertainments, receptions," and too much time spent on "gaieties and amusements."[3] They'd never get any studying done.

How Sullivan made her final decision is unclear, but it asserted her independence. She may have wanted to stay away from Boston, wishing to avoid the city of Perkins and Michael Anagnos. She explained to Pratt that she lacked "full faith" in the methods used to teach oral speech at Northampton's Clarke Institution or at the Horace Mann School, where Helen's previous articulation lessons had not succeeded as hoped. Wright-Humason, however, was not necessarily a logical choice. The school had not yet even opened—and while Bell had been "favorably impressed" with the two men, they had no long-standing educational reputation. In fact, prior to 1895 neither man was even mentioned in the pages of the *Silent Worker*. Why they started a school for deaf students, and why they considered themselves eligible to do so, is unclear. In a photo taken at the 1894 AAPTSD meeting, both men appear mustached, dapper, and substantially younger than the other "well-known educators" pictured. In 1895, the *Silent Worker* characterized them as "young, energetic, scholarly, progressive."[4] Perhaps they were highly persuasive. Perhaps they simply impressed Sullivan. Perhaps she thought they would be more easily manipulated than some of their counterparts.

Funding appeared easily. John Spaulding offered to pay the eight hundred dollars required for board and tuition. Spaulding, Pratt, and former Perkins housemother Sophia Hopkins formed "the Helen Keller Club" in order to collect and disburse "funds for the use and benefit of 'the twins.'" Hopkins served as secretary and treasurer. Helen's father quickly agreed, signifying to Bell that "as much depends upon" Sullivan's preference, the Wright-Humason choice should be followed.[5]

Sullivan and Helen spent the next two school years, starting in October 1894, at the Wright-Humason School at 42 West 76th Street in New York. Keller's 1903 autobiography explained that she went to Wright-Humason "for the purpose of obtaining the highest advantages in vocal culture and training in lip-reading." In November of the first school year Bell visited Helen, Sullivan, and the school. The school's directors impressed him: "They are doing a good work." Humason's efforts to "improve" Helen's voice had "remarkable" results. Bell told his wife, Mabel, "I should not be at all surprised to find her singing some day, for it is her ambition to sing." Keller later reluctantly wrote that at Wright-Humason she did not gain the lip-reading and speech skills for which she had hoped. "It was my ambition," she wrote, "to speak like other people, and my teachers believed this could be accomplished." "I suppose we aimed too high," she wrote, the disappointment reflected in her words even ten years later.[6]

Though Helen's articulation never developed as she and Sullivan had hoped, the teachers at Wright-Humason (most likely Thomas Humason) taught Helen the lip-reading method she relied on for the rest of her life. She placed the index finger of her left hand on the speaker's lips, perpendicular to the lips, and her thumb on the speaker's throat. She read the vibrations of the throat and the movement of the lips, reportedly to comprehend at least the majority of what was said. This left her right hand free to fingerspell quick exchanges with Annie.[7] Though Sullivan encouraged Helen's articulation lessons, and though the media made much of her articulation skills, she and Helen relied almost exclusively on fingerspelling.

At Wright-Humason Annie thus served primarily as an interpreter. With other teachers, Helen studied German, at which she excelled, as well as French, arithmetic, and geography. Sullivan nearly always sat close, interpreting at least part of the intellectual exchange. She and Helen could fingerspell faster and more accurately than Helen could read a moving lip and throat.

Wright and Humason—or perhaps Helen—quickly established a

strong reputation for the new school. In January 1896 the *Silent Worker* reported, "This private school is believed to be one of the most fashionable schools for the deaf in New York." On several occasions the school held teas or receptions, one in honor of Helen. As with the receptions staged at Perkins, Wright-Humason invited local dignitaries to the events so they could meet its students—including, of course, their famous student, Helen Keller.[8]

Helen and Annie savored the metropolitan life of New York. The students sometimes attended the theater. During the winter of 1894–1895 Helen sought permission from her parents to learn to ice-skate, a novelty to the Alabamian. In February of 1895 Helen reported to her mother that "Teacher is quite dissipated nowadays, and goes out in the evening very often," attending performances by Sarah Bernhardt and a Wagnerian opera. Helen didn't tattle to her mother about who Annie's companions were at these performances, but in this case, it obviously hadn't been her. Together they attended tamer events such as an afternoon dog show and a "poultry-show." They also walked Central Park, visited the new Statue of Liberty, and sailed on the Hudson River. A local reporter made much of Helen's January 1895 acquisition of a cat named Topsy, and at one point she and Annie even housed a pet rabbit in their room.[9]

Though Sullivan and Helen didn't see much of John Spaulding, the tycoon who provided the bulk of the funds used to pay for their presence at Wright-Humason, as primary funder he was omnipresent. He also provided funds for incidentals—such as a typewriter of Helen's choice in early 1895.[10]

Boston's John Spaulding, "King John," had made his substantial fortune in sugar, as well as railroads, banking, and property, and built his philanthropic reputation by flamboyantly distributing his money. On holidays he was known to give five-dollar gold pieces to porters. The publicity he received after giving $30,000 to each of seven young women employed at the Boston hotel where he lived caused him to receive thousands of financial requests. Keller described him in *The Story of My Life* as someone "who made every one happy in a beautiful, unobtrusive way." Spaulding had assisted in many ways since 1890. His death in January 1896 saddened Helen tremendously. She wrote to

Caroline Derby, one of the Boston elite who continued to support her, that "it was so hard to lose him, he was the best and kindest of friends, and I do not know what we shall do without him."[11]

Sullivan also didn't know what they'd do without him, perhaps because of emotional ties, but primarily due to finances. Spaulding adored Helen and doted on her; Sullivan was a necessary auxiliary. They had rushed to his side after learning that he was seriously ill in the fall of 1895, soon after their return from summering in Tuscumbia. "I cannot but feel very anxious should he die without making provisions for Helen," Sullivan wrote. "I do not know what would become of us." Spaulding had given Sullivan the impression that he would provide for the pair in his will, but that didn't happen. After his January 1896 death Spaulding's heirs not only weren't interested in continuing to fund Helen Keller, but they also demanded repayment of the $15,000 loan Spaulding had made to Arthur Keller in early 1893, around the time of the Frost King trial.[12]

Financial panic thus dominated Sullivan's life during Helen's last year at Wright-Humason. In February Arthur Keller wrote to Sophia Hopkins. The Spaulding heirs had offered to settle his substantial debt, now $17,000 including interest, for a payment of $10,000 cash. He thus wanted whatever remained of the money held by Hopkins for Helen's education. He held the sugar company stocks valued at $2,500 given to Helen by Spaulding several years earlier and as her guardian planned to use those to repay the loan. (Hopkins held the $1,000 certificates Spaulding gave to both Helen and Sullivan the previous Christmas and assured Annie that she would not tell Captain Keller where they were.) If there were no funds available for him, he asked Hopkins to see if any of her "acquaintances" would loan Helen $7,500 for him to use. If nothing could be done, he threatened, he would have to "have Helen raise the money by doing [that] which I have always opposed her doing—that is giving the public a chance to see and hear her from the platform," or, in essence, putting the now fifteen-year-old on paid display.[13]

Annie had wrestled with the sorry state of the Keller family's financial affairs for years, and had repeatedly expressed scorn for Arthur Keller's financial management. The financial strain must have upset her, for she knew poverty well. On at least one occasion she had loaned him money, and she knew that frequently he had spent money earned by Helen. Relying on his deaf-blind daughter to support his family must have infuriated and humiliated Arthur Keller. Like many other formerly stable white landowners, the proud Confederate captain had few financial resources. The regional economy was weak, and the entire nation wrestled with high unemployment, business failures, and generally miserable economic conditions in the 1890s.

Hopkins responded "kindly" but negatively and brought Annie Pratt, and thus Alexander Graham Bell, and Sullivan into the conversation. Her letter indicates that she and Sullivan still exchanged confidences frequently. "Does he think people at the North are fools," she asked Annie. Arthur Keller's threat to take "Helen out of school and show her as you would a monkey" was proof to Hopkins of his poor character. She cautioned Annie to protect her few assets. She suggested that Annie request Captain Keller to return to her the certificates given her by Spaulding and others and put them in Hopkins's safe-keeping instead. If he could treat his daughter like this, he might treat Annie badly as well.[14] It is unclear how much any of Sullivan's certificates held by Arthur Keller were worth, or whether he ever returned them to her.

Home life in the Keller household in Tuscumbia must not have been pleasant. While both parents keenly felt the effects of their financial decline, they strongly disagreed on how to deal with it. Kate Keller did not want her daughter appearing on stage. Decades later Helen explained to her sister, "Mother wrote a heartbroken letter to Teacher declaring that she would die before this happened." Vaudeville king Benjamin F. Keith had offered her father five hundred dollars per week, a substantial sum, if she would appear on his circuit. [15]

While nearly everyone but Arthur Keller considered Helen above such a display, it was not a completely ludicrous idea. B. F. Keith had established himself as the most respectable of vaudeville stagers and enforced his own strict decency standards (as he defined them). The acts he sponsored, however, ranged from singers to lecturers to Baby Alice the Midget Wonder. The line between vaudeville and freak show ran dangerously thin, as many who knew Helen feared. Though performing on the circuit was considered the option of stigmatized, lower-class people, it also served as one of the only and probably the most lucrative means of making a living for people with atypical bodies. Helen's education and fame made many consider her a step above those other people with disabilities, but she actually shared much in common with them—most of all, the stigma of disability. Like them, she had few financial resources and even fewer options for making a living, and someone in her situation could easily have been institutionalized permanently or shunned by her family. Only a decade later, when Helen was twenty-six instead of sixteen, she and Annie would choose to join the vaudeville circuit in order to support themselves.

Sullivan, only a decade out of the almshouse, likely recognized the economic precariousness of Helen's situation, and her own, more than anyone—and greatly feared it.

While worrying about money, Sullivan also had to decide not only what Helen would do next but what *she* would do next. The years at Wright-Humason, and subsequent conversations about college for Helen, left Sullivan's status vague. Now that she no longer formally *taught* Helen, was she merely a hired interpreter? Was she a paid companion similar to those respectable but poor women who accompanied wealthy young women on their travels? Was she an educational professional? And if so, why sit around and interpret for Helen in the classroom while someone else taught?

Did Annie want to attend college? Helen had gained all she could from the articulation lessons at Wright-Humason, and Sullivan, Bell, Hitz, and Helen shared the hope that she would attend college. While everyone spoke of the option for Helen, no one seems to have discussed such a possibility for Annie. John Hitz alone recognized that attending class alongside Helen, interpreting lectures and reading materials for her, would require Sullivan to learn the materials.[16]

Annie attempted to use the two academic years at Wright-Humason to solidify and define herself after her tumultuous exile from the life of Perkins. She was approaching thirty, likely felt she would never marry at that old age, and through Bell saw a chance to remake herself as an educational professional.

The worries thus piled up for Sullivan. Where would Helen go to college? How would everything be paid for? What would *she* do—both in the upcoming fall and for the rest of her life?

In early May Helen excitedly reported to her mother that "plans for the summer and next year are slowly beginning to take shape." She and Sullivan were going to Cambridge, Massachusetts, in the fall of 1896 to prepare for Radcliffe College, the female counterpart ("annex") to Harvard. This time Sullivan didn't even pretend to ask Arthur Keller's opinion. Helen successfully pleaded with her mother to let her stay in the North for the summer: "I should feel so lonely without Teacher," she wrote, assuming that Annie would stay as well, "though of course I wish to see you." They could again summer with Sophia Hopkins in Brewster. "To help pay expenses," Sullivan was seeking to teach "a little deaf child."[17]

Financial details didn't distress the nearly sixteen-year-old Helen as they did Annie. But Helen cheerfully reported to her mother that Bell soon would meet with "several gentlemen and arrange with them about the money for my education." He even invited Arthur Keller to the meeting. Bell stepped in once again on Helen's behalf, undoubtedly warned of the events and corralled by Annie Pratt. Over late spring and summer he attempted to generate a group of philanthropists to support Helen's continued education. Bell kept Sullivan updated on his efforts but she felt that his efforts were inadequate and his leadership minimal, and expressed this to Hitz—which likely meant that her complaints were communicated to Bell. Once she, Helen, and Bell lunched with William Spaulding, the heir of King John.[18] Bell and Sullivan hoped that if he met Helen, he would agree to continue his father's contributions.

By moving to Cambridge, Sullivan was stepping back into Perkins territory. She and Anagnos had had little contact over the previous two years. The 1894 and 1895 Perkins annual reports hardly made mention of Helen, and virtually none of Sullivan. Both reports instead glorified deaf-blind student Edith Thomas. Anagnos praised Thomas's teacher, Fanny Marrett, enthusiastically. In a not very oblique reference to Sullivan, he wrote that Thomas's teachers, "instead of striving to impress upon her their own personalities," had "endeavored to lead her to express the truth that is in her, and to enable her to observe and to compare, to reason and to judge, to resolve and to do."[19] The rest of the thought went unfinished—a comparison between Marrett and Sullivan, whom Anagnos now believed had manipulated her student to tell a falsehood in the Frost King trial.

Such comments undoubtedly pained Sullivan greatly. Not only did Anagnos dismiss her as a liar and an unethical teacher, but he did so by comparing her with Fanny Marrett. Marrett had been one of her teachers during her last years at Perkins. In Sullivan's view, Marrett had double-crossed her by interrogating Helen about the Frost King story on the evening before Washington's birthday in 1892 and running to Anagnos with her mistaken tale of Helen's confession; she was a tattle-tale of false information as far as Sullivan was concerned. Anagnos's praise of Marrett served as salt in a still sore wound.

Before Sullivan stepped back into the lion's den of Boston, how-ever, the summer of 1896 beckoned. Upon leaving New York she and Helen spent three weeks at the home of their friends Edgar and Ida Chamberlin. They then went to Philadelphia for the AAPTSD meet-ing. Since they'd last attended, sometime during the years at Wright-Humason, Sullivan had taken it upon herself to write a paper on the importance of using the natural world to teach children, particularly deaf children. She was confident enough to step forward as a pro-fessional educator of deaf students but hesitant enough to send it indirectly to Bell, through John Hitz, qualified by statements of her inadequacy. She suggested that Bell take her ideas and "use his great influence" at the yearly summer meeting of the AAPTSD to convince educators that "what their pupils need is more out-of-door lessons—lessons about living things . . . things they love and are curious about."[20] Bell had more confidence in Sullivan than she had in herself. Or else he simply didn't want to deal with it. Through Hitz, he suggested that *she* present at the AAPTSD meeting.

The summer 1896 meeting of the AAPTSD featured Helen, but not Sullivan. She left no record of her feelings on these matters. Per-haps still uncomfortable with public speaking, she chose not to follow through on Bell's suggestion that she present her pedagogical ideas. Perhaps she felt no one would listen, or that her lack of educational training or her age, gender, or class background would put her at a disadvantage. Humason presented a paper at the 1896 meeting encouraging educators to teach language to deaf students naturally. The *Silent Worker* considered his methods similar to those of educational theorist François Gouin. If so, Humason's method was markedly similar to that articulated by Sullivan. Perhaps the adulation it and Humason received frustrated Annie. Though Bell and Hitz praised her enthusiastically, other deaf educators never embraced her as a pedagogical professional.

While she was undoubtedly proud of Helen's oral presentation at the meeting, Helen's unequivocal success among educators of deaf students may have prompted contradictory feelings for Annie. In reportage that allocated no more than a paragraph to any other person or event at the meeting, Helen earned two lengthy paragraphs in the *Silent Worker*. The paper's reporter considered Helen's address, "The Advantage of Speech to the Deaf," "the great wonder and treat" of the entire event. And the superlatives went on: "For clearness of statement, originality of illustration and beauty of diction, the address could hardly have been bettered."[21] Undoubtedly the praise of her student pleased Annie. Helen, however, had succeeded in doing what she had not: speaking before the AAPTSD crowd of educators and receiving their enthusiastic praise.

After the meeting, the pair went to Sophia Hopkins's house in Brewster, whereupon Annie made a brief trip to Boston to visit with Bell about financial details. While she was gone for only four days, the separation pained Helen. "I miss her greatly. Her departure made a great gap in my life," Helen reported to her mother, from whom she'd been separated for almost a year. "Love is our very life, and Teacher seems part of myself."[22] Perhaps Sullivan suffered similarly through the four-day separation. Perhaps she experienced it as respite, despite the stress of continued financial discussions. She had little time away from Helen.

Annie and Helen remained with Hopkins for the rest of the summer of 1896. Hopkins and her home on the beach, the endless sandy shores and their summertime flowers, had provided retreat and solace to Sullivan for almost a decade. She trusted Hopkins as she trusted and would trust few people. Once again Hopkins and the place served as home. In many ways, it was the only home Annie knew. From there she could look back on the years at Perkins and Wright-Humason, at how far she had come from Feeding Hills and the Tewksbury Almshouse, and ahead to Helen's preparation for and entrance to Radcliffe.

The years at Wright-Humason had not been a waste, despite the dissatisfaction with Helen's articulation skills and Sullivan's increased searching. While there she had built relationships with powerful people that went beyond Michael Anagnos. Some of the relationships—particularly those with John Hitz, Laurence and Eleanor Hutton, Joseph Edgar and Ida Chamberlin—became quite meaningful and continued for years. Other individuals provided important financial assistance, institutional legitimacy, and advocacy. While some of those she depended upon were primarily interested in Helen, others recognized Sullivan as an individual.

Laurence Hutton and Joseph Edgar Chamberlin both occupied important and powerful places in the U.S. literary world. They and the connections they provided to Keller and Sullivan assisted in the sale of Helen's writings. From 1886 to 1898 Hutton served as literary editor of *Harper's* magazine. He and his wife, Eleanor, drew both Annie and Helen into the active social world of their New York home, introducing them to literary figures such as Samuel Clemens. In 1895, after an afternoon at the Hutton home in which she first met Clemens, Helen had written to her mother, "I wonder that I, only a little girl of fourteen, should come in contact with so many distinguished people."[23] Sullivan, though older, undoubtedly had the same thought. Eleanor Hutton managed Helen's finances throughout the years at Radcliffe and beyond, indeed, succeeded where Bell had not in establishing a financial trust adequate to pay for the years at Radcliffe. Sullivan would rely on her in the years ahead for business and financial advice.

Joseph Edgar Chamberlin and his wife, Ida, (referred to as "Uncle Ed" and "Aunt Ida" by Annie and Helen) also lived in a rich literary circle. Both became important and genuine friends of Annie's and welcomed her to their Wrentham, Massachusetts, home "Red Farm" for decades. She had first met Chamberlin in his capacity as associate editor of the *Youth's Companion*. During the tumultuous March of the Frost King trial he had thrown her an emotional lifeline, asking that she and Helen write an account of Helen's instruction for the magazine. Unlike many, he and Ida recognized Sullivan as an individual and not simply a paid auxiliary to Helen. At another difficult moment, in April 1893, after she had left Perkins to align herself with Bell, he wrote, "Sometimes I fear that in our interest in Helen, some of her friends fail to express the great sympathy that they feel with you personally."[24]

Decades later, near the end of Sullivan's life, Keller thanked the man she called "Uncle Ed" for all he had done for her teacher. "That you included us in the circle of your charming hospitality, we entered the intellectual atmosphere of which Teacher had dreamed. Through you she enjoyed satisfying conversation with persons who had seen or written or traveled or done large things. Eagerly she drank with me the fresh, sweet waters of thought that flowed under the old linden in the yard at Red Farm. . . . We both have ever looked back upon those days as the richest and brightest experience of our lives." The Chamberlins frequently hosted large parties of literary figures, including one party of forty while Sullivan and Helen visited in June of 1896.[25] Red Farm lay along King Phillip's Pond, where they frequently boated, swam, picnicked, and talked and talked. When the pair later bought land, they did so very near Red Farm.

In June, while at the Chamberlins', Sullivan called upon Arthur Gilman of the Cambridge School for Young Ladies (sometimes referred to as the Gilman Training School for Radcliffe) to ask if Helen might attend in order to prepare for the Radcliffe entrance exams. As Gilman later put it, "the proposition startled me." Sullivan, however, was persuasive. She and Gilman made plans for Helen to begin in early October with the rest of the incoming students. By so doing, Sullivan admitted that she did not have the knowledge and skills to prepare Helen for college. Strategically, the Cambridge School brought them both closer to Radcliffe. The *New York Times* twice reported Helen's admittance.[26]

Before the two could leave for Cambridge, amidst what must have been hurried efforts to prepare clothing and housing, they received telegraphed news of Arthur Keller's death. Neither knew of his illness. They immediately made plans to leave for Tuscumbia, but Kate

Keller insisted they remain in Brewster with Sophia Hopkins due to "the beginning of their sickliest season." Sullivan never recorded her own feelings, but the death devastated Helen. "She is still inconsolable," Sullivan wrote to John Hitz. "I never dreamed there was the possibility of such great sorrow in the dear child's nature." Helen's grief revealed to her teacher a misconception she'd held about her student, a misconception illuminating more than she admitted about her continuing and demeaning views on disability. She had assumed that Helen's "peculiar limitations had dulled her emotional nature so that she did not feel as intensely as many. But I see that I was wrong and I am sorry." The summer preceding Helen's October 1896 entrance to the Cambridge School for Young Ladies had not been "free from mental effort," as Gilman later characterized it.[27]

At the end of Helen's first semester Gilman declared the novel strategy of placing Helen in college preparatory classes alongside hearing and seeing girls a success. In a *Century* magazine article he reported in detail on Keller's coursework, shared her marks, reproduced several of her essays, and assured his readers that "she keeps up with speaking and hearing girls." Being sure to state that "the direction of Helen's intellectual work has been committed to me," he thanked Sullivan for her "loving superintendence" and the "ministrations that she has so willingly rendered all these years."[28] He considered himself in charge.

Sullivan put in lengthy hours. She went to each class session and spelled its entire contents into Helen's hand (although Gilman and the German teacher eventually learned fingerspelling). Few of the books were brailled or embossed (raised print) so studying demanded that Sullivan "read and reread" class notes and books to Helen.[29] At Christmas, the first Christmas after Arthur Keller's death, Helen's mother and sister Mildred joined them in Boston. Mildred remained to attend the Cambridge School. This thrilled Helen, but created more work for Sullivan.

Helen finished her first academic year at the Cambridge School in the summer of 1897 with a fanfare of public reporting. She had passed the Radcliffe preparatory exams in elementary and advanced German, French, Latin, English, and Greek and Roman history. Proudly she received honors in German and English. Her presence brought publicity and credit to the Cambridge School, just as it had done for Wright-Humason and Perkins, but she considered the credit Sullivan's. "I consider my crown of success is the happiness and pleasure that my victory has brought dear Teacher," she wrote to Hitz after the exams. "Indeed, I feel that the success is hers more than mine; for she is my constant inspiration."[30] Arthur Gilman, however, did not agree.

Despite the public praise, or perhaps because of it, tensions had been growing between Sullivan and Gilman over who was in charge of Helen—just as they had between her and Anagnos. At the end of April he'd sent a letter to Sullivan, who lived with Helen and all the other students in a house directly attached to the school, requesting a meeting. "It has come to me emphatically," he wrote, "that we must have some explicit understanding in reference to the management of Helen. . . . The present arrangement is loose." What event, if anything specific, precipitated the letter is unclear; as is the immediate outcome. In the June reports on Helen's exams he indicated that while Helen wanted to and could attend Radcliffe after two more years, studying with him for three more years would be better for her health.[31]

After summering in Wrentham at the Chamberlins' home, Annie, Helen, and Mildred Keller returned to the Cambridge School for Young Ladies in the fall of 1897. War soon broke out. Annie called it "unrighteous warfare."[32] Everyone—Kate Keller, Ida and Joseph Edgar Chamberlin, Eleanor Hutton, John Hitz, Mildred Keller, Alexander Graham Bell, Annie Pratt, Sophia Hopkins, William Wade, and Helen—entered the fray.

Sullivan and Gilman first disagreed over the number of Helen's courses. Gilman argued that for a student with Helen's disabilities the rigorous course load Sullivan advocated was physically risky.

Helen had started the school year at a disadvantage. Her French, geometry, algebra, and physics textbooks showed up very late. The necessary alterations had delayed the arrival of her Greek typewriter. Because of the late textbooks and the complexities of creating embossed math problems, geometrical designs, and astronomy figures, Sullivan fell behind in brailling and preparing materials. Gilman wanted to change the course load immediately. Sullivan convinced him to wait until after Christmas.[33]

On a Friday in early November Helen experienced a difficult menstrual period (referred to as "natural causes" by Sullivan and Hitz). Sullivan sent her to bed. She returned to school on Monday and when Gilman asked her to give a recitation, not originally scheduled for that day, Sullivan intervened—how is unknown. Or, as Hitz later characterized it more blandly, she "demurred." Rarely, however, had Sullivan ever demurred in her life. Likely she protested forcefully and loudly. As Keller later wrote about her, "it was a point of honor with her to pound her arguments into those who differed from her instead of trying to win them over with tact."[34] Sullivan considered herself the ultimate authority regarding Helen and acted as such. Gilman interpreted this as a direct challenge to his authority. And it was. He owned and ran the Cambridge School for Young Ladies. In his own classroom, as the teacher, he had asked a student for a recitation. Instead of getting it, an uppity young woman with a slight Irish lilt in her voice had asserted her own authority over the education of that student.

After this Gilman began a campaign of letters to persuade Kate Keller, Sophia Hopkins, Eleanor Hutton, and perhaps others, of the necessity of separating Annie and Helen. Sullivan, he argued in numerous and repeated letters, pushed Helen beyond her physical capabilities. Helen was overworked and ill. Sullivan had lost her "mental balance" and treated Helen cruelly. Sullivan was "behind her in knowledge" and "constantly irritated with her." Sophia Hopkins apparently took his concerns seriously, and wrote of them to Kate Keller, repeating that Annie and Helen needed to be separated. Hutton had serious hesitations about Gilman's charges and sought the opinion of J. E. Chamberlin. Mrs. Keller took them seriously enough that she wrote letters to Annie, urging her to follow the advice of Gilman and reduce Helen's workload.[35]

On campus Gilman and Sullivan continued to disagree, and on December 8 tensions between them boiled over. They exchanged ugly words. Sullivan insisted she knew what was best for Helen and that she would make the ultimate decisions. Gilman, however, knew something Annie didn't. His repeated letters to Kate Keller, along with at least one from Sophia Hopkins, had convinced Helen's mother to act. As she later explained to John Hitz, "one letter after another kept coming until I lost my temper and by telegram authorized Gilman to act as Helen's guardian."[36] Gilman displayed his trump card.

That very day, perhaps before his meeting with Sullivan, but more likely after, Gilman sought to fortify the powers given him by Kate Keller. Perhaps he believed, probably accurately, that the telegram would not hold up in court. He sought to establish full legal guardianship of Helen and her sister Mildred via the county probate courts. He thus composed three letters that he sent to Kate Keller, urging her to rewrite them in her own hand, sign them, and deliver them to him. The first was a letter to him and gave him guardianship of both girls. The second was a letter to Mildred, explaining that she and Helen should from that time on "go to him [Gilman] for advice, and . . . do what he wishes you to do." He would now care for them; by so doing, Kate Keller was only "carrying out wishes that your dear father would have expressed, were he here, for he told me what he desired, especially for Helen." The third letter was for Sullivan. It stated that Helen was to be put "fully in Mr. Gilman's care, in school and out of school" as Mrs. Keller's "representative." It directed her to submit all of Helen's books, money, and other property to Gilman.[37]

Gilman's proposed letters reveal much about his relationship with and attitudes toward Helen. At the time he wrote them, Helen was seventeen years old, preparing for college and all it entailed. Yet, he did not suggest that her mother write *her* a letter of explanation—only one for eleven-year-old Mildred. Perhaps he feared her response, but the more likely explanation is that her disability caused him to disregard her.

Why would Gilman seek guardianship of Helen? Guardianship would have given him immense power, and access to the funds provided Helen and to the people who gave those funds. It also would have brought prestige to the Cambridge School for Young Ladies. Guardianship, however, would have rendered Helen legally incompetent—*non compos mentis*, determined her "incompetent to have the charge and management" of her property, and incompetent to make legal decisions. Whether or not Helen, with her disability, would have been able to regain her legal competency upon adulthood is a historical unknown. John Hitz believed, and later reported to Bell, that Gilman acted only out of self-interest. He had allowed "his ambition to get the better of his judgment." With disgust Hitz noted that Gilman had offered to pay a reporter to publish notices of Helen's attendance when she'd first arrived at his school.[38]

On top of it all, Sullivan annoyed Gilman fiercely, as she had and would many others. She had no advanced education, gave little credence to the authority he claimed, refused to back down in an argument, and was female.

While Annie later wrote and spoke of Helen's emotions on the matter, she didn't record her own. The possibility of being exiled from Helen must have infuriated and terrified her. Like Anagnos, Gilman challenged her authority and legitimacy, in the only sphere in which she had it. He threatened her livelihood. She responded territorially to the threatened loss of Helen—the only one, since the death of her brother, who loved and adored her without question, who assuaged her fear of isolation, and who took away her self-doubt. And when crossed, Annie had a vicious temper. Displaying the determination of will that had taken her thus far through life, she garnered every bit of cunning she had, every sliver of a resource she could think of, and responded to Arthur Gilman.

With Helen and Mildred in distress, Annie fled to the home of Lucy Derby Fuller and her husband, the Reverend S. Richard Fuller, seeking advice, rescue, and solace. Long after Sullivan's death, in her 1956 biography *Teacher*, Keller wrote that Annie had nearly thrown herself in the Charles River that night, "overcome with despair." Helen may have been right about Annie's distress, but Annie's actions indicate resourcefulness and cunning rather than despair. The next morning, December 9, she sent telegrams to Kate Keller, Alexander Graham Bell, J. E. Chamberlin, and Annie Pratt. She returned to the Cambridge School for Young Ladies and insisted on seeing Helen. Gilman refused. Sullivan threatened to stay until she could see Helen, saying that she would not leave, "except by force." After a several-hour period—one can imagine the tense stand-off that occurred—he allowed Annie to see Helen in the chaperonage of a housekeeper in the student boardinghouse.[39]

By mid-afternoon the reinforcement troops that Sullivan had called for arrived: Chamberlin from Wrentham and Pratt from Chelsea. Chamberlin easily took Annie, Helen, and Mildred home with him to Red Farm. There they stayed. The drama continued on Sunday, December 12, when Kate Keller arrived in town on the first train, hastily responding to Sullivan's telegram: "We need you." In curious order, she first visited Mrs. Hopkins (likely in Brewster) and the Cambridge School the following day. Gilman informed her that those she sought had gone to Wrentham, where she traveled on the 14th. Within one or two days John Hitz, sent once again by Alexander Graham Bell to investigate charges leveled against Sullivan, also showed up at Red Farm. Kate Keller quickly became convinced of her errors, John Hitz took written testimonies from nearly everyone involved (including Mildred) for his "report" to Bell, and Annie emerged victorious once again.[40]

In her written report prepared for Hitz, Kate Keller maintained that even before receiving Sullivan's telegram she had realized "the injustice" and the "cruel" nature of what she'd done. Upon her arrival in Wrentham she found Helen "in perfect physical condition," with no evidence of "nervous prostration or over-work." "Mr. Gilman had made cruel use of the authority I [had] given him," she complained, "to distress my children and Miss Sullivan. After ten years of service I certainly never dreamed of Miss Sullivan being forced away from Helen." The whole affair had left her "in such a state of worry."[41]

The guardianship decision that Gilman foisted on Kate Keller had been the first major decision she'd had to make about Helen since the death of her husband. She had voiced her opinion about prior questions, such as Helen's threatened appearance on the vaudeville circuit, but her husband had held the legal authority. She'd parented her children alone for only a little over a year, attempting to provide them emotional support while meeting their legal and financial needs. And she was parenting a deaf-blind child, whom many considered defective by definition, long distance. Since 1888, over eleven years, circumstances had forced her to share Helen with the young woman nearly the age of her stepson. Rushing to Boston in response to Sullivan's urgent telegram, she left toddler Phillips at home.

Indeed, Helen spent more time with Sullivan than her own mother over these years. Less than a month earlier Mrs. Keller had written to Annie, "I always think of Helen as partly your child." Years later J. E. Chamberlin wrote that the day Helen and Annie arrived at his Wrentham home he spoke with Helen privately, perhaps being one of the few to ask her about her own preferences. As he remembered it, she said that if she had to choose, "I will go with Teacher. She has meant more to me than my mother has. She has made me everything that I am."[42]

Helen's lengthy report, couched in the melodramatic language of a seventeen-year-old, exemplifies the rhetorical blend of drama and moralism that she would use the rest of her life. She twice characterized Gilman's reduction of her course load as "humiliation." She had borne it bravely, she insisted, until Gilman attempted to force the separation from her teacher. "Only a true, loving heart can understand the agony I suffered," she wrote, "when I thought of my teacher, insulated, betrayed and driven away from me, and for what offence?" She would have suffered silently had not her teacher been involved: "my dear, faithful teacher has never deserved the cruel things Mr. Gilman has said about her." For even when Sullivan's "poor eyes were aching so she could scarcely see the letters of the lesson" she did "her duty faithfully."[43]

Furthermore, Helen characterized the event as a loss of innocence. The seventeen-year-old wrote, "this terrible experience has made a woman of me." She had been twelve at the time of the Frost King trial, less able to comprehend the threat made to Sullivan. This time, however, she understood the implications of all that had been said. "My childhood," she went on, "has slipped away with its simple, unreasoning trust in human goodness, and its dreamy unconsciousness of the evil there is in the world. I know now that men can be false and wicked, even while they seem kind and true. I have found that I cannot always put my hand in another's with a trustful spirit." Then she picked up themes she would repeat over and over again in later years, in more sophisticated terms: "Yet I know that Goodness is mightier than Evil, and my heart still tells me that Love is the most beautiful thing in the world, and must triumph in the end."[44]

Throughout December Gilman had continued to attempt to persuade others that "to bind the child for life to her Teacher would be a calamity." He corresponded with Eleanor Hutton, who directed the fund supporting Helen's education, J. E. Chamberlin, and at least several others. He traveled to New York, likely to speak with people at the Wright-Humason School. Nothing worked. By December 11 he stated that he desired nothing more to do with the education of Keller, due to the "erratic doings" of Sullivan and the advice of his doctors. He asserted to Eleanor Hutton that while she knew "the agreeable side of Miss Sullivan," she did not "know her as those do who have worked with her." "No one who has studied Miss Sullivan in her work with Helen," he went on, "would think of her as a suitable guide for a young woman." He avowed to Edgar Chamberlin that if those who saw Sullivan "in her agreeable social guise" saw her at work, "there would be a revulsion of sentiments."[45]

Sullivan's written report to Hitz is a dry summary of events. She presented herself as a professional educator and refused to acknowledge hurt feelings. She portrayed the conflict as one of pedagogical differences in which she attempted to "cheerfully" comply even when in disagreement. Privately the conflict infuriated her. "What have I done to deserve it?" she lamented to Hitz. "God only knows I have tried to do my duty to the best of my ability. I have given Helen all that I had to give—myself, my service, my love, and she has given me in return the tenderest love in the world. We are both satisfied. Why should people persecute us?"[46]

But she had won. Mrs. Keller and Mildred returned to Tuscumbia, leaving Sullivan "in full charge of Helen and with full authority to do what seems best to me in regard to her studies," as Annie explained to Hitz. Dean Agnes Irwin of Radcliffe would help find tutors for Helen's continued college preparatory work.[47] She and Helen would stay with "Uncle Ed" and "Aunt Ida" Chamberlin until July 1898. They then summered in their own rental cottage, as they would for many future years, on the nearby shores of Lake Wollomonapoag.

The surprising individual in this story is Sophia Hopkins. She had believed Gilman's words. She considered a response so necessary that she wrote to Kate Keller of the importance of removing Annie. Perhaps the accusations did not surprise her. Perhaps she simply worried about

Helen. Because of the later loss of letters we don't know whether the correspondence between the housemother and Annie decreased after these events. Annie, however, was not one to easily forget a grudge or forgive a real, or even an imagined, slight.

Ed and Ida Chamberlin took incredible care of Helen and Annie. As Helen remembered it almost half a century later, Annie thrilled to the boisterous household as if "under the spell of the Celtic fairy," "once more in the place of clouds dear to her nature." The rich cultural life created by the actors, writers, artists, and other intellectuals circulating in and out of the house opened up a "new world" for Annie. She flirted with men, laughed, and thrilled to conversation. "[T]his was the nearest she had come to self-possession," Helen wrote. "The melancholy which had oppressed her slackened its hold upon her." Not only that, but the relationship between the two of them, as Helen turned eighteen that summer, slowly began its transformation to one of friendship. "She ceased to treat me as a child, she did not command me any more."[48]

Annie invited the rest of Helen's family to join them at the summer cottage, where Kate and her three children were together for the first time since Arthur Keller's death. Sullivan paid for the cottage and other summer expenses, most likely using some of the certificates Hopkins had warned her to secure from Captain Keller. They swam and boated constantly. Once Annie swam so far she exhausted herself, and needed rescuing. She also rode her horse Lucky Star; she loved speed, but her limited eyesight made it dangerous. Helen believed that had Annie been able to see well, "she would have ridden a race horse, matching the fire of her soul with his own."[49]

Annie, however, was not well. In mid-June Ida Chamberlin confidentially sought John Hitz's help with the thirty-one-year-old. Her eyes were in "a most aggravated state." A doctor warned her that unless she had another surgery she would lose all vision. Annie vowed to Mrs. Chamberlin that she would not be operated upon, nor would she live blind. Chamberlin believed this to be a warning of suicide. "I know her so well now that I know this is no idle threat," she wrote to Hitz. "Her sight has failed noticeably since last winter and within the last week symptoms have come which I recognize and fills me with alarm. . . . A crisis is on us through her agony, and God only knows the outcome."[50] Could Bell find someone to pay for the medical treatment?

Chamberlin understood Sullivan well. "I know my girl," she warned Hitz, probably needlessly in his case, "and know that she is to be treated tactfully." They must *"persuade"* Annie to undergo surgery, for "no one else can *make* her do what she should do now." She asked him not to seek Eleanor Hutton's advice on the matter, for she feared that Hutton would "try to use authority" with Annie. Such efforts would undoubtedly fail with the stubborn, recalcitrant, and depressed Annie Sullivan.[51]

Sullivan made erratic plans that spring and summer. No evidence indicates that she ever had surgery. After the United States declared war on Spain she applied to be an army nurse. Only months before she had insisted that Helen needed her, but now she sought escape. Keller later tried to explain that Sullivan gave up the idea because of the lengthy training time, but undoubtedly Annie knew that her vision would have disqualified her. Perhaps, she proposed quite unrealistically to Helen, they could grow oranges or lemons on a Cuban plantation.[52]

Assessing Sullivan's state of mind is difficult, particularly since the limited evidence from this period was filtered through others, but melancholy haunted her. Twice in this six-month period others referred to her potential for suicide—even Helen, who always sought to make her look good. Despite Annie's comments to Ida Chamberlin it's unlikely that her threatened blindness alone caused her depression, for her eyesight had fluctuated for over two decades. Sadly, she now had much more to worry her. She had accomplished so much by the summer of 1898, yet had no assurances about her future. The frequent eye pain she experienced likely bothered her more than blindness. She had no family to claim. Helen had become her entire life, but Helen was on the verge of adulthood, about to succeed in college—which her teacher had not even had the opportunity to attempt. Despite having escaped Tewksbury, having thrived at all she and Helen attempted, despite having defeated both Anagnos and Gilman, she still felt herself lacking a definition, a reason. Ever vulnerable despite her pragmatism, she feared that Helen would either leave or be taken from her.

In the fall the rest of the Keller family returned to Tuscumbia, and Annie and Helen returned to a Cambridge boardinghouse at 12 Newbury Street. Merton Keith, who had been tutoring Helen in algebra, geometry, Greek, and Latin since her departure from the Cambridge School, continued to do so five days a week. In these early days of women's collegiate education many doctors and educators warned of the dire physical and mental consequences of a college education for any woman. Keith reported warnings that "with Helen a break-down might be fraught with more terrible consequences than in ordinary cases, that total collapse might ensue." Helen, however, thrived. Annie's physical health proved to be his concern. Lengthy sessions, some of which required her to interpret for up to three and a half hours, caused her to be "well nigh exhausted."[53]

Helen always claimed the drive for college success to be her own, never placing credit or blame on Annie. It's difficult to believe, however, that Annie was not equally driven. Helen's successful graduation from the most prestigious women's college of the time would prove false all that had been charged about Helen's intellectual failings and Sullivan's manipulation of her. Perhaps then Sullivan would no longer have to worry—about money, about what others thought of her and Helen, or about her place in the world.

Annie left little documentation about the 1898–1899 academic year. Strenuous work, as well as the concern and pain caused by her eyes, dominated the year. The Radcliffe preparatory exams were scheduled for the end of June. Poor conditions, certainly, for emotional or physical healing.

The stress affected both Annie and Helen. In February Helen shared her "sad dilemma" with John Hitz. "I really dread going to college next fall on her account," she wrote. "I cannot bear the thought of the constant and terrible strain upon her [Annie's] poor eyes, which I fear will come with our new studies." Helen imagined escaping. "How I wish we could slip away, and live in the peaceful country for a year at least, away from every one we know and just be happy, and free from care and anxiety!" They would tell only Hitz and Mrs. Keller of their hideaway. "Perhaps her eyes could get better there, and we would be quite ready for any amount of college work." In March she complained, "It is awfully lonely here at times, and Teacher and I hope that we shall not have to come here next year."[54]

The college entry exams, however, beckoned. Because Harvard authorities would not allow Sullivan to interpret the exam materials, an instructor from Perkins, who could only communicate with Helen by using Braille, administered the exams. Several days later the long-desired, long-sought-after certificate of admission to Radcliffe College arrived. The two women must have felt immense relief as well as joy. Alexander Graham Bell sent money that they might have "a nice time in the country this summer," undoubtedly at the instigation of Hitz. They returned once again to the shores of Lake Wollomonapoag near Wrentham. Helen wrote to a friend that her "dear teacher has not had a vacation for twelve years. . . . Now her eyes are troubling her a great deal, and we all think she ought to be relieved, for a while, of every care and responsibility."[55]

Again, however, things were not as easy as they might have seemed. Of the next academic year, 1899–1900, both women would say little. In *The Story of My Life*, Helen gives it merely one sentence: a vague statement that "Before I entered college, however, it was thought best that I should study another year under Mr. Keith." That fall Helen began to explain to friends that though she had long dreamed of attending college she was not going to do so. She had already "shown the world that I could do the college work." To "pursue a four years' course of study at Radcliffe, simply to be like others girls" would be "very foolish."[56]

The reality differed. Despite Sullivan and Keller's reluctance, Dean Agnes Irwin of Radcliffe persuaded them to enroll Helen in a "special course." As Keller reported, the college dean made the unlikely claim that "she did not consider a degree of any real value, but thought it was much more desirable to do something original than to waste one's energies only for a degree." Instead Keller should study translation and composition, languages and literature, for which she had a "gift." "I found it very, very hard," Helen confessed to John Hitz, "to give up the idea of going to Radcliffe." When Helen and Annie returned to meet the proposed tutor, they discovered that Irwin instead had arranged for a young female student to tutor Helen. The two women were insulted and furious, and they rejected the idea.[57]

Nearly each day that school year both women must have walked by Radcliffe. They lived at 138 Brattle Street and would have walked first by the Episcopal Seminary and then the lawn of Radcliffe as they went to shop in Harvard Square. It was a daily reminder of Radcliffe's refusal to admit Helen. Yet, they stayed in Cambridge. Helen continued to work with Mr. Keith.

Sullivan seethed, and wrestled with continued gloominess. "Helen is restless and disappointed and I am utterly discouraged," she lamented to Hitz in late October. He and Bell were in the midst of publishing a new Volta Bureau *Souvenir* celebrating Helen's admission to Radcliffe. Annie considered it farcical: "Here is the subject of it clamoring at the door of a nineteenth-century institution for instruction and getting splendidly snubbed for her audacity." She wondered if Gilman had negatively influenced Keller's marks on the entrance exams, but she didn't push the issue as she had in so many other circumstances with so many other issues. She simply had no energy or fire to do so.[58]

Annie's despondency, her disillusionment with the world, her self-hatred, and her overwhelming feeling of being undeserving permeated her letter to Hitz. She thanked him for his love but warned him that she did not deserve it. Such affection "makes me wretched and rebellious sometimes. I would much prefer to have people despise me as they certainly would if they guessed how full of distrust and contempt my heart is towards my fellow beings." She wanted him to know just how "detestable" she was. "I find people hateful and I hate them," she wrote.[59] Ida Chamberlin, who might have offered emotional support, spent most of the school year ill, in pain, and confined to bed.

Though the reluctance to let Keller begin at Radcliffe apparently came from Agnes Irwin, Keller's successful college entrance exams had unleashed a fury of skepticism. Even her supporter William Wade complained to Bell of the "ridiculous exaggerations" in circulation. He believed her success "a lot of utter bosh." He charged, "Even her wonderful mentality cannot accomplish impossibilities, and her exquisite beauty of character is deformed by such stuff about her being published."[60] To top it off, he repeated such charges in the Perkins alumni magazine the *Mentor*.

Helen, now a twenty-one-year-old woman, responded with a steaming letter. How dare Wade "shower" such "cruel indignities" upon her and "those who are dear to me!" It brought "bitter tears" to her eyes to call him friend, for he had now "taken up position" among her "enemies"—Michael Anagnos and Arthur Gilman. She implored him "not to attack my friends anymore" and bade him a "sad farewell."[61] His attack on her was insulting, but his attack on Annie worse.

Bell and Hitz's publication of the 1899 Volta Bureau *Souvenir* tried to address skepticism such as Wade's. It minutely detailed Keller's college preparations and reproduced the Radcliffe admissions certificate. Sullivan had no enthusiasm for the effort, only hopelessness. "Helen and I have suffered more than you or anyone else in the world can ever understand, through the publicity that has been given to her education," she wrote to John Hitz. "I cannot think the new Souvenir will unravel the tangled web of truth and falsehood that over-zealous friends and enemies have drawn about us. Time only can do that."[62]

Both women, for both were now adult women, sought a purpose, a task, a calling that would take them away from the pressures they experienced. Ida Chamberlin continued to fear for Sullivan's mental health and suggested the creation of the Helen Keller Home as a solution. There Sullivan could teach deaf-blind children, and Helen could assist. The idea interested neither Annie nor Helen. Helen continued her tutoring with Mr. Keith, necessitating Annie's assistance. Helen also noticed her friend's emotional and physical difficulties and wrote to Hitz of them repeatedly. "Poor teacher is very tired and nervous after her winter's work," she wrote in March. "Her eyes trouble her constantly, and the heat of the fire in our study room aggravates them sorely." In May she, and presumably Sullivan, garnered determination enough to once again approach Radcliffe about enrolling in regular courses. The "condition," of course, was the classroom presence of Sullivan.[63]

Why the two women insisted on Radcliffe is unclear, other than its prestige. During the summer of 1900, both Cornell and the University of Chicago offered Helen admittance. At the end of August Edgar

Chamberlin pled their case once again with Radcliffe's dean, Agnes Irwin. Certainly, he implied, Radcliffe would not want the world-famous Helen Keller to attend a competing school.[64] The administration of Radcliffe relented. Helen Keller could attend the regular first-year courses with other students and Anne Sullivan could interpret for her. Both women would get their way.

CHAPTER 9

Radcliffe, 1900–1904

WHEN KELLER entered Radcliffe College in the fall of 1900, she and Sullivan lived in a boardinghouse at 14 Coolidge Avenue. It was a longer walk to Radcliffe than from their home the previous academic year, but the new house stood on a quiet street, overlooking and directly across from the beautiful serenity of Mount Auburn Cemetery. Helen's dear friend Reverend Phillips Brooks, her brother's namesake, had been buried there in 1893. Ambling through the cemetery's quiet walkways they may have strolled past the resting places of poet Henry Wadsworth Longfellow, former slave and abolitionist Harriet Jacobs, reformer and early disability activist Dorothea Dix, or even Perkins's founder, Samuel Gridley Howe.

Imagine Sullivan walking past the gravesite of Samuel Gridley Howe, perhaps with a bit of glee, perhaps sadness, perhaps even kicking a bit of dirt at the headstone on a particularly bad day. Since 1888, when her education of Helen had first been publicized, she had been endlessly compared to the larger-than-life Howe in terms both positive and negative. Some dismissed her: all she'd had to do with Helen was mindlessly follow the clear pedagogical path laid down by the genius Howe. Some praised her: she'd exceeded Howe exponentially in Helen's education by developing her own pedagogical methods. She'd never even met the man.

The years of Keller's enrollment at Radcliffe, October 1900 through

June 1904, brought profound changes to Annie's life. Helen's adulthood granted Sullivan greater freedom. She dared to start falling in love. Her relationship with the elderly John Hitz deepened. She started to realize that both she and her reputation would survive Michael Anagnos and Arthur Gilman. At the same time, Helen's adulthood left her without a definite purpose in life. What was she? No longer could she pretend to be Helen's teacher.

Helen, John Hitz, Eleanor Hutton, and other friends grew increasingly aware of Sullivan's visual disability and its resulting pain during Helen's years at Radcliffe. For Helen, her growing awareness of her teacher as a human being and friend went hand in hand with her growing awareness of Sullivan's disability. At one point a doctor recommended that Sullivan temporarily give her eyes a complete rest. At first no one else could be found to fingerspell the materials to Helen. The Radcliffe student thus often lied when asked if coursework materials should be reread, telling her former teacher that she remembered everything in hopes of sparing her eyes.[1]

Part of the difficulty of documenting Sullivan's life and emotions in this period comes from her worsening eyesight. While in earlier periods she had written letters that historians of later generations could depend on, in this period she wrote little. According to Keller, "it was almost impossible" for her to do so: "She could not see much farther than the end of her nose and she had to concentrate on her pencil and the word it was tracing."[2] Over and over again as Helen wrote to their friends, she sent Sullivan's greetings and apologies for not writing. Sullivan could use Braille, but badly. That she did not use Helen's Braille-keyed typewriter in order to write her own letters is noteworthy—for she easily could have improved her Braille skills. It may have been impossible for Sullivan to write letters using a pencil, but it was not impossible for her to write letters.

Sullivan's relationship to her disability is difficult to entangle. I'm convinced that she often experienced her partial blindness, and the physical pain that accompanied it, as more debilitating than Helen experienced her deaf-blindness. Near constant pain combined with the waves of melancholy that confronted her throughout her life. And because of Helen's star status, Helen got to be *the disabled one*, indeed a disabled superstar. Accompanying such a person left Sullivan little social space in which to claim her own disability and the accommodations it required. Finally, her status as Teacher made claiming disability difficult. The powerful social definition of disability, one that classified disabled people as markedly different from others, precluded the status of Teacher. Such sentiments assumed that one could not be disabled and be a prominent teacher. Sullivan's efforts to create a livable self-definition in this period, as in other periods, were intricately linked to her ongoing efforts to integrate her disability into her public and private sense of self.

Everything that Keller left behind about her Radcliffe years indicates that she thrived. Occasional flies flirted with the ointment certainly, but the young adult loved the intellectual challenges, the greater personal freedom, the college life of sleigh trips and endless debate. Philosophers Descartes, Kant, Emerson, and her beloved theologian Emanuel Swedenborg taught her that the senses themselves were untrustworthy. Her deaf-blindness didn't matter. What mattered was intellect and spirit, and she had plenty.

How much Sullivan appreciated those same elements of Radcliffe is unclear. She was thirty-four years old when Keller started college, older in years and with vastly different experiences than most others in the Radcliffe and Harvard community. Since eight years of age Helen had been told that she was amazing, but Annie had received dramatically different messages while growing up. She never achieved the carefree spirit, the welcome abandon that made it possible for Helen to savor life and assume goodness.

While the pair tried to maneuver through the studies and practicalities of Helen's first year of college, plans made for them by Ida Chamberlin, with little interest and support from them, commandeered much of their time and energy throughout October, November, and December of 1900. Chamberlin believed it her mission to create the Helen Keller School for deaf-blind children. Sullivan was to teach and Helen to help care for the children. Sullivan and Keller's efforts to maneuver out of the situation without offending Chamberlin, and thus their hesitation to say an explicit *no*, worsened things. Without their approval, she began soliciting students and board members. Sullivan and Keller once again turned to Bell and Hutton, who tried to save them from the situation by speaking to Chamberlin.

Ida Chamberlin believed her plans best for everyone. They would spare Helen the strain exacted by a college education and would ease the demands on Annie's eyes. The Helen Keller School would address the unmet needs of deaf-blind children across the nation. Chamberlin argued to Helen that it would even meet the call of God: "She told me that God had laid this work upon me and that it was my duty to hearken to His voice."[3]

These efforts distressed Annie and Helen tremendously. Neither had much interest in the endeavor, but both feared insulting "Aunt Ida." Sullivan feared that Chamberlin would "banish us out of her life" and told Bell's friend and assistant Annie Pratt that such an action "would have been the saddest thing that could happen for all of us concerned." Ironically Mrs. Chamberlin feared the same. A month earlier her husband, Edgar Chamberlin, had written to Pratt that she was "racked and torn with the thought that Annie and Helen have turned their backs on her." When Annie and Helen visited the Chamberlins for Christmas, after a long fall of evading plans for the proposed school, Annie felt great relief that the holiday went smoothly: "A great load is lifted from my heart." "Well dear little Aunt Polly [as she called Pratt]," she wrote fondly, "I guess the worst of the tempest is passed and we shall get to shore safely."[4] The unwelcome distraction dissipated, perhaps, as they would see, helped along by future events.

Health problems had plagued Mrs. Chamberlin since at least the fall of 1899, and Christmas of 1900 found her in dire shape. At the end of November she had been confined to bed, "quite ill . . . exceedingly nervous, very much disturbed and excited." Sullivan thought she looked "dreadfully" at Christmas.[5] She hosted the holiday meal though unwell and with limited eyesight, blamed on the combination of a kidney problem and a difficult pregnancy.

In January a Chamberlin family conflict exploded, further involving Sullivan and Keller in the family. Mrs. Chamberlin's health failed rapidly; she lost her vision entirely and started convulsing, and doctors forced the delivery of her baby. The baby boy died. Approximately a month later Edgar Chamberlin disappeared. His wife assumed suicide.

The two youngest children went to live with other family members and the oldest, fifteen-year-old Beth (Elizabeth), moved in with Annie and Helen. Beth could fingerspell classroom readings to Keller and did so for five dollars a week. Helen enjoyed her presence immensely and Annie must have appreciated the reading respite. The pair had received so much assistance, so much charity, that they cherished being able to offer their own. "Both Teacher and I are glad we can offer Beth a home, and thus return the generous kindness Aunt Ida showed us three years ago when she opened her home to us after the Gilman affair," Helen wrote to Hitz.[6]

Edgar Chamberlin resurfaced in April, alive but in New York. At first the trauma seemed only to make Ida Chamberlin more resolute about her plans for the proposed school. Keller wrote to Hitz, "we despair of being able to make her see the impossibility of carrying it through." She later considered the effort one of many in which "the would-be directors" of her life attempted to make her decisions for her.[7] Resisting these took considerable time and energy away from Radcliffe, where she wanted her time and energy to go. Chamberlin soon gave up her plans—perhaps because of the lack of support, perhaps because of her own family situation.

With Beth still living with them, that Easter Annie and Helen hosted Ida Chamberlin at their home on Coolidge Avenue. For so many years they had gone to the Chamberlins' for holidays. Perhaps this was the first time they hosted a holiday celebration in their own home. They must have shown off the home proudly, for they savored it.

The house at Coolidge Avenue provided a true home for the women. Annie rented a piano and pianola, which she played in the evenings. She likely remembered the neighbor's piano she had coveted as a child in Feeding Hills. They maintained lots of plants, decorated with lace curtains, secured more and more bookshelves, and eventually enjoyed a new Franklin stove. John Hitz gave Helen a statue of Venus that featured prominently in the parlor. Behind the house a florist grew pansies, marigolds, geraniums, and carnations. Italian immigrant women and their children who grew the flowers provided a background of laughter and loud conversation. Helen loved it, and the pastoral combination of Mount Auburn Cemetery and a flower farm was also a perfect fit for Sullivan.[8]

For several of the Radcliffe years, perhaps even there on Coolidge Avenue, an Irish woman named Bridget served them—whether as their own maid or as owner, cook, or manager of the boardinghouse is not clear. She made good coffee and muffins. Sullivan's parents had listed a "Bridget Sullivan" as her baptismal sponsor so many years earlier, likely her father's sister. Perhaps Annie remembered the prior relationship; perhaps not, but an Irish brogue and the name "Bridget" would have sounded familiar to her ears. And the housekeeping help must have been a blessing.[9]

Sometime during these years Annie repaired her relationship with Sophia Hopkins, her former Perkins housemother. In the past she often had looked to Hopkins for maternal care. However, by her belief in Arthur Gilman's allegations about Sullivan's treatment of Helen at the Cambridge School for Young Ladies, and her subsequent letter to Kate Keller based on this belief, Hopkins undoubtedly damaged the fond relationship between the two. In a letter dated December 26, 1900, Sullivan indicated that Hopkins spent Christmas with her and Helen, referring to Hopkins's presence as if she were a member of the family.[10] How the two women reconciled, and how deeply they did so, remains unknown. Hopkins did not die until 1917, but after 1900 little evidence remains of significant contact between the women. Sullivan had other people in her life after that point—John Macy, John Hitz, and the adult Helen. As someone who long remembered personal slights, perhaps Annie was unable to let go of the pain of Hopkins's betrayal. Also, Sullivan was an adult now and may not have needed Hopkins in the same way as before. All of these factors likely ended their relationship.

Sullivan found other friends who were more like peers. Lenore Kinney, a boardinghouse friend from the year before, learned to fingerspell—slowly at first, then proficiently, and then quite well. Like Beth Chamberlin, she eventually provided respite for Sullivan. Lenore and her fiancé (and later husband), Philip Smith, socialized with both women and, in Keller's words, "brought some nice young men to see us." Lenore Smith's friendship and fingerspelling skills mattered, but perhaps her most consequential act in this period was to introduce Annie to John Macy—undoubtedly one of those nice young men.[11]

John Albert Macy entered Annie's life, as nearly everyone else did, because of Helen Keller. Keller had written the beginnings of an autobiographical piece for a Radcliffe course—English 22 with Professor Charles Townsend Copeland. The *Ladies' Home Journal* learned of her efforts, and its editor, Edward Bok, sought to publish her autobiography in serial form. He would pay the stunningly large sum of $3,000. Sullivan initially tried to do all the editing herself. Her remaining letters bear witness to her strong literary skills. Living amider the educated of Harvard and Radcliffe, however, she may have felt inadequate due to her lack of academic credentials. She certainly lacked the visual acuity necessary to help Keller prepare, shuffle, read, and reread materials. Someone else needed to help them. John Macy lectured in English at Harvard and lived in the same boardinghouse as Philip and Lenore Smith. Lenore recommended him as a possible editor to help prepare Keller's autobiographical essays for publication. Possibly she sought to play matchmaker as well.

John Macy thus arrived as a hired hand around Christmas 1901— but a young, handsome, and exciting *male* hand. Helen adored him. In her first mention of him to her mother she called him "one of the noblest men I ever knew" and compared him to Alexander Graham Bell. "He is very bright; so in most cases we hearken to his advice as to an oracle." Later she referred to him as "extremely clever, and just the sort of knight errant to deliver me from the jaws of this [publishing] dilemma."[12]

And so he did in 1902. Learning fingerspelling, sitting with both women for hours at a time, bringing the authority of a Harvard lecturer to the project, John Macy helped prepare what would become the memoir *The Story of My Life*—a book eventually published in so many languages that keeping track became nearly impossible.

As early as March of 1900, even while Keller's entrance to Radcliffe had been uncertain, Sullivan had intended to publish her own chronicle of Helen's education. She had started to collect materials, likely planning a compilation rather than a prose narrative of her own. Keller glibly called it the "little book she proposes to publish" and claimed that Sullivan was too busy to work on it. Most likely her eyes didn't allow it.[13]

The Story of My Life is a radically different book from what Sullivan originally had in mind, even based on just the little bit known about her unrealized plans. In her imagined book she would have been the primary actor, the focal point from which the story was told. *The Story of My Life* tells the story from Keller's vantage point as Keller's story, with Keller as the authorial voice. As the book has come down to us since 1903 it has remained Keller's story.

However, *The Story of My Life* as it first appeared was a more complicated book than its cover and title page suggested. The text authored by Keller, which today is generally considered *The Story of My Life*, occupies only one-third of the book. While most editions since then have deleted the rest of the material, the original book included two additional sections.[14] Part Two included excerpts of letters to and from Keller between 1887 and 1901.

Part Three can be viewed as part of the Sullivan–Macy courtship process. John Macy wrote much of Part Three, "A Supplementary Account of Helen Keller's Life and Education," but Sullivan wrote substantial segments, mostly taken from earlier reports she had written for Bell or Anagnos. The longest sections focused on Keller's education and included one titled "Literary Style" giving Keller's version of the Frost King events. These vigorously defended Sullivan (referred to formally in the book as Anne Mansfield Sullivan) against charges that she had manipulated Helen or lied about her student's intellectual prowess. The book was, as John Macy stated, "Miss Keller's and is final proof of her independent powers."[15] If Keller's intelligence was real, Sullivan's skills were real. She had not produced an intellectual puppet. The Frost King allegations of Anagnos were false; it was all a misunderstanding, the error of an unknowing and innocent child, an error that, ironically, proved her intelligence. John's recasting of her as a pedagogical heroine must have been very appealing to Annie.

John not only helped to prepare the book, but throughout 1902 he also began to handle publishing house negotiations. He had experience approaching publishers and negotiating royalty details and legal contracts. It may even have been his idea in the first place to create a book out of Keller's *Ladies' Home Journal* articles. Sullivan introduced him to Alexander Graham Bell as a publishing assistant, casting herself as in charge of the publication process. To Bell she defined him as "a young man who seems peculiarly adapted to do this work well, especially as he will have my advice and assistance and all the material we have."[16]

John's father, Powell Macy, was born in Massachusetts of a longtime Nantucket whaling family and his mother, Janet Foster Macy, was born to an English family in New Brunswick. His parents had been living in Detroit, Michigan, at the time of his birth in 1877, but by 1880 they were in St. Paul, Minnesota, with young John, his older brother, Oliver, a sister of his father's, a boarder, and a servant. They stayed there through at least 1891.[17] John was the second of five children. He was only three years older than Helen but eleven years younger than Annie. At the time of his birth Annie had already lost both of her parents and her brother Jimmie, and was savoring her brief respite away from Tewksbury with the Sisters of Charity in Lowell.

When Annie and John met he had already graduated from Harvard (1899) and published his own poetry, and was lecturing at Harvard and establishing a reputation as a respected literary critic. As a scholarship student at Harvard, he had excelled, becoming a member of Phi Beta Kappa and editor in chief of the *Harvard Advocate*, the prestigious literary magazine. He lived and socialized in a lively intellectual circle, likely overlapping with or similar to the literary world of the Chamberlins but building on the elite literary networks of Harvard and the *Advocate*. Photographs present him as a forthright, relaxed, and self-assured individual, physically confident, handsome, and unafraid of facing the camera directly. His relationship with Sullivan and Keller quickly grew beyond the terms of their business agreement, and he became a vital and intimate member of the household. He advised them on which courses Helen should take and read to her as often as he could to help spare Annie's eyes. From 1901 to 1909 he served as associate editor of the *Youth's Companion*, the same position held by Edgar Chamberlin—that is, until Chamberlin disappeared briefly and resigned his position in 1901. Perhaps Macy knew Chamberlin prior to knowing Sullivan.

We know frustratingly little about the courtship between Annie and John. When did the spark begin? Was it real, or was his attraction to Helen, as many later alleged? Were they able to woo one another in privacy, away from Helen? When did they first kiss? Did they speak about their age difference? How did he respond to her limited eyesight? This was Annie's first serious romance. Did John have previous relationships? Did he bring her flowers from the flower stands at Harvard Square? Did he write her love poems?

He attempted to look after Annie, and she undoubtedly thrilled to that. Never before had a young man, or perhaps anyone, taken care of her in the same way. She had long had foot problems and during Keller's senior year began to limp badly. John persuaded her to see a doctor, when no one else had been able to do so. The doctor, Dr. Goldthwaite, considered surgery urgent. They lacked the money necessary for hospitalization so Goldthwaite agreed to perform the surgery—her ninth surgical procedure—at their home, and provided a nurse and ether. Reliable Bridget repeatedly scoured the kitchen table in order to transform it into an operating table. Within a month Annie walked better "than she had ever done."[18] Was she then able to take long romantic walks with John along the Charles River?

The almost overwhelmingly positive responses to *The Story of My Life* must have increased John's appeal. Alexander Graham Bell, to whom the book is dedicated, sent hearty congratulations to both Macy and Sullivan but apparently not to Keller—reflecting his opinion about who deserved credit. Samuel Clemens also loved the book, expressing his admiration for Sullivan's character: "How she stands out in her letters; her brilliancy, penetration, originality, wisdom, character, and the fine literary competencies of her pen—they are all there."[19]

Kate Keller served as the lone harsh critic. Helen, she believed, had betrayed her family by presenting them negatively in some of the original *Ladies' Home Journal* articles. Oft-told stories of Helen's violent childhood temper, of a whipping by her mother, or of broken dishes may have been permissible or even entertaining around the family table, but Mrs. Keller did not consider them appropriate for public consumption. Keller responded with a contrite apology. Macy and Sullivan left no response.[20]

Throughout the Radcliffe years, and especially after the publication of *The Story of My Life*, Alexander Graham Bell attempted to convince Sullivan that she should dedicate her life to teaching deaf children. In late 1901 he told her of two deaf siblings from Texas and encouraged her to consider taking them on as students. After the publication of *The Story of My Life* his opinion of her only expanded. It was her "duty," he pleaded, to use her "brilliant abilities as a teacher FOR THE BEN-EFIT OF OTHER TEACHERS." He warned her that once Helen graduated, he would pursue this possibility wholeheartedly. "You must be placed in a position to impress your ideas upon other teachers. YOU MUST TRAIN TEACHERS so that the deaf as a whole may get the benefit of your instruction."[21] Sullivan evaded Bell's plans for her, just as she had those of Ida Chamberlin. The passive-aggressive act of pay-ing him no heed worked, for Bell let it drop.

Keller's graduation from Radcliffe should have been the culmination of Sullivan's work since 1887. While so few women achieved a higher education, and while doctors debated the advisability of a college edu-cation for any woman, her deaf-blind student graduated from presti-gious Radcliffe. Sullivan was proud, but Keller's achievement failed to satisfy her own desire for success, for adulation, for accomplishment. Always the question lingered: was the accomplishment Keller's or was it Sullivan's? Now that Helen was an accomplished adult, did Annie matter? If Keller proved herself a capable and independent intellect she had no need for her teacher. If not, Sullivan was a fraud.

In many ways, and probably due to these contradictions, Helen felt it was impossible to satisfy Annie's drive for accomplishment. Like a child prodded relentlessly by an ambitious parent, years after Sulli-van's death Keller still considered herself a "failure," a "disappointment" to her beloved Teacher, because she did not graduate with the label *summa*—only *cum laude*. This supposed failure made Sullivan "rent with emotion and overwrought."[22]

Keller's June 1904 graduation reflected Sullivan's uneasy status. John Hitz recorded that the crowd gave a standing ovation as together both women crossed the stage while Helen's name was read, but Sullivan received no official mention at the event. Keller remembered it as quiet and anticlimactic. Kate Keller remained in Tuscumbia due to illness.

Bell remained with his family at their vacation home in Nova Scotia, and even his promised telegram failed to arrive. A few friends came to see Keller walk the stage—certainly Hitz did, but the rest remain unknown.[23]

After the graduation ceremony the two left for Wrentham as immediately as possible. Keller implied they went nearly directly from the stage to the streetcar.[24] Wrentham had provided sanctuary for many years, both at the home of the Chamberlins and at the cottage the two women rented on Lake Wollomonapoag. It would do so again.

What was Annie Sullivan to do with the rest of her life? By the time of Helen's graduation she was thirty-eight years old. Though she never stated it directly, the many years of intense college preparation and coursework, the constant pain and anxiety caused by her eyes, and the nearly continuous emotional strife of the previous decade had undoubtedly exhausted her. Bell had ambitious plans for her, but she never took substantive steps to take on another student or to train teachers. The success of *The Story of My Life* and the continued support of philanthropists assured her financial security as long as she stayed with Helen. No one else could guarantee her comparable financial security. The ambitious possibilities presented by Bell, however, illustrate that she had other options, such as an expanded teaching or teacher training career.

Primarily, however, I believe that Annie was afraid to leave Helen—and did not want to leave her. Though publicly her status alongside Helen remained vague, Helen loved her. No one else in her tumultuous life ever provided love and support, or tolerated her moods, as Helen did.

Sullivan eschewed all other options by purchasing a beautiful old farmhouse on seven acres of land on the northern edge of Wrentham, conveniently located on the trolley line. Hitz stated that Sullivan purchased it; Keller stated that she and Sullivan purchased it together. They paid jointly for the $3,000 house and its renovations by selling sugar stock John Spaulding had given them years earlier. Helen described it as "a small, old farmhouse, long and narrow, decidedly Puritanical in appearance, with a neglected field of seven acres." Its yard held both fruit and shade trees. Hitz approved of it entirely. At Annie's direction, workers painted and papered it before their arrival and converted a dairy room and two pantries into a study for Helen. Helen's bedroom contained its own balcony, surrounded by evergreens, apple trees, and wisteria. No one ever bothered to describe Annie's quarters.[25] The purchase, however, publicly tied her to Helen and showed everyone that the two planned to remain together.

Both women left little information about the first year at their home in Wrentham. John repeatedly proposed marriage and Annie either turned him down or didn't answer. He visited them often and sometimes served as Keller's interpreter at meetings in Boston. He once stayed for two weeks, playing handyman and household patriarch: he repaired steps, cleaned the barn, lengthened a walkway for Helen, and read to both women. In October 1904, Sullivan, Keller, and Macy together traveled to St. Louis for "Helen Keller Day" at the World's Fair, timed to coincide with the International Conference on the Deaf and the Dumb. Crowds swarmed to see Keller just as they did at the Chicago World's Fair eleven years earlier. Her uncle, a physician already living in the area, joined her. John's parents appear in the 1910 St. Louis census; perhaps they were there in 1904, introduced by John to the famous Helen Keller and the woman he was courting, the almost as famous Annie Mansfield Sullivan.[26]

Sullivan's state of mind is difficult to ascertain. Hidden away in Keller's 1956 biography of Anne Sullivan Macy, far away from her section on the early years in Wrentham, is a statement that "a breakdown overtook Teacher soon after I graduated."[27] What that breakdown involved and what it meant we don't know.

Sometime in these years John Hitz accompanied Annie on a literal walk through her past, back to the haunting terrain of Feeding Hills. John Macy's absence during the trip, and the fact that Annie had time to do it, suggests that the trip took place during the year after Helen's Radcliffe graduation. The bearded old man Annie called *mon cher père* was in his mid-seventies in 1904. That Annie relied on him in this time of personal crisis is not surprising. Since the Frost King allegations he had proved a steady and loving presence. He accepted her inconsistencies, her sometimes erratic emotions and turbulent moods, and considered her a brilliant teacher. We don't know who initiated the visit they took together to Feeding Hills, Massachusetts, the home of her Irish immigrant parents. Neither Annie nor Helen left a written record of the visit.

Nearly twenty years later, as Nella Braddy Henney researched her eventual biography of the famed teacher, Annie revealed this visit, likely for the first time. Henney chose not to include it in her biography. The timing of the visit suggests Sullivan felt that either the cause of or the solution to her breakdown could be found in her early life. She had had no substantial contact with any family members since her arrival at Tewksbury, none at all since her father's brief visit to Tewksbury in order to say goodbye.

Hitz and Sullivan traveled through Feeding Hills anonymously. Hitz explained their questions by identifying himself as a researcher of Civil War pensions. Sullivan likely appeared to be his secretary. They spoke with former neighbors and at least one family member—an aunt. Even after twenty-five years Annie remembered enough of the neighborhood to find the church where her mother's funeral had been held in nearby Chicopee, to search out the already gone school of which she had been so envious, and to find the house in which her family lived at the time of her mother's death. Hitz sketched the house for her. Did she find her mother's gravesite? Presumably it bore little resemblance to those of the venerated buried at Mount Auburn Cemetery near her Radcliffe home. The pair must have asked specific questions about the Thomas and Alice Sullivan family, for according to Henney they heard stories of the naughty and blind daughter whose mother had died and whose father had left.[28]

The research Henney did for her biography leaves frustratingly vague the question of whether or not the Feeding Hills Sullivan family knew of the life the young girl Annie went on to live. Some believed she had died. Others knew this to be false. It would have been impossible for them not to hear the stories of Annie Sullivan and her student Helen Keller. But did they know that Keller's Annie Sullivan was their Annie Sullivan? Did they suspect that the middle-aged woman who traveled through asking questions in the early 1900s was the daughter of Thomas and Alice Sullivan?

And because Sullivan provided so little information about this visit, it leaves us with many questions and few answers. If she recognized buildings and neighborhoods, did she recognize family members? What were her thoughts as she spoke to Feeding Hills residents? Did she and Hitz take the next step and travel to Tewksbury? Did the visit help to heal her wounds or did it exacerbate them? Both before and after this visit John Macy sought her hand in marriage. What did she tell him of the visit and of her past? The biographical information included about her in *The Story of My Life* was deceptively simple and brief. Henney believed that when Annie spoke to her in 1928, the only others with whom she had ever shared the details of her past were John Hitz and Sophia Hopkins—not her dear friend Helen and not her husband, John.

CHAPTER 10

John, 1904–1914

IN 1896, just a first-year student at Harvard, John Macy had published a charming and good-natured poem about the refusal and acceptance slips both dreaded and hoped for by authors.

> To-day art comes at Traffic's call,
> A victim to commercial sway,
> When poet, novelist, and all,
> Who give their budding genius play,
> Must wait for magazines to say
> If Fortune's scale shall rise or dip;
> And, good or bad, they all convey
> Their answer in a printed slip.

He went on to mock, but sweetly mock, the marriage proposal made by such an author.

> Dear Princess, for proposals pay,
> No sweet reply, by word of lip,
> But send, as promptly as you may,
> Your answer in a printed slip.[1]

In December of 1904 Annie agreed to marry him. Did she do so in a printed slip? Did he call her "Princess"? Since Helen's graduation and the purchase of the Wrentham home, a trolley ride and the demands of his job often had separated John and Annie geographically. Both individuals loved words. John was a writer. Annie also wrote her own poetry. They almost certainly exchanged letters, perhaps many printed slips.

Annie changed her mind about marrying John so many times that he purportedly threatened to print "Subject to change without notice" on the wedding invitations. When Keller reflected on the couple's relationship almost half a century later she wrote, "Annie never wholly acquiesced in the fact of her marriage. She gained greater self-control—she held her darker moods well in hand like an animal trainer, but now and then she could hear them growling, and she said she needed me to keep her quiet and reasonable."[2] The courtship, indeed the whole relationship, was not an easy one.

What would it have meant for a thirty-nine-year-old woman like Annie Sullivan to *acquiesce* to marriage? The reasons against the marriage were numerous, and she rarely acquiesced to anything. Many of the marriages around her didn't offer examples of female self-fulfillment, joy, or even fun: Edgar and Ida Chamberlin's, her parents', Arthur and Kate Keller's. The professional women she knew were single. Marriage to John would have limited the fiscal independence she had attained in her life with Helen and made her more vulnerable and dependent economically. Her career successes had come because of her refusal to follow others unquestioningly, especially men. Allowing someone other than Helen to experience the extent of her disability meant more vulnerability. Moreover, although older men frequently married younger women, women did not marry younger men, and John was significantly younger than her. Did she have to convince herself of his sincerity? Did she worry about what others would think? And what about sex? If she had any prior sexual experience, likely it was abusive and inflicted at Tewksbury.

Marrying John, giving in to someone else, and tying her happiness to that of another person, embodied tremendous risk. Except for her relationship with Helen, such risk had only failed her in the past. And here was a handsome man eleven years her junior, likely the object of many women's desires, cocky in his self-assured critiques of

Helen Keller, John Macy, and Anne Sullivan Macy in Wrentham, circa 1905. Courtesy of the American Foundation for the Blind, Helen Keller Archives.

contemporary literature, who wanted her to marry him. It disoriented and bewitched her.

At the time those around Sullivan, including Helen, assumed her reluctance was due to real or perceived obligations to Helen. Keller recorded that one time, after reflecting on how beautiful Helen had looked onstage, Annie proclaimed she would never marry. Helen replied, "Oh, Teacher, if you love John, and let him go, I shall feel like a hideous accident!"[3] Though Helen thought that Sullivan's reluctance to marry reflected the weight of Annie's obligation toward her, it could just as easily have come from feelings of inadequacy. John had interpreted for Helen at the event where these remarks were made. It's just as likely that watching them together left Annie feeling maternal, old, ugly, and duty bound to remain so.

Annie desired the blissful contentment, the normality, the easing of her perpetual strife promised by love. She scarcely, however, dared believe in it. She did not handle tranquility well. Sometime before the marriage, in one of the few love letters she left behind, she wrote to John on a beautiful summer evening: "I felt out of sympathy with the calm loveliness of the night. My heart was hot and impatient—impatient because the repression and self-effacement of a lifetime—and my life seems a century long as I look back upon it—have not stilled its passionate unrest."[4] The women at Tewksbury had portrayed men as dangerously risky, but they'd also described them as immensely enticing and pleasurable. Perhaps John could still the unrest of her passionate heart, or bring to fruition hopes she had repressed for so long.

The woman who had had no personal home found hers in him: the sense of "being at home comes to me so deeply when I am near you that I am always a little shivery when you leave me." Did the spiritual home he provided also include the pleasures of sex, of touch, of physical satisfaction? The shivers he left her with provide hints of a strong attraction between them, at least on her part. His love for her bewildered yet thrilled her. "How wonderful it is! And how impossible to understand! Love is the very essence of life itself. Reason has nothing to do with it!" She even, momentarily, gave herself up to "supreme happiness . . . and in that moment all the shadows of life become beautiful realities." She, who felt herself so undeserving, so deeply unlovable, could scarcely comprehend or even trust the happiness before her.[5]

Yet the letter contains moments in which she abandoned all concerns. "Dearest Heart," she called him. "I kiss you my own John and I love you I love you I love you." In another letter, likely written during Helen's last year at Radcliffe, she called him "My own dear little Johnny" and herself "Nan."[6]

Did John love Annie? Macy family stories, as they came down to Keller biographer Joseph Lash in the 1970s, claimed that John's real love was Helen. He only married Annie after Mrs. Keller had refused to let him marry Helen. The family stories weren't completely unfounded. In the year preceding the marriage, Boston newspapers noted John's frequent presence with the women and speculated about romance between Helen and John, failing even to consider Annie as a possible love interest.[7] It's possible that, as in so many things, Keller was the main attraction. My hunch, however, is that John's family claim was a defensive response, stemming from later events in the marriage.

Reconstructing the relationship between John and Annie is hard, for Annie left so little about it and John left virtually nothing. I believe John did love Annie. However emotionally volatile and demandingly needy she could be, she also was engaging, witty, profoundly caring at times, and charming. Her undaunted response to all of life, outwardly completely unfazed by the prestige of Harvard or the weight of the past, may have thrilled him. Her accomplishments with Keller impressed him profoundly, as is reflected in all he did to praise her with *The Story of My Life*. Few other women like her existed.

John and Annie publicly released news of their engagement in mid-January of 1905. They must have committed themselves to one another earlier, for Helen went to Alabama alone for Christmas, an unusual event, presumably to give the couple privacy. The news reports appeared in newspapers from Boston to Davenport, Iowa, to Sandusky, Ohio. One wrote glowingly, "It is characteristic of the love and friendship the bride and groom bear the blind girl that after their marriage they will reside near Boston, with Miss Keller as a member of their household."[8] The bride and groom felt it important to reassure the public that Sullivan would not desert her former student, though Keller was now an accomplished adult herself.

For Annie, legal and fiscal matters came first. She arranged these through Eleanor Hutton, principal fundraiser and director of the Helen Keller Fund, which had provided the women's primary support since Keller started at Radcliffe. In what was essentially a prenuptial agreement that excluded the groom, she made a will that left to Keller any money she had and her half of the Wrentham home the two women jointly owned. The complicated financial arrangements between the women regarding book royalties and lecture fees, in which all money earned was earned jointly, illustrate their dense fiscal and legal entanglements. At that point, March of 1905, Sullivan expressed hope that Helen's mother and younger sister, Mildred, could join the household—"for it would make Helen's happiness, giving her a congenial young companion." As far as this letter revealed, the bride-to-be said nothing about her future groom in her will. Ironically, her marriage made Helen her primary legal and financial life partner rather than tie her more closely to John legally and financially, as nearly all other marriages did. The arrangements reinforced prior practice between the two women. She reassured Hutton that "one thing is certain, my marriage shall make no difference in my love and care for Helen, and as far as is possible I shall share every happiness with her."⁹

Keller offered her own public and private acts of reassurance. To Bell she wrote that she was "delighted." First she sang John's praises: "I am very fond of John (that is Mr. Macy). He is kind and helpful to every one, and has a personal care for me which I love. Besides, he is cheery and good-natured, and home is most truly home when he returns from town of evenings full of news." She then reassured him, and perhaps herself, of her place in the forthcoming marital household: "I shall not lose her, and I shall also gain a brother, and thus I shall be twice blest in giving and in receiving." She supposed that she would "'give away' the bride," explaining, "you see, she belongs to me more than to any one else in the world."¹⁰ This would become the problem, or at least one of them.

The Reverend Dr. Edward Everett Hale traveled to Wrentham to perform the May 3, 1905, wedding. John wore a gray suit and Annie a dark blue dress with a white silk waist. She made salads, punch, and the cake, and since her friends later remembered her as an excellent cook, the food must have been good. They decorated the house with flowers, perhaps with early-blooming lilacs, and provided a bouquet of carnations for each guest. Helen served as Annie's attendant, and Lenore Smith interpreted for Helen so that Annie could focus on getting married. Kate Keller, Sophia Hopkins, Annie Pratt, John Hitz, and Lenore and Philip Smith attended, as did unspecified family members of John's. In 1900 John's older brother, Oliver, lived in Boston; by 1910 his sister, Elsie Rockwell, lived in New Jersey. Perhaps in 1905 both lived close enough to attend easily.[11]

Now Mr. and Mrs. Macy, the couple traveled to New Orleans for a honeymoon, stopping on their route home in Florence, Alabama, to see Helen at her mother's home (where she had gone after the wedding). From there, Annie wrote to Hitz with a joy and playful glee rarely reflected in anything she left behind. The letter from her included John's comments in parentheses. "I am much the same person that I was (I agree to that, both as to the good and as to the naught—J.A.M.)—just as perverse, just as unreasonable, just as full of love for my friends, just as adverse to writing them. Yet when I realize what has happened to me it seems as if the great happiness which is mine should make me better and wiser in every way and a good deal more of a Swedenborgian (who ever heard of an Irish Swedenborgian? J.A.M.)."[12] She was happy.

Beyond their happiness, we know virtually nothing about the honeymoon. Perhaps, however, happiness was the most important thing. Years later, writing of the fictional Johannah, Macy wrote that after Tewksbury she had wanted to exact "some terrible vengeance" upon men. Marriage, however, taught her that men provided "compensations which she had never expected."[13] Compensations? It's hard not to laugh at the likely euphemism. She lived a sensual life, attuned to the physical world of nature, observant of the world around her, in near constant and very intimate physical contact with Helen. Certainly sex became part of her relationship with John. The very limited evidence available indicates that she enjoyed sex, sexuality, and the physical and emotional intimacy that came with it.

Kate Keller embraced the role of mother-in-law—loving but fierce. In a chatty letter written not long after the wedding she made sure John knew that marrying Annie meant a life with Helen. Referring to both adult women as her children, she thanked him for his presence in their lives. "Always before," she wrote, "when I . . . left the big child and the little standing at that gate it has been with such a heavy heart." Knowing he was there provided her "comfort." He would provide "ballast for the big child and the little." "It would have been cruel if you had not loved Helen," she reflected, for she "is horribly alone in the world." Helen was without father or husband, and she expected the man only three years older than her to act as her male defender. "I am glad I adopted you and feel very sure I should always have another member to my family," she told him, but included a threat that he could only "abide with us until you behave unworthily." Clearly Mrs. Keller did not expect the older son from her husband's first marriage, or Helen's much younger brother Phillips, to play the patriarchal role in Helen's life.[14]

Thus the three adults began their unorthodox household in the Wrentham home.

Reconstructing the household dynamics is difficult. In a rare letter from Annie to Helen in September of 1904, Annie addressed her as "My dear little woman." As if she were addressing a child, Annie wrote, "I am homesick for my little girl—there is nobody like her anywhere in the wide wide [*sic*] world. There is a little picture of her over the piano that I sometimes look at, but it is not much like her; it does not speak or laugh or tramp back and forth on the piazza." Earlier that day John had read to her, and his mother was visiting, but Annie hid in her room and "tried to imagine" what Helen was doing. Though written before the wedding, indeed written before their engagement was public and perhaps even official, the letter suggests efforts to position their home as a traditional heterosexual nuclear household in which John and Annie served as parents and the adult Helen as child. It also suggests the significant presence of John's mother, who appears rarely in either Helen or Annie's record.[15]

Keller always described these years, at least from 1905 to 1911, idyllically. They had numerous dogs, chickens, horses, and at one point a litter of eleven Great Dane puppies. On weekdays Annie drove John to the train station for his commute to Boston and then did the daily shopping. Helen tidied up the breakfast mess as well as the rest of the house. Though Keller later wrote that during "many years" in Wrentham they had no servant, they had one during the 1910 census. Books filled the house; trees, birds, flowers, and the rest of the natural world surrounded it. Years later Keller wrote, with words too saccharine to be taken entirely seriously, "my thoughts still wander back to those days and dwell with sweet longing on the affection of those two friends sitting beside me in the library, their hands in mine, dreaming of a bright future of mutual helpfulness."[16]

They hosted parties. Friends remembered Annie as a consummate and vibrant host in these years. Keller considered her the "moving spirit in many a gathering at our Wrentham home. She was always contriving something unusual to make her guests happy." In later years Philip and Lenore Smith spoke not only of her excellent cooking (which she'd learned in Tuscumbia from Kate Keller) but of her "fascination," a charisma and appeal that once experienced was missed when one left her presence.[17]

So many contradictory expectations surrounded the three of them. They were to remain famous public figures. They were to forge a new frontier. They were to emulate the patriarchal heterosexual household, though they failed to embody it literally. No viable models of alternative household arrangements existed for them to follow. Helen seems to have expected an idealized life of intellectual pursuit, camaraderie, and service lived out by a partnership of three.

And what of John and Annie? What did each, and both together, want? In different ways both had to deal with John's frequent and intimate physical contact with Helen, the attractive and famous young woman so much closer to his age, as they conversed, as he read to both women, and as he edited Helen's writings. Did they speak forthrightly of what it meant to forge a marriage with Helen in the house? Perhaps he and Annie snuck away on occasion to talk in private, away from Helen, or used the privacy of the bedroom to do so.

In many ways, the setting was an author's dream. John and Helen spent these years writing. John edited and critiqued Helen's materials, "weeding out the chaff." He continued the work that he had done with *The Story of My Life*, negotiating the financial and legal details of her publishing contracts. Annie also did her part for Helen: "She could ease my wrestling with the angels and demons of authorship by letting me talk to her, thus airing my ideas." John did well in these years, serving as associate editor at the *Youth's Companion* until 1909. His 1907 literary biography of Edgar Allan Poe received a positive *New York Times* review and his literary criticism came to be regarded highly.[18] Annie always read as much as her eyes could tolerate. It can be assumed that she and John read together and discussed the literature about which he wrote.

Keller increasingly began to research and write about blindness—its population, its causes, the available social welfare resources, employment opportunities—and in July of 1906 the Massachusetts state government appointed her to the Massachusetts Commission for the Blind. Macy sat beside Keller and fingerspelled for hours on end, just as she had done at Radcliffe. However, the lengthy meetings involved multiple and sometimes overlapping speakers, which made fingerspelling nearly impossible to maintain. Keller often had no idea what was going on and struggled to contribute. After several months she resigned.[19]

The public recognition of Keller as an expert on blindness and its accompanying social issues thrust Keller and Macy back into the public arena. In Boston that meant, of course, a renewal of the emotions surrounding Perkins. Many of those affiliated with Perkins continued to be angry at its former star student—for her perceived betrayal of and ingratitude toward the institution, as well as for her claims that she and not Samuel Gridley Howe deserved credit for Keller's education. While serving on the Commission for the Blind Keller met—and therefore Macy met once again—Franklin B. Sanborn, then editor of the Springfield *Republican*. As inspector for the State Board of Charities in 1881 Sanborn had "rescued" the young Annie from Tewksbury and arranged for her placement at Perkins. He, the abolitionist supporter of John Brown, had been her hero. Now the former collaborator of Howe, obviously angry at her for her supposed slighting of Howe's memory, "insulted" her. He told others of her history as a public charge, her stay at the Tewksbury Almshouse, and her supposed ingratitude toward Perkins. Macy, once again unable to escape her past, never responded publicly. Keller did. She, rather than John, rushed to Annie's rescue—responding to Sanborn with an angry letter.[20]

Perhaps Michael Anagnos's October 1906 death stirred in Sanborn a sense of duty to defend Perkins and Howe. Anagnos and Annie had not been in significant contact since 1892. No evidence indicates that she went to his funeral at Boston's Tremont Temple, and she likely did not. Most certainly, however, she knew of his death. Just as he believed her to have betrayed him, so she must have felt betrayed by the older man with whom she'd shared such a long-standing, complex, and intense relationship. Other than Sophia Hopkins, few knew the transformations undergone by the fourteen-year-old almshouse girl as well as he did.

Macy attempted to maintain a very private life. In January of 1908, however, public reports circulated that she was in "grave danger" of going blind. John practiced deceit. In his role as public spokesperson he told reporters, "Mrs. Macy's sight is as good today as at any time in twenty years."[21] John's claim was undoubtedly true, but certainly misleading. Did he or she initiate the denial of her partial, and likely growing, blindness? Whoever initiated it, it continued her ability to "pass" in the public arena as sighted.

Unstated assumptions on the part of the general public that a blind woman could not teach a deaf-blind girl, and that blindness meant incompetence, blended with reports that childhood surgeries had "healed" Macy of blindness to create an impression of her as able-bodied. John's denial of her blindness reaffirmed this assumption. And Macy had her own reasons to claim able-bodiedness. She wanted to maintain the prestige she'd garnered as "Teacher." Her disability made her deeply uneasy. Just as some gays and lesbians have passed as straight, she would pass as sighted—as the nondisabled companion and aide of Helen Keller.

In March 1908, about a year and a half after Anagnos died, the other major paternal figure in Annie's life, but one much more loved and appreciated, died also: eighty-year-old John Hitz. Nowhere is there a record of her feelings on the matter. Other than Helen, no other individual had remained as consistently supportive. He knew her intimately—her past, her foibles, her weaknesses, and all she disliked in herself—and yet he believed in her goodness wholeheartedly. His death was a huge loss.

Despite the unfounded and almost routine newspaper reports on Keller's ill health, the private and ironic reality was that Annie's physical condition dominated the household. Unspecified ill health often restricted her activities and travel, and thus Helen's and presumably John's. The scar tissue of trachoma continued to grow over her eyes, causing pain and limiting her vision, and at least once John brought her to treatment.[22]

And more uprooting was under way. John left the *Youth's Companion* in 1909 for unidentified reasons. In February news reports circulated that the trio intended to leave Wrentham in the spring for a home on the coast of Maine, near Brunswick. Their present proximity to Boston created too many distractions and interruptions for Keller to write, the reports said. To friends Keller explained that the opposite was true: the commute had become too much for John. The *New York Times* reported that John had purchased the coastal home in November of 1908. Writing to Lenore Smith with enthusiasm about the move, Keller referred to the house that "we" had purchased. John, Annie, and Helen spent part of the summer of 1909 at the Maine home, but the move never happened.[23] The likely explanation is that growing marital stress between Annie and John derailed their plans.

Increasingly by 1909 Annie and John spent time apart. John must have been busy during these years, for he did well professionally and published several more books and a large number of articles. His 1913 *The Spirit of American Literature* became his most well-known work. He involved himself, and subsequently Helen, in the growing Socialist movement in the United States, participating in its intellectual life and in strike activities and galvanizing other New York and Boston radicals. He accepted a position in the Socialist city government of Schenectady, New York, spending considerable time in the city—and, thus, time away from Wrentham. In 1912 newspapers reported that Keller had also accepted a position in the Schenectady city government and that all three intended to move there. Neither claim was true.[24]

Annie didn't involve herself in the activities of the Socialist Party. She had such a deep distrust of politicians that she scorned political matters and public affairs. Radical politics became one more thing that her husband shared with Helen more than with her. The two women continued their social relationships with wealthy donors, the very wealthy that John (and sometimes Helen) criticized.

In 1910, for at least the month of August, Annie, Helen, and Helen's sister Mildred and her child stayed at a nearby cottage on Lake Pearl (in Wrentham) while John stayed at their home doing major household repairs.[25] Perhaps he simply wanted to escape the overwhelmingly female household that afforded him little time with his wife and even less personal privacy. Perhaps it was an excuse for a temporary separation from Annie.

In late 1910 Keller sought to expand her public presence by starting oral lessons again, now under the direction of Boston singing instructor Charles White. With a grounding in voice pedagogy rather than deaf education, White worked with Keller to develop the muscles of her vocal chords so that her voice might be clearer and louder. She hoped to earn a consistent and sufficient living on the lecture circuit if her oral skills could be improved. Keller considered this vital to the future of both herself and Annie. As she explained to her mother, if she was to help Annie "later on and make things easier for her," she had to "go on" with her "voice work."[26] She left unstated the assumption that neither John nor Annie would earn the amount required for their standard of living, and Keller's writings had not had the financial success for which she'd hoped.

Though not made public, Annie's physical discomfort continued to be omnipresent. Throughout 1910 and 1911 Helen's letters to her mother nearly always included references to Annie's unspecified poor health. Both women, once again apart from John, spent some of the summer of 1912 at the Cresson, Pennsylvania, summer estate of the wealthy widow Mrs. William Thaw. Thaw had supported Keller and Macy financially for years as a patron of the Helen Keller Trust, directed by Eleanor Hutton. Helen wanted Annie to "have a long rest, free from household cares and other worries." All hoped that a summer of luxurious care and rest would heal all that ailed her. In early August, however, Helen's career trumped concerns about Annie and they returned to Wrentham so that Helen could continue with her voice lessons. In mid-August, Helen reported to her mother that Annie was "pretty well for her"—a lukewarm assessment.[27]

In September Annie went in for emergency surgery. John resigned his position in Schenectady to be with his wife. The immediate cause and purpose of the surgery are unclear, but it had nothing to do with her eyes. Nella Braddy Henney, who undoubtedly knew its true nature, wrote in her biography of Macy only that it was "major," "the only serious operation she has ever had that was not on her eyes." "It was by no means certain," she went on, "that Mrs. Macy would live." It involved multiple weeks in the hospital. Her weakness scared Helen, for at her first postoperative visit Annie could barely muster fingerspelling.[28] She was then forty-six years old.

Before Annie returned home Helen went to Washington, D.C., to stay with Lenore and Philip Smith for most of October. The circumstances inserted forced cheer in her letters to Macy, but they are among the few documents that remain from written exchanges between the two women (Macy's letters are now lost), and they reveal much about the household relationships. Helen usually tried to hide it, but her homesickness and concern for Annie are clear. "Do tell me promptly, both of you," she insisted, "ANYTHING that happens to you. I can't rest easy or come home well or live through another such experience as this if you don't." Annie had no energy to write, nor did she dictate a letter to John, but John telegrammed news of her arrival at home.[29]

While Helen loved Lenore Smith, the political and social atmosphere of Washington annoyed her. She yearned for her conversations at home with others who understood her political ideals. She praised the local Camp Fire Girl troop for its creation of a new feminine ideal: "They will not have so much need to cry and fret and waste their energies in failures as most young women seem to." She looked forward to life "under Socialism" when "every girl will have an opportunity for such training." She wanted to visit the Bureau of Child Labor but feared her questions would embarrass Smith, who held very different political

views. "I don't feel free to talk about social questions obviously unwelcome in this atmosphere."[30]

From Annie she sought advice, but didn't get it, about what to visit in
the capital. "You're too vital," Helen wrote, "too full of pent-up genius,
and that's a precious trouble, you know. . . . They ['dull people'] don't
enter into my scheme of living, much less of loving you and finding you
a perpetual fascination." She wanted updates on the Lawrence strike
and the trial of strike leaders Joseph Etter and Arturo Giovannitti.
"Please, please don't throw me out of it all, it makes me too homesick."
In nearly each letter Helen signed herself some variation of "Your own
Helen" or "Your own and John's." Once she used the nickname "Billy."
When discussing arrangements for her to return home, she referred
to herself as "your 'kiddie.'"[31]

Unfortunately, we have no record of the responses, joint or personal,
of Annie or John to Helen and her letters. Did they experience Helen
as smothering? Annie so needed Helen to need her that it's doubtful
she found Helen's concern and desire to return to Wrentham overwhelming; but it could have been a burden. John, on the other hand,
had just quit his job in Schenectady to care for his very ill wife. Perhaps, despite the circumstances, they appreciated the period of traditional coupledom. It must have been brief, however; by mid-October
de facto mother-in-law Kate Keller arrived in Wrentham to assist.[32]

In November John left his ill wife in the care of Mrs. Keller to spend
two weeks in Little Falls, New York, assisting striking textile workers.
Perhaps his political beliefs motivated him; perhaps he simply needed
an excuse to get out of the house. Keller supported the strike with a
public letter. John failed at getting arrested, "GREATLY to our relief,"
according to Helen. Annie, vulnerable to feelings of abandonment,
would have experienced his departure, no matter how noble the cause,
as rejection. By late November she still wasn't sleeping.[33]

Though doctors told Macy to "be careful" for a year, she and Keller
ignored the advice. In early 1913 they began a nearly ten-year run on the
lecture and then the vaudeville circuit. Once again they embarked on a
task that excluded John, and likely didn't even consult him when they
discounted the medical directives of his wife's doctors. Perhaps the

Wrentham home remained so full of tension and memories that both women sought to leave it. Perhaps the financial stresses overwhelmed health considerations. Moreover, Annie rarely denied Helen anything, and it's likely that the younger woman desired the public arena.

Keller enjoyed being the primary breadwinner—the sense of competence, the independence, and the respect given her in public appearances. Her speech lessons never accomplished all she desired, but they were far more successful than those of earlier years and made lecture income possible. In February she debuted on the lecture platform in Montclair, New Jersey, under the sponsorship of the local Socialist Party. In her 1929 biography Keller wrote of this speech exclusively in terms of her first public use of her oral voice, but the newspaper reportage focused on her radical politics. Macy, identified as Keller's "teacher and companion," interpreted the questions posed to Keller.[34] John, the original and most active Socialist of the trio, was not mentioned.

For most of 1913 and 1914 Macy and Keller traveled. At times John joined them briefly or they met him at home in Wrentham or in New York, but primarily they traveled alone. Nothing came easy. They constantly worried about money but didn't expect John to provide. He found a tenant for the home in Maine, the one they'd never even lived in. Macy had not fully recovered from whatever ailed her, for while in Bath, Maine, in April 1913, she collapsed at the local hotel. Keller then reluctantly accepted a monthly stipend from Andrew Carnegie. As she explained to Carnegie, she had sought "to earn my own living" in order to "make things easier for those that I love." Doing so, however, resulted in "another burden upon the dear shoulders of those who were already heavily burdened."[35]

In May, only a month later, John left for a more than four-month sojourn in Europe. While he traveled abroad, Annie and Helen would continue on the lecture circuit. All three dined with his parents, sister, and niece the night prior to his departure. Helen wrote to her mother that after the "hard" parting, "we felt better afterwards because we had seen him begin the first real holiday of his life."[36] Did he and Annie have any private moments before he boarded ship? They already spent significant time apart, but traveling meant they could pretend that they were not separated.

None of John's or Annie's letters from those four and a half months remain, though the couple did exchange letters. Annie's limited vision, and her inability or refusal to learn to type, involved Helen in the most intimate and painful moments of the marriage. Annie fingerspelled her letters to Helen, "often with her tears running over my hand," Helen wrote to John months later, and Helen then typed them.[37]

Years later Helen wrote about this period, "For some time the lack of money had been only a small part of our worry. Mr. Macy was considering leaving us. He had wearied of the struggle. He had many reasons for wishing to go."[38]

Leaving *us?* The struggle?

Scattered remaining letters from 1914 provide glances at the continuing deterioration of the marriage. In early January, Annie, Helen, and Mrs. Keller took to the road for continued lectures, starting out in Canada, while John stayed behind, likely in a recently rented Boston apartment. While traveling through John's birthplace of Detroit in late January, Annie received a letter from an attorney employed by her husband. John sought a divorce.[39] She refused it. It had been almost ten years since their marriage. Over the next months there was some correspondence between the couple, but few letters remain and they give no evidence of other unsaved letters. The primary remaining perspective on the marriage is Helen's. The circuitousness of the negotiations and bickering must have made it worse. John wrote to Helen, Helen wrote back, Mrs. Keller read it all, and then the de facto mother-in-law also contributed to the correspondence—expanding the marital relationship from an unlikely triangle to an even more unlikely square.

Though these letters provide hints of the issues tearing John and Annie apart, at least as John and Helen debated them, the overwhelming but never stated issue jumping forth from the letters is the complete lack of privacy and private intimacy between John and Annie, husband and wife, even in their marital strife. Helen completely assumed her place to be between and/or alongside John and Annie. When John wrote to Helen that he could never explain to her what *his life with*

Annie had been like, she responded at length about the wonderful life *"we three"* had had. Similarly, responding to his complaint that *Annie* had "never been a wife" to him, or "done any of the things that a woman might be expected to do," Helen wrote indignantly that "*we* have shared everything we had with you." Was John implying that he and Annie no longer shared a sexual relationship, or that they never had? If so, Keller's response was willfully naive and ignorant.[40]

Later Helen disingenuously wrote, "I do not want you to think, John, that I am trying to interfere in a matter which concerns you and Teacher." She explained that because "the relationship of us three is so close, so unusual," she should speak her mind, "as a sister might to her brother." After receiving a letter from John that made her "wretched," Helen repeatedly discussed the matter with her mother and they both agreed: "Your attitude towards Teacher is hard and unreasonable." Weeks later mother and daughter conferred once again and concluded that he was "harsh and unreasonable, and unjust."[41] The unified barrage from his wife, Helen, and Kate Keller, even from halfway across the continent, left John little chance for rebuttal.

Money, of course, and the underlying power it involved was another issue. In a period long after the passage of women's property laws, but in which husbands effectively continued to control their wives' finances, Annie had clearly and legally separated her financial affairs from John's. Indeed, she and Helen acted as much more of a financial unit than she and her husband. And despite Annie and Helen's financial concerns, they had access to more financial resources than John did. Apparently the women had provided funds on and off to some of his family members since before the marriage. Money recently sent by him to his mother had prompted rows. He'd never sent money from his job in Schenectady, and both women had grown never to expect his help in supporting the household. On top of that they'd paid off a debt of his to Sophia Hopkins (who'd refused to lend money to Arthur Keller decades earlier). As the breadwinners the women considered themselves the appropriate financial decision makers of the household, revealing an attitude that, coming from John, might have been called paternalistic and demeaning. John expected, presumably as an adult and as an adult male, that he should make financial decisions. Indeed, Kate Keller had asked him to be the patriarchal head of the household. Instead he found himself a financial supplicant. His anger made Helen indignant: "All these years ALL the money we had has gone to pay our expenses, yours as well as Teacher's and mine."[42] She considered his complaints an insult to their generosity, and the money theirs to disperse.

Helen admitted to John that Annie was "imperious, changeable and quick-tempered" but insisted that those very traits had made her successful. She also responded to John's complaints about Annie's lack of involvement in the social issues that drove her and John. Helen tried to convince John that he had successfully "helped her [Annie] to see the world, the workers and economic, social and moral conditions as she never saw them before." Really, Helen implored, Annie had "new aims, a new conviction, a new vision of life, a new ideal and a new inspiration to service." She likened John to "three selfish men, whom neither you or I respect"—presumably Michael Anagnos, Arthur Gilman, and Franklin B. Sanborn.[43] It was the most vicious insult she could imagine.

The relationship between John and Helen complicated the floundering relationship between husband and wife. Her letters to him read like those of a child caught between divorcing parents, who loves both but feels forced to choose a favorite. Her letters seem to hint that both John and Annie, like stereotypical divorcing parents, attempted to use her in order to inflict pain on each other. No, she once wrote to John, "You are wrong . . . in thinking that Teacher has tried to influence me against you." Helen once tried to spur him to reconcile with Annie, as their conflict caused her great angst. "You," she charged him, "and you alone can lift this burden of sorrow from my heart."[44]

She called John a "dear brother and generous friend." He made her literary and political life possible at that point, for all her direct connections to Socialist activities and personalities came through him. And she would never find a better editor, as her later books made clear. Though he must have expressed a desire to continue working with her, in early March she asked, "How do you think we could work together with advantage when you keep saying that Teacher is dishonest, that you cannot be harassed by a woman you cannot trust, that she has lied and deceived you!" The existential problem lay in the pronouns: Who was the *we?* John and Helen? John, Annie, and Helen?[45]

A month later, energized by meetings with the Los Angeles Local of the Socialist Party and similar groups in San Francisco, Helen struggled more explicitly with her dependence on John for the intellectual and political ties she craved. "I am feverishly seeking for new channels of usefulness, and I need you more and more," she said. "No, dear, we cannot do our best work without you. We have tried, and it is just as if you had died. Do write to me about things that really interest us all, tell me what you can of Socialist news, and suggest how I can help the workers as you used to."[46] Once again, however, the pronoun problem summed it up: Who was the *we?*

Helen ended this letter by saying, "Even so do two aching hearts send out thoughts of you and a prayer for pity and for a home."[47] In the early days of their love Annie had once called John her home. Now Helen, even if only speaking literally, did so as well.

Perhaps predictably, Annie's health prompted a ceasefire of sorts—temporarily. In May, still on the lecture circuit, she stumbled and fell while descending stairs in Buffalo, New York. She broke several bones in her arm. It must have been her left arm, for if it had been her right she would not have been able to fingerspell and that would have been commented upon. Helen hastily alerted John. The fall quickly sent both women (and likely Mrs. Keller also) running home to Wrentham. "It does seem a shame," Helen wrote, trying to induce guilt in John, "that she should have this in addition to all the worries she has had the past few months." A month earlier she had written him, "She [Macy] is very, very tired, though she will NOT admit it. At times she trembles so much that we marvel how she gets through the lecture, and nothing happens."[48]

We can only imagine the tone of life at Wrentham that summer of 1914. Did Annie and John attempt to reconcile, or did they only endure one another? Did they share a bed? Presumably the healing of Annie's bones took time and energy, and offered a pretext for general lethargy and avoidance of intimacy. They did some remodeling of the house, John worked on the yard, and Thora the Great Dane joined the household. By early October Kate Keller had returned to Alabama, and Helen sent her chatty letters omitting any mention of household tensions.

In November Macy and Keller began another lecture tour. This time John joined them, but only for a few weeks. During the first week the car broke down twice—not a good sign. John, Helen told her mother, "worked and worked with the engine until he was worn out, and swore like a trooper." John, Annie, and Helen spent Thanksgiving with friends Arturo and Caroline Giovannitti in New York. During the famed 1912 Lawrence strike, John had met Arturo, one of the strike leaders. The two men had become friends, and Giovannitti supported Keller's Socialist activism. She would write the introduction to his 1914 book of poems, *Arrows in the Gale*. After the holiday, John, Annie, and Helen returned to Wrentham together, and Annie told Helen to reassure her mother: "Tell Mother, John has begun his book, and he seems much better in some ways."[49] The unenthusiastic, vague reassurance could not have been persuasive.

Annie and Helen tried a different strategy to resolve their problems: they hired Polly Thomson—a "spirited Scottish lassie." The immigrant woman joined the household in late October 1914. The public explanation of Thomson's presence was that she had been hired to assist Keller. Perhaps this is so, but the previous lecture trip had proved that both Helen *and* Annie needed personal assistance in their daily lives: its highlights included Annie's collapse, Helen's appeal to Carnegie for money, and Annie's tumble downstairs. Helen's letter to her friend Lenore Smith hinted that by hiring Thomson she and Annie also sought to improve the Macy marriage. "I know we [Keller and Thomson] have great fun together," she wrote to Smith, "and that gives Teacher and John more time for each other, of which I am truly glad."[50] In mid-January 1915, Helen, Annie, and Polly Thomson would leave for a lengthy tour culminating in the Southwest. They were scheduled to appear in Ohio, Indiana, Kansas, Missouri, Texas, Arizona, and California, and then continue their travels almost nonstop until late fall of 1916. John would not join them. The hiring of Thomson resolved many difficulties, but it would not be enough to save the Macy marriage.

CHAPTER 11

On the Road, 1914–1924

THE DISSOLUTION of her marriage shook Annie profoundly. "It became," Helen wrote later, "her greatest sorrow." At the end of 1914 Annie would "shut herself up" in her room, "almost stunned, trying to think of a plan that would bring John back or weeping as only women who are no longer cherished weep." She gained weight, quit exercising, and "refused to be comforted."[1]

Once again, we are largely left with Helen's version of the story. Annie made sure of this, for she wrote few letters and at one point during the Wrentham years burnt her diary. Frustratingly, Helen didn't date the event, but remembered the smell of burning paper that prompted her to question what was going on. "I have burned my diary," her friend told her, "and I am relieved." Helen remembered Annie writing in it as far back as their early days in Tuscumbia and assumed that the diary served "as a kind of mediaeval self-mortification" that Annie might "come back to the world friendly, compassionate." Annie had often insisted to her former student that she was not "good," and pointed to the diary as if it held proof of her undeserving nature.[2] Burning the diary may have helped, but it couldn't erase Annie's past.

Whether or not Keller's description of Macy's profound melancholy is correct in all of its details, we can trust the general spirit of her account. The relationship between the two women may have involved more rockiness than either acknowledged publicly, but Keller unwaveringly sought for all to love and respect Macy. She never would have fabricated such information. In her 1956 biography of Macy, Keller's observations echoed the spirit of what Macy had earlier authorized for Nella Braddy Henney's biography.

Helen acknowledged that in 1915 "the melancholy which had now and then seized Teacher overwhelmed her with a despair that made it misery for her to exist. Actually she feared insanity for a while."[3] *Misery for her to exist.* Does this mean that Annie considered or threatened suicide? Ida Chamberlin had considered her capable of it in 1898. It's not impossible that in 1915 Helen had similar concerns.

The transformation from student to trusted companion must have been both a blessing and a curse. "As I grew more mature," Keller later reflected, "she let loose upon me all her varied moods, and because of this I was not taken unawares by the storms of destiny." And Annie's storms could be fierce. Only in the "silence of night," and only with Helen, did she "speak of her anguish or the terrible dreams that pursued her."[4]

Even before early 1915 Annie's mental and physical health had not been stable—and each seemed to contribute to the deterioration of other. Besides marital stress, Helen blamed the weakening of "Teacher's robust health" on "her periods of nervousness, the never ceasing torment of her eyes, her enormous disappointment in not having a baby."[5]

A baby? Nowhere else does either Annie or Helen hint, even ever so slightly, at Annie's desire for a child. John later fathered a daughter with another woman, and even dedicated one of his books to the child. If Annie's childlessness pained her, his later fatherhood must have intensified her sorrow.

It made sense for Keller to blame Macy's "melancholy" on her chronic pain and the dissolution of her marriage, but this was not the first time that the older woman wrestled with such feelings. Keller recorded frequent, but never long-lasting, episodes of "melancholy." At times, perhaps in Tuscumbia or in Wrentham, Annie hid in the woods or concealed herself under an overturned rowboat for hours at a time, until she felt capable of reemerging. Keller assumed "those dark moods" had haunted Macy as early as her years at Perkins and later acknowledged that they "continued to harass her every once in a while until her death."[6] It's possible they began even earlier than Perkins, perhaps at Tewksbury or Feeding Hills.

Keller sometimes explained Macy's mood swings away as an inevitable side effect of her brilliance and creativity. She unquestioningly forgave Annie any slights, intentional or otherwise. "Teacher's many-colored temperament," she believed, "puzzled simple folk." Only friends with wisdom, intelligence, and "genuine affection" could "decipher some of the lights and shadows of her character."[7]

Friends tried to assist. Labor organizer, Socialist, and poet Arturo Giovannitti, who considered both John and Annie dear friends, tried to ease the marital tensions. In an undated letter Giovannitti grumbled to Annie about her refusal to cooperate. He had seen John in Boston, he reported, and had "complied" with her request not to speak of the marriage and its problems. "I could hardly do otherwise," he complained, "under the circumstances, especially when said request came in the form of a telegraphic ultimatum with the threat of breaking all diplomatic relations with me in case of non compliance with your demand." In another letter, apparently reflecting on a visit with both of them, he wryly observed, "I felt rather foolish . . . that a confirmed sower of discord like me had to act as a sort of country justice of the peace."[8]

"I am sure," Giovannitti went on, referring to the escalating world war, "that it was you and John who precipitated the horrible European cataclysm, for once you two are at odds for any reason whatever, the whole world must necessarily be at war. You see, I am still a pagan at heart and I believe that when Jupiter and Juno quarrel, not only the whole Olympus shakes and all the minor gods quail, but the entire constituted order of the universe is kicked upside down."[9]

These words suggest fights of awesome proportions. Living with and loving the mercurial Annie Sullivan Macy would have been difficult. She was stubborn, defensive, and fiercely proud. She struggled emotionally. The lack of good pain management hindered her. For a man in love with her, and unable to solve her problems, observing her frequent mental and physical pain would have been its own form of anguish. Living with her *and* Helen would likely have been even more difficult. And John had his own faults—including abuse of alcohol, just like Annie's father, Thomas Sullivan.

John stayed away. For most of a decade, from 1915 on, Macy and Keller traveled. Interruptions occurred, of course, most often necessitated by Macy, but not periods of respite—with one exception. Rarely in their home for very long, always moving from place to place by train or by car, and assisted by Polly Thomson, Annie struggled to keep herself together. The realities of traveling—inconsistent food, the demands of social niceties, unpredictable sleeping schedules—must have made her personal battles harder.

Macy's physical and mental health continued to decline. In the fall of 1916 she and Keller returned home to Wrentham after a "disappointing and exhausting" lecture season. John had left. He was not there for her to return to; the home was no longer the home she wanted. Not long after their return, she and Helen also both left Wrentham—each woman drowning in her own crisis, each entangled in the crisis of the other.

The timing and details of the following events are not completely clear and the accounts that remain are sometimes contradictory. Neither woman dated all her materials; both sought to keep these events from the press and general public and later spoke of them only in vague and often misleading terms.

In her 1929 autobiography *Midstream*, Keller explained vaguely that upon their return home Macy "fell ill . . . succumbed to fatigue and anxiety." Due to "pleurisy and a tenacious cough" her doctor advised she spend the winter in Lake Placid.[10]

It was more than that. Macy had tuberculosis—the very disease she'd watched her mother die from so many years earlier.[11] The memories of her mother's slowly emaciating body, the hacking cough and its spittle of blood, the eventual loss of bladder and bowel control, as well as the resulting desertion of her father and her own exile to Tewksbury, must have haunted her. She thought she was going to die.

Meanwhile, Peter Fagan, a Socialist who had learned fingerspelling to provide secretarial assistance, professed his love to Helen. As he held her hand, she listened, "all a-tremble." She had known him for more than two years. Initially hired by John, Fagan had periodically assisted with her correspondence since March 1914. The two women had hired him to interpret for Helen and to accompany them during the last part of their Chautauqua tour in the summer 1916 so that Polly Thomson could visit her family in Scotland. "All a-tremble," Helen agreed to marry him, later blaming it partly on her "imperious longing to be part of a man's life." They decided to keep the news a secret. Macy was too ill, they told themselves, to withstand such excitement.[12]

The acquisition of marriage licenses, however, is difficult to keep secret—especially for those with a high level of name recognition. The paparazzi of 1916 were just as determined as those today. On November 19 news of their application, with both of their signatures, hit the newspapers. Kate Keller confronted her daughter. Helen denied everything to both her mother and to Annie. The angry mother kicked Fagan out of the household. Fagan, in turn, also denied everything to the papers. Macy issued a vehement and irate statement, casting the thirty-six-year-old Helen as her continuing student: "The story that my pupil of twenty-seven years is to marry her secretary or anyone else is an abominable falsehood.... She has scarcely been out of my sight. Besides this, her mother has been with Miss Keller ever since last June. If she had any affection deeper than friendship for her secretary or any one else we would have known about it."[13]

Annie and Kate Keller, however, had apparently *not* known about it. Annie was already depressed about her failed marriage, and the news of her tuberculosis undoubtedly depressed her even further and diminished her observational skills. And Kate Keller's fears for Annie, along with her inability to imagine such a relationship for her daughter, would have made it easy for her to miss the warning signs of an emerging romance. As early as June Helen had told a *Chicago Tribune* reporter of a possible "heart affair," and the reporter referred to the possible existence of an "attentive" young man.[14] Perhaps Helen had favored Peter Fagan for months.

The very next day, November 20, amidst this chaos, amidst the tensions and lies of the household, Annie left. Keller's biography, *Teacher*, explained that Macy went to a retreat at Lake Placid, New York, accompanied by Thomson, to cure a "long siege of coughing brought on by the rundown condition of her body." "Lake Placid," however, served as a code word, particularly for public usage, for Macy's tuberculosis and its treatment. Nearby was Saranac Lake, the epicenter of tuberculosis treatment in the United States. At the time of Macy's visit, the region included more than twenty tuberculosis treatment facilities. In the early 1880s physician Edward Trudeau, convinced that the climate of the region had cured him of tuberculosis, had built Adirondack Cottage Sanatorium (renamed the Trudeau Sanatorium after his death). Trudeau's treatment system became the model for the nation, and his determination "to expose" the illness "for the purely physical syndrome it was and to conquer it" transformed public perceptions of tuberculosis.[15] If not to Adirondack Cottage itself, Macy went to one of the numerous surrounding facilities. She eventually became a patient of Dr. Lawrason Brown, a longtime physician at Adirondack Cottage who by 1916 was in private practice, though still affiliated with Trudeau.

The very same day Annie left, Helen issued her own statement regarding her publicized engagement to Fagan. "It is a great pity that Mrs. Macy and I have been subjected to annoyance," she said indignantly. She denied everything. "Such a thing has never been even remotely contemplated by me." She attempted to quell rumors that the separation between her and Macy was due to anger, without mentioning tuberculosis. "Mrs. Macy and I," she insisted, "are on the warmest terms of affectionate friendship."[16]

"Dearest Teacher," she wrote the next day, "I don't know how I stood the pain of you going last night. As we walked to the car, I felt suddenly overwhelmed with loneliness and nameless dread. It seemed as if some grim destiny would take you from me forever. But of course that was just a spell of 'blues.'"[17] Helen certainly had reason to feel blue. She feared Annie's death and had denied the engagement about which she'd been so thrilled. In the process she had lied to both her mother and Annie. A few days later she and her mother left for Montgomery, Alabama.

The remaining letters between Annie and Helen over the four months of their separation, the longest they'd ever been apart, never mention Peter Fagan. At some point she told the truth to her mother, who begged her not to tell Annie. "The shock would kill her, I am sure,"

Mrs. Keller reportedly said. Annie didn't learn the truth for months.[18] Neither woman recorded her response to Helen's eventual revelation.

At least, it's likely the letters never mentioned Peter Fagan. The letters Annie wrote to Helen over this four-month period she wrote in Braille—which she was never very good at and couldn't read well. Though this took her longer, and though she complained to Helen about it, this allowed the women privacy, for Helen did not have to have someone else read the letters to her. Brailled letters, however, don't store well; nor do they make easier the work of many historians or archivists. Only typed copies of these letters remain. Presumably the unnamed typist of the American Foundation for the Blind did not edit, delete materials, or make errors when transcribing them. History, however, is full of examples of well-meaning individuals who edited the letters of those whose memory they sought to shape or protect. A few of the letters contain a small line of penciled Xs—"XXXX." Perhaps they indicate the typist's omission of additional boring verbiage. Perhaps it was Annie's way of signifying that she didn't know how to transition smoothly to the next paragraph, or just a sign for kisses. Perhaps Annie simply made errors using her Braille writer, for she often speculated about the possibly ludicrous results of her imperfect skills (Helen said she could read them best "with the aid of sympathy and imagination").[19] And it is hoped that neither Helen nor Annie burned any of the letters. Whatever the reason, the remaining letters never mention Fagan.

At the sanatorium, Annie's primary concern became what would happen to Helen. "Dearest," she wrote. "You are never out of my thoughts. They keep me awake at night, and daylight brings no satisfactory answers to them." She'd thought she'd solved the issue of caring for Helen upon marrying John, but the dissolution of the marriage left that uncertain. "He promised me that in case of my death . . . he would be a brother to you, look after your happiness, and take charge of your affairs." Did he even know of his wife's tuberculosis diagnosis? It's probable; he likely knew enough to read between the lines of the coded public language about Lake Placid. Annie claimed that her illness had removed the "bitterness" from her thoughts of him, and she pleaded with Helen to "forgive and forget." "Would it not be better in every way to let the suffering, the unhappiness, that has come to all three of us die with me?" she went on. "You still love John. I am sure you do love him. Such love as we have felt for John never dies altogether."[20]

If forgiveness was impossible, the ever-practical Annie suggested, they would turn to lawyers to manage Helen's affairs after Annie's death. Or Helen's younger brother, Phillips. Perhaps, she directed, Helen should start writing her brother more regularly in order to get to know him better.[21]

Annie did not take to sanatorium life. Though we don't know which sanatorium she attended, we know that eventually she became the patient of Dr. Lawrason Brown. Brown's tuberculosis cure involved a "minutely calibrated system of rest, exercise, and diet." Upon her arrival Macy likely was given a rule book and instructed to read and sign it. Most sanatoriums allowed little reading during rest and limited contact between men and women. Brown typically recommended a strictly regimented daily schedule, such as the following:[22]

7:30	Awake. Take temperature. Milk (hot if desired) if necessary.
	Warm water for washing. Cold sponge.
8:00	Breakfast
8:30	Out of doors in chair or on bed
10:30	Lunch when ordered
11–1	Exercise or rest as ordered
1–2	Dinner. Indoors not over one hour, less if possible.
2–4	Rest in reclining position. Reading, but no talking allowed.
	Take temperature.
3:30	Lunch when ordered.
4–6	Exercise in prescribed amount.
6:00	Supper
7:00	Out on good nights
8:00	Take temperature
9:00	Lunch and bed.

He detailed the type of chair she should sit in while resting on an outside cure porch—the chair now commonly referred to as an Adirondack—and how she should fold the blanket around her body.

It's no surprise that the woman who had resisted every effort of Michael Anagnos or Arthur Gilman to control her did not respond well to such a regimen. Nor was she the type of woman who responded well to the social demands of the sanatorium's summer camp atmosphere. Sick people reminded her that she might die, that she too was sick. And those sick people had many of the same symptoms experienced by her dying mother. She hated the place. Helen, undoubtedly saddened about her own disastrous engagement and the frustrations of keeping that agony private, tried to encourage her. "I am grieved to hear from Polly [Thomson] that you find it so depressing at Lake Placid," she wrote. "I don't wonder that you do with such a trying combination of bad weather, medical bugbears, 'elderly stodgy people' and loneliness, and the worn-out feeling you speak of."[23]

Between the time of her mother's death and Macy's own diagnosis with tuberculosis, the place of tuberculosis in American culture and medicine had changed profoundly. Robert Koch's 1882 identification of the germ that caused tuberculosis, and wider comprehension of germ theory, intensified fears of contagion but also raised hopes for cure. Macy had genuine reason to want to keep her diagnosis private. The stigma of tuberculosis remained strong despite the growing visibility of sanatoriums, and those who could afford to tended to keep their diagnosis and treatments hidden. Since 1900 some cities and states had banned those with tuberculosis from employment as teachers and in other trades where the germ might easily, at least in theory, be transmitted.[24] Kate Keller could have been worried for her own health as well as for Helen's.

Helen worried, but about Annie. "I know I am rather nervous," she wrote on Thanksgiving Day. "I shall not feel easy until Polly can say you are free from pain, and don't cough any more."[25] It was the first Thanksgiving they'd spent apart since 1887.

Annie's next actions attest that, though depressed and ill, she was not immobilized. Already considering deserting the New York sanatorium for Alabama and Helen, in early December 1916 she saw a steam-ship company's advertisement for cruises to Cuba and the West Indies. She packed her bags. On a Monday she told the doctor of her plans, and on Wednesday she and Thomson left New York harbor on the SS *Carolina*, bound for Puerto Rico. Helen may not have even known they were gone until after they'd set sail.[26] Not only had Helen and Annie spent their first Thanksgiving apart, but their first Christmas apart would follow a month later.

"I do want you to understand, Helen," Annie wrote, "that I had to leave Placid. I couldn't endure the cold, the snow, the frozen face of the lake and the forlorn people one sees everywhere. . . . I simply hated that place—I could never have got well there." She still coughed each morning, but otherwise felt "all right."[27]

After initially staying at a hotel in San Juan (with a "fat, lazy, stupid, and good-natured" proprietor), Macy and Thomson rented a "little shack in the hills" near Bayamon for fifteen dollars per month. They called the shack, elevated on sticks, "the camp." An orange and grape-fruit grove surrounded them; immediately in front sat a pineapple patch. "I believe I can be happier here than any place I can afford to go to," Annie told Helen.[28]

But Puerto Rico? Those with tuberculosis who wanted warmth went to San Francisco, not Puerto Rico. Perhaps that was its appeal. No one knew her there. The chances of running into someone she knew, or who had even heard of Anne Sullivan Macy, were less than on any street in the United States. No one had social expectations of her. No one knew of her marital troubles. No male doctors told her what to do. Indeed, at fifty-one years of age, for the very first time in her adult life, she had four months without daily obligations to Helen. She could almost ignore the growing world war. She had run away—and run away to a place that thrilled her.

Rather than sit on a cold cure porch in a line of Adirondack chairs filled with other tubercular patients amidst sometimes swirling snow, she sat in privacy on her own porch that wound around three sides of their shack. Every evening she sat, with obligations only to herself: "We . . . watch the sunset melt from one vivid color to another—rose asphodel . . . to violet, then deep purple." "Polly and I," she went on to

Helen, "hold our breath as the stars come out in the sky—they hang low in the heavens like lamps of many colors—and myriad fire-flies come out on the grass and twinkle in the dark trees!"[29] No wonder she preferred it.

She luxuriated in her idleness. "I'm glad I didn't inherit the New England conscience," she wrote without regret. "If I did, I should be worrying about the state of sin I am now enjoying in Porto Rico [*sic*]. One can't help being happy here, Helen—happy and idle and aimless and pagan—all the sins we are warned against."[30]

Kate Keller tried to convince Annie to return to the sanatorium. Annie resisted strongly, and sent the message through Helen that she intended to stay in Puerto Rico through April. "I'll march right into the Lion's den rather than return to Placid," she insisted. "To paraphrase Emerson, the chambers of the 'club' are jails. Paul Bunyan went to jail rather than attend the parish church. George Fox went to jail rather than take off his hat in the presence of the magistrate, and I'll be martyred somehow before I return to the Adirondacks."[31] Humor and melodrama buffered her resistance, but it remained there all the same.

She settled in. She bought a car, secured a driver, and adopted a few dogs, and she and Thomson often traveled the island. Most of the time, she left it to Thomson to transmit to Helen the necessary affairs of business. Instead, she sent Helen meandering, happy travelogues that included stories of picturesque neighbors, marauding but comical goats, tropical foods and flowers, and the daily scenes of Puerto Rican life. She felt at home—"like stepping upon my native heath after a long, distressful absence"—and often had sensations of having been there, or in a similar place, before.[32]

Annie wanted Helen with her, and tried to convince her and her mother to visit. "I want to see you so very, very much," she wrote once. "I am sad despite all the beauty that billows about me," she wrote in another letter, "because you aren't here to enjoy it with me." She sent details of what clothes to bring: "old blouses and one nice dress for calls."[33]

She considered Puerto Rico a paradise, not in the stereotypical way of contemporary billboards but in a manner described by Socrates: "Isles [where those] who had lived in beauty sailed to after death. . . . Here I find freedom from the vexations of war and politics and duties that have never [left] me." She could escape from the demands of "silly fads and sillier conventions."[34] This escape worked far more effectively than the lecture or vaudeville circuit.

Sometimes Macy turned to poetry. Perhaps poetry provided solace. In her 1930 essay "On Being Ill," Virginia Woolf wrote that during illness, "indeed it is to the poets that we turn. Illness makes us disinclined for the long campaigns that prose exacts." Macy left no evidence of what she read, but penned her own definition of poetry as "the exquisite fusion of image and emotion in words."[35]

Despite Annie's happiness, or perhaps enabled by it, she and Helen continued their preparations for her eventual death. Both women gave up on John. Instead they used an attorney and made the necessary legal arrangements via the mail. "Dear," Annie wrote, "I do want to get well for your sake. You do need me still. Your letters make me realize it more and more. This separation is teaching us both a number of things, is it not?"[36]

While Annie's references to her death became more contented, Helen's remained slightly hysterical. "If anything should happen to you suddenly, to whom would you wish me to turn for help in business matters? How could I best protect myself against anyone who might not be honest or reliable? Mother loves me with a deep, silent love; but in all probability she will not be with me constantly. Another thing, if you should be taken from me, or be unable to attend to our affairs, what should I do with all our papers? Whom could I trust to go over them with me? . . . Oh, Teacher, how alone and unprepared I often feel, especially when I wake in the night!"[37]

Annie simply became more and more philosophical about death. "You must not worry about the future," she reassured Helen. "I am not going to die yet. . . . But even if I should die," she went on, "there is no reason why you should not go on with life." In the long run they as individuals did not matter, she believed, but that did not bother her. "The merciful Providence—or whatever power there is in the universe—has so ordained things that our little world will go on without us. Indeed, it will not miss us long. It is a comfort to know that the waters close over us quickly. Only a few remember the splash and struggle, and fancy it important, really. . . . I daresay we are making all this fuss for nothing." Her words, almost aloof and uncaring, undoubtedly failed to assuage Helen. "Cheer up," she said without real concern and with a mischievous dash of glee, "the worst is yet to come."[38]

Discussions of death brought on discussions of religion, and of essential differences between the two women. "It pains me deeply, Helen," Annie wrote starkly, "not to be able to believe as you do. It hurts me not to share the religious part of your life." She appreciated the Bible as poetry, but nothing more. "With you," Annie went on, "the belief in a future where the crooked places will be made straight is instinctive." To Macy, in contrast, "the future is dark."[39] As the months wore on, she became less and less concerned about herself and increasingly turned her attention outward to the ongoing European war, U.S. politics, and Puerto Rico. She considered President Wilson an "egotist, a tyrant at heart who wants to be Bismarck without Bismarck's intelligence." She feared, but assumed, that the United States would enter the growing fracas in Europe. At least she said, in reference to Helen's lectures against the war, "we, as individuals, have done all we can to keep America out of the maelstrom." The massive violence shocked her. She remembered back to labor activist Bill Haywood's argument that "our high refinement was a thin veneer concealing liars, swindlers, and murderers." Earlier she'd considered his words "wild," but now believed "the abominations of this War make his statements appear mild."[40]

Increasingly she critiqued U.S. imperialism in Puerto Rico, recasting herself as a reform-minded activist. "The white man's greed," she wrote, "is boundless." Sugar cane crops gave Americans "fat profits" but left Puerto Ricans with little land to grow food crops. She noted the frequent appearances of small coffins. "These children would eat and live if some people we know in New York had only their fair share of earth's bounties." Though she didn't mention the 1916 Jones Law specifically, she was aware of its March 1917 implementation. The controversial (at least in Puerto Rico) law made Puerto Ricans U.S. citizens and limited their political and economic independence. She characterized the U.S. presence as an occupation. "We Americans," she noted contemptuously, "can't seem to understand that when burglars break into a house, the family can't regard the intrusion as a friendly act, even if the burglars take only a little of what belongs to them."[41] The knowledge that John would have been proud of such sentiments must have made them bittersweet.

Helen fretted more about Annie's return than Annie did. Would she even return at all? She seemed happier than she'd ever been. Once Helen closed a letter, "With a heart of love, and with fear and trembling, lest you should lose your heart to Porto Rico forever."[42] And if Annie tried to return, would she be in danger from wartime German submarines? And if she arrived home safely, where would they live? And if they found a place to live, how would they support themselves? The worries, at least for Helen, seemed endless.

Helen begged that they not return to Wrentham, and took it upon herself to make the decisions. "The truth is, neither mother nor I could abide Wrentham and you ill. Believe me, a hut in the mountains somewhere in California would be better for us all, there would be fewer worries and no sad associations there." She would find work, but first had to figure out what it would be. "You're my precious trust now," she vowed to Annie, "and God and the world call upon me to act." A few days later she had it figured out: translating, since "John used to say I translated very well." She would immediately start to study all the languages she could.[43]

Annie expressed little concern. "My plan is to return home—alas! There is no home for us, but we shall find one, probably in New York—in April. First, I shall go to Saranac and have myself examined." Then they would settle somewhere. Indeed, she expressed little concern about anything. At the end of one letter she wrote lackadaisically, "P.S. I am hazy on dates, and there isn't a calendar in this cabin. So I am writing this letter any day of the week or the month you fancy."[44]

For a biographer, the Puerto Rican letters are a prize. The relationship between Annie and Helen was a defining feature in their lives. And for a relationship of such importance, we have very little direct evidence of the nature of their exchanges. The crises in which both women found themselves at that time perhaps lent greater truthfulness and urgency to their reflections.

Years later, in 1931, when Nella Braddy Henney was working on

Macy's biography, Annie wrote to Henney about the letters exchanged between Puerto Rico and Alabama. Her letter reflects her unease with Henney's ongoing biographical efforts—or perhaps, more accurately, Helen's unease. A "troubled" dream had prompted Annie's letter. In the dream, as Henney read to her from a manuscript, Annie realized that "by mistake" she had given her biographer the letters she had long ago written to Helen from Puerto Rico. "Helen," she said in her dream, "will never forgive me." When she awoke she shared the dream with Helen, who replied, "Why, that's just what you would do if I let you have the letters."[45]

What Annie revealed is confusing and multilayered. It's a warning to Henney that Helen did not want the biographer to have access to the letters—followed by a paragraph explaining that the typist of the letter was Helen, for by 1931 Helen served as Annie's personal assistant, typing communiqués that Annie fingerspelled to her. It was perhaps Annie's way to reassure Helen that Henney would never get access to the letters.

However, why would Helen, in 1931, not have wanted Henney to include the Puerto Rico letters in Annie's biography? To today's reader nothing in the letters appears damaging or particularly revealing. Henney eventually gained access to the letters, at whose direction we'll never know. Keller referred to them and included excerpts in her 1956 biography of Macy. Speculation is all that's left to us today, speculation made more titillating by the possibility of a secret Helen did not want revealed, though that's unlikely. Perhaps some of the letters are missing. Perhaps one or both of the women discussed their tumultuous romances in ways they wanted kept private. Perhaps it was simply a bad time that Helen, or Annie, did not want to revisit in depth.

When Annie returned to the U.S. mainland in April 1917, she and Helen first faced the task of finding and creating a new home. Fortunately Annie returned at least somewhat renewed, both mentally and physically. She, Helen, and Kate Keller prepared the Wrentham home for sale. In June they sold and then left the house, traveled the Northeast for a while, and received a positive report on Annie's health. Dr. Brown said she had improved tremendously and would recover. The physician advised them to go to southern California for at least a year.

California, however, lay too far away from everything they knew. They landed in Forest Hills, New York.

John didn't move with them. Leaving Wrentham symbolically closed the door on the marriage of John and Annie and all the dreams that had been built around it—his dreams, her dreams, the dreams they shared, as well as those of Helen. In her 1929 autobiography Keller wrote of leaving Wrentham as a great life sorrow brought about only by financial difficulties. Macy left nothing about her feelings on the matter.

John, however, remained a part of Annie and Helen's joint life, flitting in and out of the historical record. Between the time the two women left Wrentham in June 1917 and settled in Forest Hills in the fall, they saw him at least once—at Lake St. Catherine, Vermont. Yet the married couple lived apart. Perhaps he and Annie exchanged letters; though there's no evidence that she wrote to anyone, much less her estranged husband. Helen wrote—bragged?—to her mother, "He has certainly not been negligent about writing to me."[46] What did Helen and John write about? His career was then floundering. Helen's reference is tantalizing. In her latter books she always referred to John in fond terms. Did their relationship bother Annie? Or was this how the estranged husband and wife sent messages back and forth? The periodic and scattered references to him indicate that he remained aware of the events in his wife's life.

Mrs. Keller stayed with Macy and Keller until fall, after they purchased and settled into their home in Forest Hills, New York, fifteen minutes by train from Pennsylvania Station. Keller called it "a regular dovecote of a house—tiny, wee, petit, klein, pequena, piccolo, parva, mikra, and all the smallness you can imagine," but the house included a sun parlor, four bedrooms, a bath, kitchen, dining room, and a garret where Keller kept her books, and was also home to their Great Dane, Sieglinde. They stayed put for over a year. Keller explained that Macy "did not really recover" for almost a year after her return from Puerto Rico, and that during that year "she could not lecture."[47]

Could not lecture? Or would not lecture? In 1912 the women had defied the advice of a doctor and gone on the lecture circuit. Now, perhaps capable of better decision making thanks to her time in Puerto Rico,

Annie refused to sacrifice herself. For nearly a year the two women tended primarily to Macy's continued mental and physical healing.

Keller always had a hard time remaining still, and she likely struggled with the calm—whether it had been at her insistence or Macy's. The translating business never got off the ground. She dreamed of writing a book about blind people and blindness. That didn't work either. Macy couldn't provide the assistance required for that to happen, John was not mentioned as a possibility, and they could not afford paid assistance.[48]

Historically, Polly Thomson has always been referred to as a companion and assistant to Helen, but it's likely that during these years she primarily served as an aide to Annie. Keller hints at this, and at Macy's prickly temperament, in her biography of Macy. "Never has an explorer of the Arctic or the Antarctic or of darkest Africa met adventures and hazards with a stouter will than Polly in her quest of accomplishment and her effort to understand the whimsicalities of Teacher's nature," she wrote.[49] Apparently it took more courage and strength of will to face Anne Sullivan Macy in this period than it did to brave the wilds of the world.

In November 1917, not more than a few months after the trio settled in Forest Hills, Sophia Hopkins died. Neither Macy nor Keller recorded the death of Macy's housemother at Perkins, but they undoubtedly knew of it. Perhaps they traveled to Brewster for the funeral. It was not far. Hopkins had cared for the young Annie Sullivan with tremendous kindness. She had provided her a home, a family, and even a beautiful graduation dress. Macy was now over fifty years old, and her past continued to reassert itself. Much had changed in her life, however, since she had first walked onto the campus of the Perkins Institution for the Blind.

And it continued to change. While tuberculosis had not succeeded in sending Macy and Keller to California, Hollywood did. In early January, 1918, Keller received an invitation from filmmaker Francis Trevelyan Miller to discuss a film version of her life. A film offered the possibility of excitement, travel, something to do, and money. They met several times in January and continued negotiations through May. Keller's letters to Miller and his attorneys spoke of the glories that could be accomplished through the film. The film could show how she had "been saved from a cruel fate, and how the distracted, war-tortured world . . . could be saved from strife and social injustices—spiritual deafness and blindness." Macy's letters hammered out the contractual details, extracting as much money as she could from the deal and leaving as little to chance as she knew how. In May 1918 they signed the contract for *Deliverance*. Keller later wrote that "only the hope of providing for Teacher" made her agree to do the film.[50] Increasingly the former student embraced her role as household breadwinner.

John reappears in the historical record before their departure for the hills of Los Angeles. In early May Helen wrote to her friend Lenore Smith that she and Annie had just seen John off at the port of New York, saying goodbye to the man they hardly saw. "It is very lonely without John." He set sail for Italy, as the war continued to rage. "Teacher," Helen reported to Smith, "is very tired and nervous; but she stands it all better than I expected."[51]

There was no time, however, to mope. In July Annie, Helen, and Polly Thomson stepped aboard the train to Los Angeles. In August Kate Keller joined them; at some point so did Keller's brother, Phillips. Helen wrote to Lenore Smith, "The winds of destiny blew us out here." They stayed in Beverly Hills and met movie stars like Charlie Chaplin. Thomson did most of the interpreting for Keller while they were on the movie set; presumably Macy was not up to it. Thomson and Keller also rode horses every morning. Presumably Macy was not up to that either. As of late September Macy had ridden only a few times. Decades earlier it had been one of her favorite activities. "She gets very tired," Helen worried.[52] What Macy did all day is unclear—at some points she argued with the film's financial representative and met a few film stars. Keller's request that her mother join them may have been so that someone could attend to Macy.

Upon their return home in late 1918, Macy involved herself in the details of film production. The silent film required subtitles and she had firm opinions on the text and its accompanying images. She tried diplomacy, never her strong suit, but the intensity and length of her letters still must have annoyed. "We know," she directed Francis Trevelyan Miller in April 1919, "that you and Mr. Platt and others who are interested will cooperate with us in making the film in every detail the best that we can do. Our suggestions are made solely for the purpose of improving the film as a work of art and as a vehicle for conveying Helen Keller's life and message."[53]

In July, Annie, Helen, and Polly traveled to Boston. They were "much worried" about John, who'd returned from Italy. Helen reported to her mother that he'd been ill. "He looked dreadfully, and seemed like a feeble old man." How had they learned of his illness? Did he seek Annie's help? Or did someone such as Arturo Giovannitti send word? John had lived alone for several years. Having three women descend on the apartment, three women of substantial personality and presence, one of whom was his estranged wife, must have altered the mood there tremendously. While in Boston they also visited Wrentham. Helen thought she could visit their former home with "some equanimity," but sobbed as they drove away. What Annie thought as she visited both the person and the place she had once called home, and once again left each of them, we can only guess.[54]

Keller's autobiography reported that for the two years after their return from Hollywood they "lived quietly." For her, financial concerns dominated. Approximately forty years old, she embraced the role of household breadwinner and took that responsibility seriously. In the summer of 1919 they lived on credit. She lamented to her mother, "We have been frightfully 'hard up,' mother. I don't remember a time since college days when we were so much 'up against it.'" Thankfully, she wrote, "our credit is good, and people understand." She, and their creditors, believed that cash would roll in after the release of *Deliverance*.[55]

The film, however, flopped after its August 1919 premiere, despite being reviewed by the *New York Times* as "one of the triumphs of the motion picture." The creditors couldn't have been happy. "Everything seemed to be against me in my desire to provide for Teacher," Keller later lamented.[56]

Keller turned to vaudeville. Though at first it "seemed odd" to be on the same playbill as "acrobats, monkeys, horses, dogs, and parrots," Keller insisted that "our little act was dignified and people seemed to like it." She enjoyed her fellow performers, the act of performance, her sometimes boisterous interactions with the crowd (much less genteel than the lecture circuit), and the unpredictable questions she received. She performed her twenty-minute act twice a day for several days in a row. The relatively sophisticated musical accompaniment to her act derived from Mendelssohn's "Spring Song." The score included parts for piano, coronet, drum, violins, flute, cello, trombone, bass, viola, piano, horns, clarinet, bells, oboe, bassoon, and viola.[57]

Macy hated vaudeville. Keller called it a "frightful ordeal" for her. According to the scripts that remain, she was supposed to do the majority of the talking, though Polly Thomson frequently replaced her on stage. The bright footlights brought "agony" to her eyes. Thomson had to walk with her or she frequently stumbled. She consulted oculists along their routes, who always told her to give her eyes a respite or lose her remaining vision. In May 1920 she caught pneumonia while traveling through Buffalo, New York, dangerous for a former tuberculosis patient. In 1921 influenza sent her to her hotel bed in Toronto. In 1922 bronchial troubles confined her.[58] She increasingly experienced her body as debilitated and vulnerable.

After arriving home in late June at the end of the 1920 season Helen acknowledged to her mother that vaudeville had not gone as well as she had hoped. The time off demanded by illness, largely Annie's pneumonia, had eaten up most of their profits. She had hopes, however, of bigger dollars. "If we go on the long tour next season, if we don't get sick, if the bank where our money goes isn't robbed, if we don't adopt someone else, if we don't get train-wrecked . . . and all kinds of ifs—we shall be able to lay by a nice little sum."[59]

A July letter from Helen to her mother reveals how complicated things continued to be.

> We don't see John now. I was really disgusted with him, mother. He kept asking, dunning Teacher for money. Now, you know it is money I am trying to earn to provide for Teacher, not to waste on John. So I wrote him a letter repeating what I said last fall—that I didn't want to work with him, that if he persisted in coming to the house, I would go away. I begged him to go to work at anything and prove to his friends that the John Macy

they once knew was not utterly given over to selfishness and alcohol. Well, he wrote that he would terminate his relations with us and trouble Teacher no more. So far he has kept his word. I hated to write him such a letter, believe me. But what could I do. I couldn't bear to have Teacher treated thus, or to see his last spark of manhood quenched without an effort to save it. I don't know, though, what Teacher will do. She seems to feel terribly about the letter, and she says she simply can't help it. She does try hard for my sake to let things take their course, but ————. You know her warm heart and her constant remembrance of what John was to her once.[60]

John received the final boot, but from Helen and not Annie. He apparently kept his word and never contacted either woman again. Did he simply want work? Money? He had no consistent employment at that time other than authorship, not a dependable monetary source. Did he claim husbandly authority? Did he again request a divorce? Did he want to reconcile? How often had he visited the house? What then happened? How much did his disability—alcohol abuse—threaten and scare them, particularly Annie, whose father had abused alcohol? The remaining questions are more tantalizing than the few answers we have. This was not the life Annie had hoped for with John. Nor was it the life she'd hoped for with Helen.

Helen's assertiveness in the relationship between John and Annie is striking. Did she consult with Annie before dismissing the other woman's husband, or even warn Annie that it was about to happen? She claimed to her mother that she undertook the task for Annie—"I couldn't bear to have Teacher treated thus"; and for John himself—endeavoring to save "his last spark of manhood." As Helen represented the situation to her mother, Annie attempted to follow her lead. Helen, not Annie, made the final decisions about Annie's marriage.

And about money. Keller's ability to earn money, combined with Macy's inability to do so, was often the driving power behind their relationships and activities. John had been forced to recognize this from the very beginning of the marriage, but he likely had little initial knowledge of how powerful a force it would be.

More than anything else, the stark historical records of the U.S. Census reflect the changing power dynamics and relationships of the household. In 1910, when the married couple and Helen lived in Wrentham, the census listed John as "head" of the household, Annie as "wife," and Helen as "boarder." In 1920 the Forest Hills census listed Helen as "head," Annie as "teacher," John as "lodger," and Polly Thomson as "secretary." Between 1910 and 1920 John had been demoted from household "head" to "lodger." Helen's position as primary breadwinner promoted her from "boarder" to "head." Annie lost her status as "wife" and became "teacher."[61]

John did not do badly after being dismissed by Keller. He never became rich, but he had friends and he wrote. Beginning in late 1921 he went on to publish a sizable amount of respected literary criticism, both books and articles. In 1922 and 1923 he served as literary editor of the *Nation*. Working with fellow Harvard graduate and composer Frederick Shepherd Converse, he wrote the text to several operas. He met another woman, a purportedly "very beautiful" deaf woman, and dedicated *The Story of the World's Literature* (1925) to their daughter.[62] The book earned a favorable full-page *New York Times* review. Macy followed his career, as did Keller, and would later read his book *About Women* (1930) with great trepidation.

In August 1920 Keller wrote to her manager with the news that she was giving up vaudeville. That didn't last long. Perhaps the repeated appeals of her manager convinced her to change her mind. Perhaps she wanted to be begged to return to the stage. Perhaps creditors convinced her to change her mind. For whatever reason, the cycle of months on the road, months at home, continued until 1924.[63]

Like a mother skilled at inducing guilt, like a father explaining his constant presence at work, Keller always insisted that she stayed on the lecture and vaudeville circuits for her family's sake—meaning Macy. In 1912 Keller had justified her voice lessons to her mother by stating that if she was to help Macy "later on and make things easier for her," she had to "go on" with her "voice work." In 1956 she explained that at the age of sixteen she had vowed to "make a provision" for her teacher, to support her financially, to provide her reprieve from the pressures of life—because the teacher had given all she could, indeed her very self, for the student.[64]

Such claims undoubtedly reflected the truth, but they were also disingenuous. Keller had wanted her voice lessons. She enjoyed the lecture and vaudeville circuits, at least far more than Macy did. People, after all, came to see her, came to hear her, and not Macy. And financial support could have been found elsewhere.

But it's more complicated than simple disingenuousness.

Keller embraced her role as breadwinner, and the authority that came with it, as fiercely as a model patriarch. Indeed, in many ways, she became a husband to Annie. To protect Annie she resolutely exiled the erring husband and took his place. She provided the primary emotional support and the principal income. There is no evidence that the two women shared a sexual relationship, nor is there evidence that they did not. If they did, Annie's depression and physical debility likely limited the intensity of such a relationship, just as they probably had with John. Annie's scattered but lifelong yearnings for John suggest that she always cared for him romantically, and ached for what they once had. What mattered in her daily life, however, and what she and Helen made clear over and over again, is that no one made each of them as happy as the other one did. They lived intricately intertwined lives, were deeply dependent upon one another, and loved one another profoundly—even as they made mistakes. As they grew older, and as needs varied, each performed the daily physical and emotional caretaking that made it possible for the other to go on.

That pattern had been established long before the arrival of John Albert Macy. He was unable, or perhaps was not allowed, to become the emotional center of Annie's life. The child and student Helen had provided a safer love, more dependent and perhaps less challenging than the adult John. Annie's growing emotional and physical weakness, coupled with Helen's growing emotional and economic strength, pushed the married couple apart. It was easy, and comforting, for the older woman who had stubbornly resisted the authority claimed by so many men to give in to the authority—and love—claimed by Helen.

In the summer of 1924, after completing their last vaudeville circuit, and as Thomson vacationed in Scotland, Annie and Helen camped their way through New England. Annie instigated the trip. Harry Lamb, an old friend and driver, accompanied them. They took a tent, a stove, an icebox, and Sieglinde, their dear Great Dane. The car must have been crowded and chaotic. Annie was fifty-eight, Helen forty-four. Decades later, writing of this period, Helen wrote that Annie's "life seemed to always turn and turn in circles of futility as a fish in an aquarium, and her fits of melancholy did not help her." Life wasn't easy, but the trip was divine. "Every time I touched her face," Helen later wrote, "my own happiness was complete because life was sweet to her. . . . There was nothing more gratifying to us than the sense of equality between two souls communing in the breadth, depth, and height of the universe as well as in love."[65]

CHAPTER 12

The American Foundation for the Blind, 1924–1930

WHILE ANNIE and Helen prepared for their 1924 summer camping trip across New England, the board of trustees of the American Foundation for the Blind (AFB) received an account of the women's recent public activities on behalf of the organization. "When Mrs. Macy and Miss Keller appear," a staff member reported, "they are always received with marked reverence. The message and demonstration which they alone can give never fails to move the audience to great emotion, making a tremendous appeal for the work of the Foundation."[1]

For Macy, the timing was ideal. Just as she had grown incapable of continuing in vaudeville the AFB had sought out her and Keller for assistance with fundraising, lobbying, and educational efforts. Created in 1921 by the merger of several social welfare organizations for blind people, the AFB sought to better the lives of blind people by working on a national scale. Its board of trustees hoped and believed that Macy and Keller could establish it as the premier institution for the blind in the United States. Its first president, M.C. Migel, a wealthy businessman and chair of the New York State Commission for the Blind, eventually became a reliable friend to both Macy and Keller. The AFB provided Macy respectability, professional recognition, a salary, and structure for the last years of her life. She and Keller provided the AFB legitimacy and incredible star power.

The immense public recognition and esteem with which the general public beheld both women is reflected even in excerpts of the standard introductions given them at early AFB events:

> In presenting one of the most loved and undoubtedly the most marvelous figure of our century it is superfluous to say more than "This is Helen Keller" for we have all heard the story of the little girl. . . . What she has achieved as author, lecturer, and as one of the most brilliant minds in contemporary life has been a legend.
>
> In introducing Mrs. Anne Sullivan Macy, who has been Miss Keller's life-long teacher and companion, there are many things one could say, but the most striking fact of her life is that Mrs. Macy, as a teacher, has achieved greater results than any other in this country. This, with her patience, faithfulness, and devotion makes her stand alone, perhaps in the history of the world.[2]

She had finally beaten Samuel Gridley Howe.

The AFB had first contacted Macy in the summer of 1923. In March 1924 she and Keller began appearing at AFB events. They succeeded beyond anyone's dreams, and it became clear to all involved that a formal relationship would serve everyone's best interests. The women sought and received advice on salary negotiations from their friend Charlie Campbell of the Detroit League of the Handicapped. Migel wooed them. He acknowledged the financial assistance they gave the organization but reminded them of "the far greater boon you are conferring on the Blind throughout the United States toward ameliorating their material and spiritual wellbeing."[3]

Negotiations took all summer and into the fall. Macy, as always, took charge of the dirty work, leaving Keller to emerge without a stain—just as in the negotiations regarding *Deliverance*. Though Keller was the public breadwinner, Macy was a partner. In the end, the Helen Keller Campaign began in October 1924. The goal was to raise two million dollars in six months in order to provide an endowment fund for the AFB. The "Helen Keller Party" received two thousand dollars per month in salary. The contract committed Keller to four appearances a week, three with Macy, one with Thomson, but allowed for

Thomson to replace Macy in case of illness. Macy apparently won one major concession—a "readjustment of compensation" whenever they secured single donations of over five thousand dollars. The salary came from the funds of a private individual, one of the AFB's trustees (likely Migel), not the general AFB coffer.[4]

Macy's health remained a concern. Helen expressed hesitancy about the schedule to her sister, Mildred. She feared Annie wasn't "equal to all they would like us to do." Annie felt confident that despite her unpredictable health, they held the drawing card: the AFB could not succeed without Helen Keller. At least once, she so threatened Migel: "If you think other agencies can raise the two million dollars without Helen Keller, we shall be most willing to withdraw, and further negotiations will not be necessary."[5] Macy won this round. She acted with awareness and self-confidence.

But it didn't go very smoothly at first.

In early November the women had yet to be paid because the AFB meetings hadn't started. Macy wrote to Migel with an only slightly veiled request for money, mentioning the possibility of using Keller's name in other business enterprises. "We are at the end of our resources," she stated. Their house was mortgaged and because they were committed to the AFB they couldn't return to vaudeville. They owed money to doctors and dentists, had spent money on clothing and incidentals to prepare for the upcoming AFB meetings, and had their regular household expenses as well. She was forced to sell the car, "the only luxury we permit ourselves," she told him, and their "chauffeur and man-of-all-work" had left to find another position.[6]

Late December found the women traveling through Illinois. The effort had already discouraged Macy. In March 1925, her friend Charlie Campbell sent her a get-well letter, obviously responding to a note from her and hoping she would be "restored to the best health once more."[7]

By summer they had made their way to California, where they stayed recuperating, for most of the summer. Macy tried to salvage some good from what she characterized as their "unsuccessful efforts." "We have failed so miserably," she acknowledged to Migel in June, but held that attempting to raise two million dollars in six months had been "naively childish." She offered lengthy suggestions on how to improve the effort, noting that few people were interested in the AFB because they had simply not heard of it—everyone, however, had intense interest in Helen Keller. Her suggestions (which included placing a Catholic on the board so that they could more easily raise funds from Catholics) appear sound, and they also served to remind Migel that though they had not raised the desired two million, she and Keller still had much to offer. "Multitudes came to our meetings, listened to our story," she told him. "The educational value of our work cannot be overestimated. Indeed, it may be that educating the people about the needs and capabilities of the blind is the most important part of our campaign."[8] In contrast to earlier relationships with Michael Anagnos or Arthur Gilman, Migel and Macy got along well. She was older, more established, and less bristly than when she'd contended with either Anagnos or Gilman. Migel responded to her suggestions carefully, always signifying that he took them seriously.

Hidden away in Migel's June 1925 letter is a hint that Annie's past with John was not entirely behind her. It's a sign of continued social, political, and intellectual connections to John. The ever-so-skimpy hint is the location to which Migel sent his correspondence: in care of Mrs. Iva Ettor of Burbank, California.[9] In 1912, Iva's husband, Joseph Ettor, along with Arturo Giovannitti, had led the Lawrence textile mill strike. In 1924 and 1925, Giovannitti and Ettor had renewed the friendship they'd formed during the strike in order to advocate for the release of Sacco and Vanzetti. At the Ettor home Annie and Helen undoubtedly heard updates on the Sacco and Vanzetti case; but perhaps most important, they undoubtedly heard the latest gossip about John.

Though the fundraising for the Helen Keller Endowment didn't bring in two million dollars in six months, the AFB found Macy and Keller's contributions to the organization vital. The women attracted publicity and established the legitimacy of the organization in the public arena. Macy and Keller sometimes argued with Migel about strategy, and Macy frequently argued with him about money, but no one thought seriously of discontinuing the relationship.

The financial negotiations, however, were fierce. Macy had no qualms about using personal barbs and manipulation, and, at least in her letters to Migel, took any refusal or hesitancy as a personal insult. Several times she sent Migel detailed and lengthy explanations of why they required substantial amounts of money: they needed to pay Polly Thomson's salary; all three women needed to be "suitably dressed" for the many public events; "obviously" they required "the best hotels" in order to have a sitting room in which to greet the press and local committees; they needed to travel in private vehicles because Keller was easily recognized. On top of it all, their roof leaked, the leakage had damaged several rooms, neighbors were quickly encroaching on their previous isolation, and perhaps they needed a new home altogether. They could secure substantial money performing on the vaudeville circuit, she threatened once again. She did not want to appear "mercenary—to demand payment for doing what is not only one's duty but also one's pleasure" but "circumstances force one to be selfish."[10]

When Migel balked at her suggestions she lashed out. She accused him of putting "a great strain" on their friendship. "Somehow I imagined a better deed and a more generous attitude," she said. "Your words and deeds do not harmonize." He had insulted her by "expressing a profound appreciation of our endeavors" but "bargain[ing] with us like a railroad magnate employing stokers or road-menders." She tried to close with a stinging barb: "To help others is the highest blessing and happiness of life; to hurt others is the greatest unhappiness."[11] He, she implied, brought unhappiness to her and Keller.

Finally, all agreed on the contract—after an additional "two very protracted conferences" between the AFB's Robert Irwin and Macy.[12] The contract differed little from that of the previous year.

The new year was a huge success and began with a bang. The AFB had organized a major educational and publicity blitz for early January 1926. A massive public reception for notables in Washington, D.C., succeeded wildly, and the press fell all over itself in its efforts to praise Keller. She met President and Mrs. Coolidge (a former oralist educator at the Clarke School for the Deaf) at the White House, calling him "a dear President"—something only she could get away with. She then visited Minnesota senator Thomas Schall, a blind man she had known for several years, and requested that Senator Borah call on her that very moment in Schall's office. Borah obeyed without hesitation.[13]

From January through June of 1926 Keller promoted the AFB at 110 meetings in nine states and seventy cities.[14] And so it went. She and Macy would stay home for the summer and then begin again in the fall. Eventually the AFB put Keller on a yearly salary, which would grow substantially. She remained affiliated with and employed by the organization for the rest of her life. Her duties evolved over time to include less travel and more lobbying, often via letter. Occasionally she would withdraw from public advocacy due to Macy's or her own personal needs. Always, however, people came to see and hear her. She was the draw, the star, the event. Macy remained secondary.

The lives of the two women had conspired with cultural beliefs about women and disability to build for Keller a powerful public persona: a deaf-blind saint, unstained by selfish concerns, with rough work like salary negotiations left to Macy. At home, in private, however, the division of labor was not always what it appeared to be. During the fall of 1925, for example, as much of the negotiation took place, Helen was serving as Annie's secretary.[15] Thomson had returned to Scotland for a family vacation. Annie's eyes were so bad that she could not write. The fierce letters of salary negotiation were not written down by a determined Mrs. Macy, sitting at her desk and tightly gripping her pen as she scowled at the paper. Some, or even all, of those fierce letters Annie had fingerspelled to Helen, and the deaf-blind woman had then typed them. Neither woman embodied physical strength, health, or even determination in the ways anticipated by others.

Publicly Helen Keller was the disabled one. Indeed, the deaf-blind woman was a public figure because of her disability. Privately, however, by the mid-1920s Annie experienced her body as far more debilitating than Helen's had ever seemed to be, weighed down by the ever-changing multiple disabilities of fluctuating eyesight, chronic pain, and depression. Helen Keller, the world's most famous disabled person, had become Annie's personal assistant.

Annie left little direct evidence of her daily life from the mid-1920s onward. In the fall of 1925, in the midst of her AFB salary negotiations, John's latest book received a tremendously positive review in the *New York Times*. He had dedicated *The Story of the World's Literature* to

"My Daughter Margaret." Now the whole world knew he had found someone else.[16] Her past refused to stay in the past.

Other evidence indicates that all was not well for Annie. In June 1926, while she and Helen vacationed in Montgomery, she wrote to Polly Thomson. Did she have others to write to? The letter indicates that Thomson, who would soon embark for Scotland once more, had become a friend. "I'm afraid this letter is as rocky and barren as my life looks to me at present," she wrote. The problem was her, not Montgomery. "Somehow things have got a wrong twist in them—or perhaps it is true to say I have got a wrong twist in me. For the first time in my life the game doesn't interest me—doesn't seem worth while. But enough of this."

Sometime in 1926 Sieglinde, her Great Dane, died. Helen remembered Annie impulsively lamenting, "It is worse to lose such an appealing embodiment of affection that cannot speak than [to lose] a child!"[17]

Annie progressively lost her remaining vision and her eyes caused her increasing pain. "The sorrow that oppressed me," said Keller of the years 1927 through 1930, "was the knowledge of her coming total blindness." Despite prescribed eyedrops, reading for even a short period triggered "nauseating pain." A white tablecloth could cause "acute distress," "candles and unshaded lamps pierced her eyeballs." Frequent bronchial infections caused her to lose her sense of smell.[18]

Helen wrestled with Annie's blindness until her own death, long after Annie's. Whether deserved or not, whether manipulated by Annie or not, guilt lay at the core of the contradictory sentiments and analyses Helen left behind. "As I recall how Teacher gave her sight in unnumbered ways to benefit me," she wrote in her biography of Macy decades later, "I think of her eyes as 'dainty Ariels,' spirits too delicate to act out her exacting, incessant commands, and often tormented through no fault of their own."[19] She believed Annie had sacrificed those "dainty Ariels" for the cause of Helen Keller.

Keller always insisted on Macy's faith in her, and on Macy's refusal to accept "the blind" as defective. "Teacher," she asserted, "believed in the blind not as a class apart but as human beings endowed with rights to education, recreation, and employment suited as nearly as possible to their tastes and abilities." She considered Macy a brilliant pedagogical theorist and believed that if others had listened to her more often throughout the twentieth century blind people would have benefited tremendously. She praised Macy posthumously for refusing to tolerate "the sense-arrogant" and for inherently understanding the "harmful nature" of pity.[20] Keller lived and preached these messages, always crediting Macy for having taught them to her.

But even Helen recognized the threads of intellectual and personal discord. Annie, Helen acknowledged, simply could not "reconcile herself to the fact that her neglected, overdriven 'Ariels of vision' would sooner or later be unable to serve her." According to Helen, Annie "was one of the sensitive spirits that feel shamed by blindness. It humiliates them like a stupid blunder or a deformed limb. They do not count on the compassionate understanding of others, and they shrink from the comments of those who watch their struggle against misfortune. Blindness is a blow to their freedom and dignity, especially when they have always been active and industrious."[21]

Helen blamed the Perkins Institution. If only her dear teacher "had been rightly trained as a child in ways suited to the dark, she would have developed techniques that would have preserved her independence longer." The real "tragedy," Helen insisted, "was the fact that as a child she had not received the training or acquired that mental outlook that would have enabled her to enjoy far more independence, to listen to the counsels of reasons, and to use her sight prudently."[22] If only she had learned and used braille well; if only she had been taught mobility; if only, if only.

Helen also blamed the transitory nature of Annie's vision: "Since she felt so keenly in memory the darkness where she had once dwelt, her brain was 'fierce with light,' and she could not easily accept a return of her exile from that light."[23] First sighted, then partially blind, then partially sighted, then slowly, completely, blind again—even the labels and categorizations don't work well.

Once Macy told reporters, "Helen is and always has been thoroughly well behaved in her blindness as well as her deafness, but I'm making a futile fight of it, like a bucking bronco."[24] But while ridiculing herself and praising Helen, she was also scoffing at her as one of those boring, well-behaved disabled people. Just as she had infuriated her teachers at Perkins, Macy embraced a belligerent attitude toward her own disability.

But the essential facts remained: Annie experienced her "sick eyes,"[25] as Helen so often called them, as extremely debilitating, and her belligerence didn't accomplish much. She who drove Helen to reject all limitations, who insisted that Helen learn to be independent, failed even to try to learn the many things that would have made her own blindness less debilitating.

Perhaps, however, the easy assessments, even Helen's, are too harsh.

Just as the public defined Keller by her disability, so was Macy defined in opposition to disability. The necessary accompaniment to Keller, as the public understood her, was the able-bodied savior who had freed her from the chains of her disability. Anne Sullivan Macy had become a public figure because of her teaching, her supposed redemption of a piteous deaf-blind girl. The general public always assumed her to be sighted—even when told the opposite. The overwhelming cultural belief that disability debilitated, that only an able-bodied person could teach and assist someone with a disability, trumped the reality of Macy's limited vision and chronic illnesses. This context probably made it very hard to accept and be at ease with her own disability. And claiming to be disabled, when standing alongside the deaf-blind Helen Keller, would have seemed petty, inconsequential, and attention-seeking. The proud Annie would never have wanted that.

But even then her multiple disabilities—both visible and invisible—would have remained: the melancholy, the chronic pain, the unresolved childhood traumas, and her fluctuating eyesight. And there were no good medical treatments for most of her problems.

In 1926 Keller agreed with enthusiasm to write a book about the eighteenth-century Christian mystic Emanuel Swedenborg, the Swedenborgian faith, and her embrace of it. Macy had little enthusiasm for the project. Keller always attributed the tepid response to the subject matter. It's just as likely that Macy's reluctance also lay in her inability to assist. She couldn't read the printed materials on which Keller depended, or repeatedly go over the manuscript. John Macy, whose eyesight and editing skills had made the previous books possible, was missing from the literary equation. On New Year's Day of 1927 the manuscript lay in an unrevised mess. As Helen reported to her sister, "We were both in despair." As they sat despairing, a "bright, capable lady" from Doubleday and Page, the editor Nella Braddy Henney, rang them by telephone. Her boss, Ken McCormick , had long been asking Keller to write a second installment of her autobiography, to continue *The Story of My Life.* The AFB supported the idea.[26]

Keller accepted the proposition, but with the proviso that she first had to finish *My Religion.* Would Henney assist? Henney reported for duty the next morning and within three weeks Keller sent the manuscript to the press.

Henney, twenty-eight years Macy's junior, would eventually learn more about Annie than any other person besides Helen. She became a trusted friend. After Annie's death she would remain Helen's confidante until 1963.

Thus the three women began work on the book that eventually became *Midstream*—at least that was the public story. The true one was more complicated. For the rest of 1927 and 1928 the three women worked on what would become three different book projects: Helen on *Midstream*, Annie on an autobiography, and Henney on her biography of Macy. (Henney's plans to write her own book did not begin until it became clear that Macy would not complete her autobiography.)

In April Annie wrote to the AFB's Migel. She and Helen desired to take "a little trip" and "it occurred to her" that he "might like to finance it." He'd offered funds at Christmas, but they'd turned down his generous offer. Could they now have $500? The trip, she assured him, involved business. "We think it would refresh our memories, and bring back incidents and events which have faded from our memories to revisit the scenes of our earlier years in Massachusetts." They planned to visit her birthplace, Feeding Hills; Cambridge, the old site of Perkins; and the new Perkins campus in Watertown. Nella Braddy Henney would accompany them. Annie reported that though the pain in her eyes was "terribly intrusive" and "interfere[d] with work," Keller's book was progressing.[27]

Migel graciously agreed, and a month later Macy asked him for additional money. They had so many doctor bills. Could he send them an additional $1,000?[28] Again he agreed. Over the next years he repeatedly sent them money when asked, and sometimes without prompting.

The literary work made the three women close friends, but it began bumpily. Henney initially didn't know fingerspelling. Helen didn't like their first efforts. Eventually Henney spent ten to seventeen hours a day in their Forest Hills, New York, home.[29] They traveled together repeatedly. Henney came to revere Anne Sullivan Macy.

During this time period Macy and Henney traveled at least once through Feeding Hills. They sought out the remaining extended family members of Thomas and Alice Sullivan, and this time Annie identified herself. They sent letters to family members they found, asking questions about the family and Annie's past. Henney interviewed friends and acquaintances from Perkins, from Radcliffe, from the Macy marriage, and left few topics untouched. She sought Tewksbury records. She interviewed Annie, formally at times, and the women shared repeated and lengthy informal conversations. For the first time, Annie tried to integrate her past into her present.

Annie likely began writing her undated, unpublished memoir materials as well as fictionalized versions of her life at Tewksbury at this time. Annie, Helen, and Thomson spent part of the summer of 1927 on a small island near Cohasset, Massachusetts. Henney joined them briefly. Annie claimed two new dogs, a black terrier and another Great Dane. In July Thomson reported to Henney that Annie worked twelve hours a day from her bed, even though she found it difficult.[30] After their island retreat she largely remained in Forest Hills until the summer of 1929, eschewing the public appearances that Helen and Thomson made.

Annie must have felt her death to be near.

The materials Annie left behind range in length from a sentence to several pages and are undated and unordered. Some life events are represented in multiple but unnumbered versions; life at Tewksbury generally is fictionalized. She chronicled her early memories from a child's viewpoint but interpreted them in the voice of an adult trying to make sense of a difficult past. Chronologically, she never made it past her early education of Helen, stopped either by physical or emotional pain. She accompanied her memories with an equal quantity of short philosophical reflections—most under the title "Foolish Remarks of a Foolish Woman." Once it became clear that she would not write her own book she handed these written materials over to Henney. Intelligence, curiosity, sometimes brutal self-reflection, occasional whimsy, sporadic self-pity, a rare regret, and a general ferocity toward life, all emerge from the written materials Annie left behind. She mixed gripping pessimism with intense optimism for herself and the rest of humanity.

Annie recognized the sporadic but overwhelming nature of the sadness that haunted her. She recognized that her life included "unexpected good," yet confessed that sometimes "melancholy without reason grips me as in a vice." She never knew when "a word, an odd inflection, the way somebody crosses the street, brings all the past before me with such amazing clearness and completeness, my heart stops beating for a moment." Though she didn't refer to it by name, the reappearance of Tewksbury in her mind is clear. "Then everything around me seems as it was so many years ago. Even the ugly frame-buildings are revived. Again I see the unsightly folk who hobbled, cursed, fed and snored like animals. I shiver recalling how I looked upon scenes of vile exposure—the open heart of a derelict is not a pleasant thing. I doubt if life, or eternity for that matter, is long enough to erase the errors and ugly blots scored upon my brain by those dismal years."[31] She blamed Tewksbury, more than anything else, for the later volatility of her spirits.

Some of the manuscript scorned the unspecified reader's desire for understanding. "Why, O curious ones," she wrote, "do you stop at my door to-day and peer into my face wonderingly. You have passed me with miserly glances for sixty years and longer. Why did you not ask your questions before my heart was cold, my hair gray? What does it matter now who my father was? Or my mother? How my childhood was nurtured?" Curiosity, wonder, and, particularly, compassion would have been easier for her to accept earlier in life. The child at Tewksbury would have embraced such curiosity, as would have the child at Perkins. She hinted at secrets still kept. "You have kept aloof, proud world, too long. The time for confidence is passed. The most safe abode for my secret is where the darkness shelters all."[32]

She was, she claimed here, too wounded for understanding, for life, even for pain. "I am as indifferent as a stone," she went on. "Love has betrayed me; friendship is a broken reed; life has pierced me in a thousand ways; but the wounds are all dry. I think I have forgotten how they used to bleed."[33]

Since her early education of Helen, Annie had steadfastly eschewed reporters for over forty years and often had let misinterpretations, errors, or exaggerations stand. She made no attempt to isolate Helen from reporters after Helen became an adult but rarely spoke to any herself. Why care now what others thought? Why attempt autobiography? She who had once burned her diary could so easily have never started the manuscript, could so easily have destroyed it after it became clear she would not publish the book. Instead she wrote, often from her bed, often via Helen, and ensured the longevity of that material by giving it to Nella Braddy Henney. Despite her lifelong tendency toward privacy, despite the many secrets she had kept about her past, she wanted others to understand her. She desired to leave a record, to define herself, and to be understood on her own terms.

Yet, she sometimes backpedaled uneasily. She belittled herself and her efforts by putting many of them under the title "Foolish Remarks of a Foolish Woman." The manuscript is anything but foolish, and while she can be criticized for much in her life, *foolishness* is a term that can never be applied to her. She fell into the far too common trap of female autobiography—accepting full blame for supposed failures but reluctant to claim ambition, success, or authority.[34] Only by dismissing herself, her thoughts, and her analyses as foolish could she claim space to voice them. It's a warning to tread carefully through what she wrote.

Embedded in Annie's memoir materials is also a ferocious desire to understand herself. It's more than an end-of-life desire to assess. It's a desperate attempt to grasp the self-comprehension that had eluded her her entire life. "Let me retrace," she vowed, "the record to the years that made me what I am."[35]

She sometimes returned to the theme of life as experimentation. "At times," she wrote, "I was terribly lost in this new experiment; but when one has challenged a strongly entrenched tradition there is no turning back." As she wrote in her "Foolish Remarks," "I still think there is not much to life, except to learn all one can about it, and the only way to learn it is to experience much—to love, to hate, to flounder, to enjoy and to suffer."[36]

The autobiographical effort sometimes hurt, but Annie left little about her feelings on her renewed family contact or on anything that Henney dug up about the past. She tantalizingly wrote that autobiography required "courage" because of the truth it demanded, contradicting her earlier statement about keeping secrets. "I am not spiteful, and I have never intentionally hurt any one," she wrote, "but in such a book I should feel bound to write without fear or favor what I think and with strict regard to veracity." Henney once passed along the same message to one of Macy's family members. "It is too bad there are so many sad things connected with it all," she wrote in 1928, "but they are there, and Mrs. Macy would rather know the truth than anything else."[37]

For the first time in nearly fifty years she met family members— learned of cousins, nieces and nephews, aunts and uncles. She and Henney asked questions about her parents, her sister Mary, and the family's memories of the young Annie.[38] Macy, via Henney, pursued her questions about her father vigorously. She had not seen him, had not even heard of him, since he appeared at Tewksbury to say goodbye, shortly before her brother Jimmie's death.

Her father, family members told her, had hanged himself. Again, Henney begged family members not to spare Macy's feelings. "She is very anxious to find out all she can about her mother and father and hopes that you will be able to tell her when it was that her father hanged himself in Chicago and something of the circumstances that led up to it." Annie, she assured them, "wants to know the truth, no matter how terrible it is." Henney explained that Annie would have taken it upon herself to write, "but her eyes are so poor that it is not possible."[39]

Annie wanted to know more. Her father had committed suicide. We know of at least two occasions when others feared she would do the same.

No one in the family could, or would, tell her more.

She would never know if he regretted leaving her, if he ever thought about her afterward, if he ever tried to reclaim her. She would never know if he had followed her eventual career and fame. Her intense curiosity suggests that despite her earlier erasure of her past, she had hungered for it all along—to be reclaimed, embraced, and acknowledged by her family. She wanted them to know her and be proud of her.

In early June 1929 Annie's longtime eye doctor, Dr. Conrad Berens, removed her right eyeball. Migel sent her and Helen $1,000 for a much-needed vacation and encouraged them to send him the hospital bills. His wife invited Annie to recuperate at their home, accompanied by Helen, but Annie declined. Helen described Annie as "reluctan[t] to accept her invitation to visit Rest Haven until the traces of what she had been through were somewhat less conspicuous." The refusal embarrassed Helen. "I suppose there must be more vanity in Mrs. Macy than in me." The only good news Helen could impart was that recent gifts in the will of Mrs. William Thaw allowed them to pay their own hospital bills in addition to many other "obligations."[40]

Helen despaired. She had been worried about Annie "a long time" and the surgery had not solved everything. She wrote to Migel nearly hysterical: "Things have gone badly with her, there is no disguising the fact. I thought the Battle of Eyes was over, and was feeling happy, even though we had lost. But we saw Dr. Berens last Friday, and he told Mrs. Macy that her other eye would have to be operated on in September for cataract. He said she must take a complete rest during the summer months, and not worry!!!" Helen didn't know what to do. She went on, "How does one not worry when there is a possibility of becoming totally blind in a few weeks? Without doubt, Fate lays relentless hands on some individuals. If Fate had perception, a soul, a heart, a conscience, it must needs blush for the pain it wantonly inflicts." More than Keller could express, she appreciated the "magic carpet" of Migel's money.[41] It would allow them a lengthy vacation and respite.

As she so often liked to do, Annie wanted to hide. They rented an isolated cabin on Long Lake in the Adirondacks, forty miles from the nearest railroad and inaccessible by road. A boat brought them provisions as needed. The icy mountain stream that flowed to the lake served as their refrigerator. Helen used a rope that extended from the cabin to the lake to walk by herself; she tied another rope to her waist, a length of fifty feet tied at the other end to the dock, in order to swim alone, and an additional rope of over two hundred feet allowed her to ramble through the nearby woods. They hired someone (Annie called him "our coloured boy") to chop wood, care for the fires, and run errands as needed. They stayed through mid-October, when the fall foliage must have been at its best.[42]

As they prepared to depart Annie admitted her springtime malaise to Migel. "I had been feeling fagged out such a long time, it had almost come to seem like a natural state of being," she conceded. But the retreat, she insisted, had renewed her. "My enjoyment has been complete." They would return to Forest Hills and Helen would return to her AFB engagements.[43]

Once again, however, running away had solved things only temporarily. The fall publication of *Midstream* might have lifted Helen's spirits, but by late fall "the Battle of the Eyes" had become a battle between her and Annie. After the June surgery the doctor had been insistent that Annie needed cataract surgery in the fall if there was any hope of preventing complete blindness in her remaining eye. While Helen's workload increased due to the interviews and public appearances for her new book, Annie refused to see the doctor. In late November Helen sought Migel's help: "Naturally, I am up in arms, but what can I do? I need your help to make her behave."[44]

By late January 1930 things had deteriorated further. Helen again expressed her frustration to Migel. "There is no disguising the fact that things are going very badly with my teacher these days," she lamented. Annie still refused to see the doctor. Not only that, but "She has not been able to read even the headlines of a newspaper for more than a week. She is very nervous, and naturally discouraged." It saddened Helen tremendously. She lamented to Migel as she could not to Annie, "I can take no interest in my work just now, my heart is so heavy. All my life I have lived in a dark, silent world, and I seldom think of my limitations, and they never make me sad; but to see the light failing in another's eyes is terrible, especially when one is unable to do anything to avert the tragedy!"[45]

Helen went on. "These days we are living at high tension, and all round us is uncertainty and the dark."[46] Not only was the sixty-two-year-old Annie inconsolable about her deteriorating eyesight, but she refused to do the little that could be done to prevent total blindness. Why was Annie so resistant? Martyrdom likely had its own benefits. And for many people, depression is immobilizing. Perhaps physical incapacity felt like the most appropriate accompaniment to emotional incapacity. Annie's refusal to act must have infuriated deaf-blind Helen, who made excellent use of all of the adaptive equipment she could either find or create.

Around them, the stock market crashed and many of the rich of Forest Hills, New York, lost much that they had owned. The lines of people seeking food and shelter grew daily—in New York, in Massachusetts, and throughout the nation.

THE 1929 PUBLICATION of *Midstream* made public material presumably both disconcerting and comforting to Annie. The book went on and on about the wonders of John Macy. Keller's introduction expressed how keenly she still felt his absence. "He was a friend, a brother, and an adviser all in one, and if this book if not what it should be, it is because I feel lonely and bewildered without his supporting hand." But her adulation went beyond the literary. She praised his "his brotherly tenderness, his fine sensibilities, his keen sense of humor, and his curious combination of judicial severity, and smiling tolerance"; his "helpful kindnesses"; his "laughter that leaves the heart light and soothes the ruffled mind." "There are no words to tell," Keller wrote, "how dear he was to me or how much I loved him. Little incidents hardly noticed at the time but poignantly remembered afterwards crowd upon me as I write."[47] This may have been a means for Keller, who was unable to lash out at Annie over current annoyances, to needle her friend. If so, it undoubtedly succeeded.

Keller, however, concluded *Midstream* with homage to Annie. The final chapter, "My Guardian Angel," reflects Helen's anxiety about An-nie—her blindness, her ill health, and her eventual death. The pros-pect of Annie's death, Helen wrote, "terrifies me." She feared she would become "blind and deaf in very truth if she were gone away." The read-ing public had no idea how likely it was that Annie's death would occur relatively soon.[48]

Keller expressed her overwhelming belief, once again, that every-thing she was and had become was due to Macy's sacrifices. "She has always abused her eyes for my sake," Keller explained, in prose that must have been written during the summer of Macy's eye surgery. How could she complain about Annie's response to blindness, when that very blindness was due to Annie's sacrifice on her behalf? Though this sentiment ignored the medical realities of Annie's early years with tra-choma, Keller repeated it often.

Not only that, but Macy had sacrificed her own personal and pro-fessional advancement. "She has closed these doors to herself and re-fused to consider anything that would take her away from me. . . . She has given me the best years of her womanhood, and she is still giving herself to me day by day."[49] The boundaries between love, obligation, and guilt are thin and permeable.

Macy left no record of her thoughts on the contents of *Midstream*.

In February of 1930 Helen decided to take charge. Annie had al-ways responded well to a complete change of scene—in Puerto Rico, in the cabin on Long Lake. They would take a ship to some "blessed isle of peace," she told Migel. "I intend to leave everything and devote myself to her the next three months." He knew how "far from well" Annie was, and perhaps a "complete change" would help her "nerves."[50] Helen, Polly Thomson, Nella Braddy Henney, M. C. Migel, and her doctor conspired to get Annie out of the house at Forest Hills. A hint of desperation pervades Helen's and Henney's short descriptions of the efforts.

Nella Braddy Henney reported another reason for Keller's perse-verance about their departure. Keller dreaded major public recognition of her upcoming fiftieth birthday and wanted no part of it. She had no wish "to have to wear a company smile and make a silly speech about feeling fifty years young."[51]

Annie dug in her heels and refused to go. In a rare admission of Annie's unpleasant behavior, Helen acknowledged later that "she became disturbed, then angry and did almost everything against good sense and courtesy." She gave the impression of yielding by not expressing resistance any longer, and Helen and Thomson made preparations to sail to England. Only hours before their departure from the house, however, Annie made her refusal clear. "No force or persuasion was of any avail," was Helen's description. As Helen chronicled it decades later, only guilt and manipulation convinced Annie to accept the departure. Thomson became silent, "sad, tired, and spiritless." Helen sat at her desk and "said nothing." Annie became "quite repentant." Not many days later, on April Fool's Day, they departed for Plymouth, England, on the SS *President Roosevelt*.[52]

Despite a tremendous storm, in which the chairs in their stateroom "flew back and forth like footballs," they arrived in Plymouth safely. Thomson's sister had arranged lodging for them in Loos, Cornwall. With her help they kept the visit from the British press. They traveled quite a bit—Waterford, Killarney, the trail of King Arthur, and much more. The trip, at least most of it, was so enjoyable that they stayed long past the planned departure date at the end of May, until sometime in August.[53]

In June they sailed on board the *Bally Cotton* for Ireland. Annie sought again to search for her past by learning more about her parents. In the memoir materials she eventually gave to Henney she left little about the nearly three months spent in England, but pages and pages about the two weeks in Ireland. Intermingled are vague and slippery memories of her father. The memoir materials she left are weighty pieces of metaphysical reflection. She experienced the country through a lens, a curtain, of her unresolved past and her current expectation of death.

For two days they traveled through Limerick, stopping at several castles, seeking information from local priests. Annie believed her parents to have come from Limerick but didn't know which parish they had lived in, and the records from the famine years were scattered and incomplete. She learned nothing.

In the small village of Cratloe the three women each made a donation to the parish priest, "feeling sure that Teacher's parents would have contributed if they could." Annie stood in the small white chapel and "wondered if my parents had been christened and married there." "The countryside," she went on, "is very poor and nearly deserted."[54]

"I have not enjoyed myself," she wrote, describing Helen and Polly climbing the ancient castle steps in Limerick. "The thought of visiting the scenes in a handsome automobile driven by a man in a livery made me very uncomfortable. In imagination I saw my forbears working in those hills . . . trudging bare-foot to their comfortless thatched cottages or, driven by extreme poverty, trekking toward a port from which they would sail to distant lands."[55]

Ireland and the emotions it wrought overwhelmed her. "Ireland disturbs me strangely . . . a fierce ache gnaws at my heart." It was otherworldly, a pull from the grave. She linked the Ireland of her unresolved past with her future death—both disconcerting, both unavoidable. "When one stops talking in Ireland, one hears the murmur of grieving and death. One feels that death and the sweet-breathing earth are one. Her forests and streams, her shores and mountain crags always leave me melancholy." To her, Ireland was separated from the rest of the world—not in geographical, but in mystical terms. "I missed the settled and ordered life of humanity."[56]

The terrain pulled her toward an even deeper misery than she had already experienced. It spoke to her with the siren call of suicide.

> The weird rocks on the hillsides watch me, and their expression is intense. I find myself waiting for them to speak to me, and deep in my soul I know their message will break my heart. The long violet shadows call to me to follow them over the rocks and cliffs down, down, down to the sea, whose cruel white hands will drag me from the light and the warm sun forever.[57]

The theme of death is overwhelming.

In her 1956 biography of Macy, Helen wrote that near the end of their time in Ireland Annie was "no longer herself." She gladly dragged the older woman out of her parents' homeland.[58]

After Ireland they settled in Essex, at a secluded country home nearly four hundred years old. Again, the letter-writing duties fell to Helen. "We dare to be dull," she reported to Henney, "to ignore time, to spend evenings that seem like eternity secure from visitors in a world where there are no uncertainties." They ate scones, gooseberries, salmon, roast lamb, and lots of butter from nearby farms. Helen felt Annie was improving. "Teacher is glad now that we carried her off to Britain. There are still times when she worries about her eyes, but on the whole she is improving in health and spirit." Helen reported that both she and Annie experienced the trip as revitalizing. "I thought we might as well wear our garments of enchantment as long as possible, and forget the strait jacket of routine and publicity which Teacher and I have worn the best part of our lives."[59]

In Essex, however, the more recent past haunted Annie.

As they were settling in there, John Macy's latest book, *About Women*, arrived in the mail. Macy had asked for it in May when it was first released, but the book didn't arrive until late July. Gossip quickly went back and forth in letters between Polly Thomson and Amelia Bond, Migel's secretary at the AFB. The remaining letters tell us only that Macy agreed with Bond's opinion about the book. Bond sent not only the book but also multiple reviews.[60]

Annie must have hated the book. Helen must have hated it. Morrow advertised it as "daring, frank and controversial." The misogyny of *About Women* is only lightly disguised. Annie must have had a hint of what was coming. *Harper's* magazine had earlier published John's essays "Equality of Woman With Man: A Myth" (1926) and "Logic and the Ladies" (1928). Annie's long-estranged husband argued that he really loved women; indeed, his book was not an "attack on women." However, the book decried their growing influence in society. The problem, John argued, was "certain kinds of women, egregiously assertive feminists, and women who pay men the doubtful compliment of imitating them, and interfering women who try to run the whole show and reform the male actors." The problem was the "feeble flabby-minded fellows that men are permitting the women to make of them." He called upon American men to act, for the country was being "enfeebled by feminization."[61]

John's list of praiseworthy women—all dead—included Julia Ward Howe.[62] He could not have designed the list to be more infuriating to Annie. As a Perkins student she had seethed at Mrs. Howe's aristocratic and haughty nature. And since leaving Perkins she'd been battling the memory of the woman's dead husband, Samuel Gridley Howe. Perhaps John did design the list to infuriate his legal wife.

Somewhere around the time of *About Women*'s release Annie wrote—on the back of a shopping list that included "Epsom salts, lavender water, Listerine, perfume"—her own, much briefer, analysis of contemporary marriage. She argued that marriage caused women's "confessed inferiority in men's pursuits and professionals." Because women were raised with marriage as the ideal and "direct aim," they were raised to "hope or expect to get their life given to them."[63] Thus men learned to depend on themselves and women learned dependency. Reading between the lines, one can conclude that she believed John's inability to accept her independence caused the marriage to fail, whereas John blamed its failure on her independence and assertiveness. In John's analysis, independent women destroyed marriage; in Annie's, marriage destroyed independent women.

Divergent intellectual analyses of the institution of marriage, however, did not erase the emotions of *their* marriage. Annie still cared for John, or at least for what he once represented. The manuscript materials she eventually gave to Henney include an undated paragraph, presumably unsent, addressed to the man she had refused to divorce. "Last night you came to me, John," she wrote.

> I do not know if it was a dream or your spirit presence. I felt your step so near and you were the very same—your manner and the smell of your clothes. I held your hand so tight and you called me Bill, but I felt the same glad thrill I always felt when you put my hand on your lips and said Hello Bill. Oh I was so happy because you had come back to me. Home isn't just the same when you are not there. We walked in the hill wood and we hunted toadstools and got a basket full that were good to eat. We walked home through the field and you said, "This is like the old times," and the way you said it brought peace to

my heart. I can't tell if it was a dream or a vision. I only know I
have been happier today because you called me Bill in the dear
old way.[64]

He could still thrill her—and thus, he could still hurt her. *About
Women* must have hurt a great deal.

Sometime in 1930 Annie revealed the truth of her life at Tewksbury
to Helen. In all probability the conversation occurred after their return
to the United States. The immobilization brought on by her depression in the months prior to their departure for Europe would have
made an earlier conversation unlikely.

The only record of the conversation is from Helen. Taking advantage of Thomson's vacation absence, Annie sent the maid and even the
dog away for the afternoon. The two friends sat "side by side" and "the
terrifying drama of her early years began to unfold in my palm." Annie
fingerspelled, "pouring out a tale of a tragic childhood spent among human beings sunk in misery, degradation, and disease." Helen recalled,
"I put myself into the exploring spirit of the half-blind, lonely child
who lived in that hideous environment and I nearly went distracted at
the dreadful sobbing with which, after the silence of half a century, she
spoke of her brother Jimmie's death in the almshouse."[65]

Annie was sixty-four. What caused her, after nearly lifelong secrecy,
to reveal herself after so long? Helen, more than anyone else, must have
assumed she knew all there was to know about Anne Sullivan Macy.
Perhaps Annie felt it imperative to tell Helen before she died, and the
conversation was a form of deathbed confession. She'd likely already
told Henney, or would soon. Perhaps she wanted Helen to hear it from
her first.

The conversation relieved Helen, for it explained what she had long
failed to understand. "It gave me," she wrote decades later, "a sense of
equilibrium." The hole in their relationship, Helen's failure to understand Annie's "peculiarities," was now filled.[66] They had lived together
for forty-two years.

Annie's decades-long refusal to tell even her most intimate companion Helen about her life at Tewksbury signifies deep trauma and
perhaps shame. Helen never would have considered her friend deserv-

ing of shame, but an almshouse childhood highlighted the family and status differences between the backgrounds of the two women. Perhaps the secrecy lay in the trauma of loss—of Jimmie, of her family, of an innocent and carefree childhood, of a family identity. Perhaps the trauma simply lay in the wretchedness, the misery, the horrid routine of daily life at Tewksbury. Perhaps Annie had repressed the memories, forbidding herself to share them until it felt safe to do so.

CHAPTER 13

Concluding, 1930–1936

BY 1930, Macy's frequent pain and ill health had aged her beyond her sixty-four years. Thanks to endurance, stubbornness, and an unremitting commitment to Helen, however, she'd outlived her critics. At the end of 1930 Charles Beury, the president of Temple University, wrote separate letters to both Macy and Keller. The university sought to bestow an honorary degree upon each of them. The invitation reflected their growing eminence. Keller had just had her fiftieth birthday. Only months later, the *New York World-Telegram* would list her as one of the ten "greatest women of today."[1] Both teacher and pupil now stood as senior stateswomen, representative of American womanhood at home and, increasingly, abroad. In public Macy appeared as an elderly matron, respectable and dignified.

Despite Keller's best efforts to convince her to change her mind, Macy declined the honor offered her by Temple University. She felt she wasn't good enough. "I do not consider my education commensurate," she confessed. "All my life I have suffered in connection with my work from a sense of deficiency of equipment." Others attempted to persuade her to accept the honor, but she refused their overtures.[2]

Her refusal is both revealing and puzzling. For decades she had fought to be recognized as a pedagogical innovator. Alexander Graham Bell had believed in her. For the first time, official and public recognition lay before her. She never, however, shook off a pervasive sense of self-doubt. In her mind, the Frost King episode taunted her, even after decades; her poverty-stricken background and limited education made her question herself. At the very core of the Temple honor lay the question that had plagued her for decades: had she simply followed the directions laid out by Samuel Gridley Howe, or had she led Helen through pedagogically new territory? Temple University considered Macy, whose admission to Radcliffe alongside Keller had not even been contemplated, worthy of an honorary university degree. The honor also made her vulnerable to physical scrutiny. The assistance she would have required to walk across the stage would have revealed her blindness, her own disability, to the audience.

On February 16, 1931, Temple awarded honorary degrees to Helen Keller and two others.[3] The AFB's Migel sat in the audience.

With the help of Nella Braddy Henney, Macy had traveled to Philadelphia without Keller's knowledge. She snuck in the door of the auditorium. Migel saw her briefly, but neither Beury nor Keller knew she was there.[4]

The resulting events affirmed Macy's worth in unexpectedly profound ways. President Beury told the crowd of her refusal to accept the honorary degree and read the painfully humble letter with which she had declined. Governor Pinchot of Pennsylvania, who also sat on the podium to receive an honorary degree, spontaneously made a motion that the audience vote on the matter. As Keller later described it to a friend, "In a moment four thousand people in the spacious auditorium had risen to their feet and, amid applause, decreed that Mrs. Macy's innate modesty should not be permitted to interfere with the purpose of Temple University to honour her with me."[5]

The moment is worth imagining. The crowd around Macy, who was by then a large woman with a manner often perceived as haughty, did not know her identity. Four thousand strong, they enthusiastically stood to applaud her and her accomplishments. We know little of how she responded, but it meant a tremendous amount to her. A week later she wrote to Beury, "I shall always 'thank whatever powers there be' that I obeyed the call of my heart that day." She had intended to speak with him after the ceremony, "but the kind reference to me moved me so deeply, speech deserted me, and I fled in a sort of panic."[6]

At the luncheon following the event someone—likely Migel or Henney—got word to Helen of Annie's presence at the auditorium. The same person told Helen the name of Annie's hotel. She and Thomson rushed out. All we have of their encounter are Helen's words of two months later: "I won't repeat what I said when I got her within my arms' reach. She pleaded guilty, saying that the desire to see me honored had proved stronger than her fear of being discovered and punished for her perversity." A friend, who had spoken in praise of Keller during the ceremony, later teased Macy about her presence in the auditorium. If he'd only known, he claimed, he would have said things to make her blush "to the roots of your hair!"[7]

After that it was easy to persuade Macy to accept the honorary degree. Beury even offered to travel to Forest Hills to confer the degree. Macy's letter of acquiescence is telling. The scene at the auditorium had "extremely delighted" her. "I had the pleasant sensation," she wrote, "of thinking that I may after all have been a good teacher." Perhaps this constituted genuine humility, but it also reflected the profound feeling of unworthiness that she had never been able to shake. "I warn you, though," she told Beury, "that the laurel crown will sit ill on my erratic head."[8] She initially embraced the possibility that the degree be given to her in the privacy of their Forest Hills home, but eventually acquiesced even further to the honor and agreed to appear at the next Founders' Day—one year away.

In the undated "Foolish Remarks of a Foolish Woman" Macy dismissed the importance of honors. Recognition, she implied, simply came to her too late. "Honors which would have transported us with joy if they had come earlier have no thrill in them, especially when they are forty years overdue." One was only "cold, sated, bored" by honors received. "In youth," she acknowledged, "I would have gone round the world for a compliment. Now I am indifferent."[9] There's no way of knowing if she wrote this before or after receiving the Temple degree.

In her 1929 autobiography *Midstream*, Keller had written, "She [Macy] delights in the silence that wraps her life in mine, and says that the story of her teaching is the story of her life, her work is her biography." Henney referred to a "twin personality . . . called Helen Keller," of "two entities, separate and inseparable, like Damon and Pythias,

Héloïse and Abélard, Beaumont and Fletcher, Plato and Socrates." She praised Macy as "a sculptress whose clay was Helen."[10]

Macy's actions, however, reveal that she cared about the Temple degree. Someone other than Keller believed in her professional authenticity. University educators, pedigreed educators in fact, considered her a legitimate and worthy teacher. She loved Keller but she also needed an identity apart. The highly public esteem bestowed upon her as Henney wrote her biography and she reflected on her own life mattered enormously.

Not long after Helen received her Temple degree ill health bothered Annie again. Helen called it bronchitis. In early April 1931 she returned from a doctor-ordered retreat at Buck Hill Falls, Pennsylvania. Frustrated and slightly angered, Helen considered Annie to be neglecting her health. "She is still far from well," Helen reported to a friend. "The doctor wants her to get away as soon as possible. I simply won't let her neglect her health as she has done during many years."[11]

They stayed home long enough for Keller to attend and help lead the first World Conference on Work for the Blind, in which delegates from thirty-six countries met in New York. The event emphasized the AFB's, and consequently Keller's, growing prominence nationally and internationally. As soon as possible upon completing the conference, however, Macy and Keller once again left the country.

Decades later Keller wrote that they went to Concarneau, in Brittany, France, in order to "rest and struggle with unanswered mail." Writing during the trip, Annie explained that they were "worn out. . . . Our nerves were fiddle-strings, and our tongues were dangerously spiked." They chose France because of Britain's strict quarantine laws pertaining to incoming animals. They stayed abroad from mid-May until mid-October. With two trunks, a hatbox, a shoe bag, four large suitcases, three rugs, three extra coats, and Annie's small black terrier Darky, they rented a beachside villa. Annie complained that the towels were hardly larger than handkerchiefs and the small bathtub "extremely hazardous" for an adult of her "bulk." She described the location as ideal, however, "granting the proposition that we don't want to see anybody or go anywhere."[12]

Concarneau wasn't isolated enough, however. Though Macy hoped "we had put the Atlantic Ocean and the French language between us and public demands," a formal invitation from the Yugoslavian government showed up at their door. They were invited to visit the country to generate interest in improving the lives of its blind citizens. Transportation and lodging had already been arranged. "There seemed to be nothing to do about it," Annie wrote to her old friend Lenore Smith, "but pack up and go." The Yugoslavians hosted them kindly and with generosity, but the trip exhausted her. She wanted to be alone. For the nearly monthlong trip she hadn't "a moment" without social obligations. While Helen and Polly considered it "an adventure" she thought it "a nightmare of the deepest dye."[13]

Keller later explained that they accepted the invitation to Yugoslavia because "Teacher refused to be spared."[14] Macy so often martyred herself for Keller's sake that the explanation undoubtedly is true, but it's also convenient. Indeed, it became Helen's standard explanation: they engaged in activities that Helen enjoyed but Annie disliked (or experienced as deleterious to her health) only because Annie insisted on it—be it vaudeville, the classroom work of Radcliffe, the lecture circuit, or the public demands of a state-sponsored tour of Yugoslavia. This enabled Annie to simultaneously savor the events while complaining about them.

Annie corresponded little in these years, but sent two lengthy letters from Concarneau (one to Nella Braddy Henney and one to her old friend Lenore Smith). As with so many things, these letters must be interpreted through the complexities of her friendship with Helen. Annie fingerspelled (she called it dictating) both letters to Helen who then typed them. Perhaps this shaped the letters' contents, perhaps not. In one of the letters from Concarneau, and in later letters as well, Helen inserted comments in parentheses, disagreeing with or editorializing about Annie's words. We'll never know if Annie knew of Helen's annotations, or if she edited herself because of Helen's listening hands. She was, however, always aware of Helen's oversight. To Smith she explained, "I am dictating this to Helen. She is laughing in her sleeve at me."[15]

Annie's early June letter to Nella Braddy Henney is the letter of a woman struggling to be cheerful. She began by describing her dream, mentioned earlier, about the letters she and Helen had exchanged during her 1916 stay in Puerto Rico, revealing anxiety about her planned biography. She reminded Henney that Helen did not want those letters shared. The letter's tone is slightly sardonic, with lengthy descriptions. The weather and fog were horrid, but liquor warmed them: "If liquor of every sort wasn't as cheap as mud, we should all mould and disintegrate." She admitted to "a touch of Irish melancholy and a trace of genuine homesickness," but downplayed it by claiming that afternoon tea would heal her. She attributed her complaints to her dog Darky, reveling in the terrier's supposed distaste for the place. "He hates everything French—dogs, people and the garden," she told Henney. "He also hates the sound of the wooden shoes, and of the language he is most contemptuous."[16]

Her early September letter to Lenore Smith, written after the Yugoslav trip, is reflective and frequently glum. She hadn't written to Smith in years but thanked her at length for her friendship. She described herself as "old and infinitely sickened of many things." Her words worried Helen, the ever-present typist. "I've come to the period of my life," Annie went on, "when I prefer the pleasure of reflection to the fatigue of action. I've become reminiscent and resigned." Here Helen parenthetically inserted four question marks with the indication that they were from her.[17]

The letter includes passive-aggressive sniping between Annie and Helen. In a slightly joking manner Annie complained about Helen's cheerfulness and health. While the food, drink, and heat had made Annie ill, Helen had insides "made of cast iron fastened down with hoops of steel" that left her unaffected. Once again Helen inserted parenthetical remarks, this time indicating that it was Annie's own fault that she got sick because she drank too much water.[18]

Elsewhere Keller told one story of their trip that reveals Macy's tremendous kindness. The Concarneau house they rented came with a servant—a woman named Louise, whom Macy described as "a good cook," "a Breton woman of a superior type."[19] Louise had worked for the house's owner for more than two decades. In all those years she'd never been more than twenty-five miles from Concarneau. When they left France Macy arranged for Louise to accompany them to Paris for an overnight and a lengthy day of sightseeing. They passed through the Loire Valley and the regions surrounding Rennes and Orléans; in Paris their sightseeing included Notre Dame, the Seine, and Napoleon's tomb. The invitation was an act of thoughtfulness that required insight and empathy toward someone whose status often rendered her invisible.

Before leaving Concarneau Macy revised her will for the last time. She left her portion of the Forest Hills house and its contents to Keller. She willed a necklace and remaining personal documents to Henney, with no mention of excluding the Puerto Rico letters. Thomson received a trust fund and various personal goods. Keller's sister, niece, and several friends were to receive specific pieces of jewelry.[20]

Upon returning home Macy, Keller, and Migel made concrete plans for Helen's care after Annie's death. The irony, of course, is that Helen had far more people to care for her than did Annie. They chose a committee of three to look after Keller's finances—Migel, banker Harvey Gibson, and editor William Ziegler of the *Ziegler Magazine*. This committee shared the task of managing Keller's trust funds, paying the salary of whoever might assist her and monitoring household expenditures. Migel's secretary Amelia Bond, Mr. O. J. Anderson, and Nella Braddy Henney were appointed to a subcommittee to serve as personal advisers when needed.[21]

Macy and those around her considered her death to be imminent.

Around the same time, Christmas Day, 1931, Keller filed a report with the police about two missing dogs. Darky the terrier and Helga the Great Dane had wandered away. The *New York Times* reported them as hers, though they were very much Annie's. The dogs eventually returned, but it must have caused Annie great worry.[22]

ONLY A FEW months later, when she finally received her honorary Temple University degree in February 1932, Macy delivered a stunningly optimistic address. The world, she proclaimed, lay at the beginning of a "renaissance"—a period in which "clear light falls upon a world previously dark.... Scholars and thinkers scrutinize events with a new intensity to learn their meaning, and the people look for a sign, a miracle." The "cry of the human spirit to be free" announced the renaissance; the "creative achievement" of Lenin, Gandhi, and Einstein (an unlikely trio) proclaimed it. She heralded the Russian Revolution, for no matter how "mistaken Communist ideas may be," it compelled Russian citizens to experimentation and effort. She worried about the fear that accompanied the U.S. economic depression and its effect on experimentation and education. The country needed education, she argued, more than ever—not just any form of education, but education designed "to open wide all the windows of the mind to knowledge, truth and justice." True education, she believed, could be achieved and could transform. However, it demanded action. "A strenuous effort must be made to train young people to think for themselves and take independent charge of their lives."[23]

On the surface, Macy's optimism appears forced when placed alongside the rest of her life in 1932. Upon digging deeper, however, it's consistent with the themes that echoed through other parts of her life. Repeatedly in words and deeds she had emphasized experimentation in the cause of a life richly lived, regardless of whether or not that experimentation came with costs. Even when struggling personally, when forlorn and discouraged, she believed in the experience and process of living a full life.

Markedly absent from her speech was mention of her education of Helen Keller. For almost forty years she'd been delivering lectures on the young deaf-blind girl, the water pump, and her early efforts to teach language comprehension to Helen. Though her address is not rhetorically brilliant, in it she purposely stepped away from the specifics of her fame to broader reflections. She embraced the opportunity to speak not about Keller, but about the world and its need for education. She wanted her life and her life's work to have meaning beyond Helen Keller.

It seems, however, that few cared about the world and its need for education. The reporters who came to the ceremony preferred to speak with Keller; indeed, Henney reported that only one even spoke to Macy. Local newspapers wrote of the event with headlines that emphasized Keller. "Even at my coronation Helen is queen," Annie reportedly said to Henney. When Henney published *Anne Sullivan Macy* only a year later, she insisted that the older woman could only enjoy "an honour which is given to Helen alone, but not to herself alone."[24] Perhaps, but it seems unlikely.

A month later the University of Rochester invited Macy to their commencement to receive an honorary Ph.D. recognizing "the very high significance of what you were able to do in opening up the mind of Helen Keller to the knowledge of the world."[25] Macy declined. She and Keller would once again be in Europe.

The very week, perhaps even the very day, that Macy declined the invitation from the University of Rochester, she wrote longingly of death to her friend Lenore Smith.

> Helen and Polly are to speak in Boston Easter Sunday at Symphony Hall. I don't know whether I shall go or not. I am almost blind now. The only way I can see anything is by using a powerful drug to expand the clear field of the pupil a tiny bit. I feel old and helpless. Otherwise I might make you a visit, I do so want to see you and the family. Perhaps, if I ever make up my mind to have the cataract removed, and the operation is a success, I may feel different. At present I only long to die out of my difficulties, but even this isn't permitted. I wish I could believe that we suffer into a better world, but I don't. I often doubt if life is worth the suffering. May be [sic] this is an illusion, as so many other things are—maybe all things. Perhaps the only peace is in yielding up one's will. I confess, this kind of victory doesn't appeal to me.[26]

But the escape of death would not come and Macy reverted to the strategy she had adopted since running to Puerto Rico in 1916: travel. In late April 1932, only six months after their return from Concarneau, the trio of Macy, Keller, and Thomson (Migel called them "The Three Musketeers") left the country for another five months. The salvation of this trip was the discovery of an old farmhouse at South Arcan, Scotland, near Muir of Ord, Ross-shire. Macy would return to it several times before her death. After that Keller would return for decades to come.

The official purpose of the visit was business. The University of

258 BEYOND THE MIRACLE WORKER

Glasgow sought to bestow an honorary Doctor of Laws degree upon Keller at its June 1932 commencement. May, June, and July passed at a frenzied pace, filled with professional obligations and public appearances in Scotland and England, sometimes up to five per day. Keller later remembered how Macy "battled against fatigue and nervousness" to interpret her speeches.[27] Why Thomson did not interpret the speeches is unclear; perhaps she spent time with family in Scotland.

Once again, of course, Macy's health deteriorated—a "bronchial siege" according to Keller. A doctor recommended higher altitudes. They canceled remaining engagements and in near desperation traveled to join Thomson's brother and his family vacationing in the Scottish highlands. The South Arcan farmhouse they discovered provided the best respite Macy found. Keller described it as having "everything we want—quiet pastures and lovely lanes, heather and honey, solitude sweet with birds, no telephones and few cars, always something new to see or hear or touch or smell!"[28]

At South Arcan Annie received a telegram, probably sent by Henney, telling her of John's death from a stroke on August 26. While in Stroudsburg, Pennsylvania, lecturing about literary matters on behalf of the International Ladies' Garment Workers' Union, the fifty-five-year-old never awoke one morning. He'd only finished three of his five planned lectures. Henney mailed numerous newspaper clippings about his death. At the time of his death he had $1.50 and a pawn ticket in his pocket.[29]

"Three thousand miles away his body, once so dear, lies cold and still," Annie wrote in her private memoir. "The dreadful drama is finished, the fierce struggle that won only despair is ended. . . . I have been homesick for many a year for his arms. Perhaps it was wrong to look too deep within. Now he is dead."[30]

She left a several-page response to John's death. Neither Henney nor Keller would use it in their respective biographies of her.

The marriage had brought her bliss that had quickly turned to pain. "What dreams! What tremulous expectations! What clouds of suspicion, of jealousy! What amazing cruelties of looks and tones and sudden denials! There is more pain than joy in the most passionate love—pain and waste for a brief ecstasy. One but glances away, and all is gone—all that golden abundance of beauty and joy, or hope, of excitement and adventure."[31]

But the memories of the bliss, a very physical bliss, remained: a bliss that came in her youth when she "dare[d] to believe all things possible!" "My heart," she acknowledged, "leaps to the whisper of a name, a touch, the first kiss that lives in every kiss. Those vanished golden hours, those warm, loving hands and lips murmuring shy words which are the sweet blossoms of life's spring-time are gone past recall. Gone? No! they flash before me more real than the realities of mature years."[32]

Annie likely hadn't seen her husband or communicated directly with him for more than a decade. They had been separated for nearly two decades. But, of course, that didn't matter. John's death forced re-flection upon her—about herself, their marriage, and what she had once wanted from life. It caused her to yearn, even more than ever before, for her own death.

"Now," she went on, "I wait for death—not sad, not heroically but just a bit tired. To love and succeed is a fine thing, to love and fail is the next best, and the best of all is to fail and yet keep on loving."[33]

At that writing, at least, she believed herself to have kept on loving John Albert Macy despite the failure of their relationship. His funeral services were held in Montclair, New Jersey, where his sister lived. He had left his five-hundred-dollar estate to his daughter, Margaret Briggs. Annie paid the burial costs, symbolically reclaiming him as her husband.[34]

Following their previous pattern, Annie and Helen returned home in the fall of 1932, likely long after John's funeral, but escaped once more to Scotland's Arcan Ridge in the spring of 1933. When they were in the United States, Keller and Thomson traveled while Macy stayed at home in Forest Hills. Keller spent the winter of 1932–1933 worrying. "My heart bled," she remembered later, "as I thought of Teacher alone in the Forest Hills house, suffering pain much of the time, trying to read when she should not, and looking after the dogs." They had no additional household help, and Helen never knew how or if Annie prepared meals when they were gone.[35]

Annie spent much of May in bed with a "racking bronchial cough." Then she had influenza. Then her arthritis bothered her. In June, only days before departing again for Scotland, Helen reported to Lenore Smith that Annie's eyedrops no longer helped her. The doctor again pushed cataract surgery. Those around Annie increasingly discussed her disability and aging body. To Helen the only consolation was that "the loveliness of Scotland caressed her [Annie's] spirit as a brooding bird gathers her fledglings beneath her wings."[36] So she hustled Annie off to Scotland. This time they would stay for a year—until June of 1934.

But there was another reason for them to leave the country: to escape "the hounds of publicity," as Keller called reporters. In the early fall of 1933 Doubleday released Nella Braddy Henney's biography of Annie—*Anne Sullivan Macy: The Story Behind Helen Keller*. Henney venerated Macy, and her biography sought to establish Macy as a brilliant educator and resolute, heroic woman who succeeded despite horrendously difficult obstacles. Though at some points the book bordered on hagiography, it revealed more about Macy's life than had anything before. It presented a damaged woman redeemed by her student, who then sacrificed herself, her marriage, and her life on behalf of that student. It presented a woman whose life included but went beyond Helen Keller. Reporters, Keller's extended family members, and friends had much to say—in anger and in praise.

Henney began *Anne Sullivan Macy* with a nod to decorum. Of course, Henney insisted, Macy wanted neither recognition nor fame. Indeed, was so "modest" that she did not want a biography written. The teacher "has never felt the need for a confidant to relieve her overcharged heart." Nor, Henney asserted, did Macy ever desire to be "elevated above Helen." The only reason for her "consent" to the biography was the threat of "one who had loved her" that he would write it. The threat "bothered" her, and thus she cooperated with Henney. Henney later admitted in a private letter that the threat was made by John Macy and derogatorily called it "practically blackmail."[37] John, however, was dead. The threat no longer existed.

Anne Sullivan Macy reflects Macy's desire to reveal all. In an era before it became fashionable to reveal a tragic past, she allowed Henney to do so for her. Rather than acts of exhibitionism, however, her effort at autobiography and her cooperation with Henney were part of an active process of self-examination. If only others could understand her, perhaps she could better understand herself.

And Henney cooperated, presenting her just as she sought to be presented—in an honest but highly crafted account. In *Anne Sullivan Macy* everything in Macy's life helped to create the teacher of Helen Keller. As Henney put it in the subtitle, the story of Anne Sullivan Macy was the story behind Helen Keller. Others figured into the story—Michael Anagnos, Sophia Hopkins, the ghost of Samuel Gridley Howe, John Macy—but Helen alone occupied the subtitle.

Before Henney submitted the final manuscript book to Doubleday in January of 1933, sometime during that worrisome winter of 1932–1933, she made sure that the book received Macy's, Keller's, and Polly Thomson's approval. Though Henney had always had Macy's cooperation, Macy had never read any of the manuscript. Now Henney twice read it aloud to Annie while Thomson spelled it to Helen. Later Thomson read it once more to Annie. Once started, Henney read aloud for eighteen hours—stopping, she explained, "only once for cocktails and once for dinner! We also stopped several times to weep."[38]

Before they could escape the country, and before the book was released officially, Helen's sister, Mildred (Keller) Tyson, complained fiercely, first to Henney and then to Helen, about the contents of a prepublication article. The Keller family pride and honor, Tyson implied, had been insulted. The prominence and wealth of her father had been underplayed. Really, she insisted, they had lived "bountifully and well"; "Helen's background was anything but humble."[39]

Macy stayed out of the dispute, but Keller jumped in with a lengthy letter to her sister just a few days before their departure for Scotland. She distanced herself and Macy from the manuscript, though not completely accurately and in misleading ways. Only a month earlier she had written to friend and *New York Times* editor John Finley praising the book and asking him to arrange for its review. Now she wrote to Mildred, "Please bear in mind, Mildred, that we have had nothing to do with Nella's handling of the material. The book is entirely hers, and we shall not get a dollar of income from it." Helen adamantly insisted to her sister that Annie "shrinks more than she can express from the

publication of her biography. Her life has not been a particularly pleasant one, and now it is ending as it began, in misery. Our only relief is
flight overseas to the hills whence cometh our help."[40]

At Arcan Ridge Keller remained active, and they received many visitors, but Macy's health continued to plague them. Over the summer
of 1933 they took trips through Sutherlandshire, Orkney, Shetland,
Aberdeenshire, the Birnam Woods, and the Pass of Glencoe, followed
part of the Caledonian Canal, called at Lord Aberdeen's, and visited
Brahan Castle. And though they hadn't been able to travel with their
own dogs, at Arcan Ridge they received two new dogs—a Shetland
collie named Dileas and a black terrier named Maida.[41] At mealtimes
they joined Annie in her bed, and she undoubtedly snuck them food.
In the fall Keller asked for and received a leave of absence from the
AFB. They would stay at Arcan Ridge for a full year, until the spring
of 1934. Macy had wanted her story told, but that did not mean that
she wanted the public attention that came with the story—especially
when blind, infirm, and in frequent pain.

In late September "the book" (as Helen referred to it) arrived at
Arcan Ridge. Despite Helen's earlier words to her sister, her words
to Nella make clear her heartfelt appreciation of *Anne Sullivan Macy*.
Once again, Annie, Helen, and Polly read the book together—this
time around a warm fire in an old Scottish farmhouse. "You can imagine," Helen wrote to Nella, "how the fire burned out as we talked far
into the night."[42]

Annie didn't record her thoughts, and as is so often the case, we are
left primarily with Helen's words. To Nella she vaguely apologized for
Annie's lack of response. "She is far from being in the writing mood,"
Helen warned. "She is almost totally blind now, and it exasperates her
that she cannot see a word. I have never known her to be so impatient
and rebellious before." Annie's doctor, Dr. Berens, had visited over the
summer but had been unable to provide much optimism. Sometime
in 1933 Polly had already written to Nella, "Teacher's sight is fast going and the problem becomes daily worse—She is difficult, oh so difficult—her spirits are low, way low."[43]

The publicity exploded in mid-December. The Associated Press,
the Standard News Service, CBS, and newspapers across the globe

melodramatically reported that blindness stalked Macy. "Helen Keller Aids Friend Going Blind," screamed the *New York Times*. Secluded in Scotland, the paper reported, Keller sought to nurse Macy and tutor her in Braille. With no apology for its lack of originality, a *New York Times* editorial entitled "Blind Leading the Blind" sang Keller's praises. "That she can now actually make some return in kind," the paper went on, "for the unprecedented and devoted ministry of one through whom alone she had contact with the life on this planet is a crowning poetic episode in this extraordinary relationship which will be remembered in the classics of friendships." Reporters in search of more information persistently phoned and pursued Nella Braddy Henney as well as AFB staff members. Reports variably circulated that Macy and Keller were financially destitute, desperately ill, and barricaded in Scotland. In March 1934 reporters even showed up at the farmhouse door in Arcan Ridge. Henney wrote to Amelia Bond, Migel's secretary, that she had no problem imagining Macy "slaying a reporter at the present stage of the game." In April a Hollywood producer approached Henney about making a film of the book. She left the decision to Macy, who quickly rejected the idea.[44] Doubleday released a new edition of *The Story of My Life*. Henney complained about the frenzy, but it didn't harm book sales.

Indeed, the exaggerated drama of Macy's sacrifice on behalf of her deaf-blind student only elevated her further in public opinion. Friends and acquaintances flooded her and Henney with letters of praise. Henney wrote to the trio in Scotland saying public sentiment ran so high that if Macy "wanted the Washington Monument now I think she could have it."[45]

What Macy thought is hard to discern, but the adulation didn't revive her mentally or physically. The public obsessed about her blindness and dependency, traits that troubled her keenly. From December 1933 through at least their September 1934 departure for home she seldom left her bed. Years later Keller wrote that her illness was "carbuncles." In January Thomson described her as "depressed and melancholy." Keller optimistically described her as "in a mood like the quiescent earth in winter," but admitted that "she does not much interest in anything, and will not discuss matters connected with her biography or reply to letters." She wasn't sleeping. By June she had virtually no sight left, but doctors indicated that nothing could be done to improve her sight until her general health improved. Keller and Thomson hoped the sulfur baths of nearby Strathpeffer would do so, but nothing dramatic happened.[46]

The three women returned to the United States in September 1934. Although Henney and Keller were loving and tolerant toward Macy's "capricious" and "unmanageable" behavior, they had their hands full. Macy's enthusiasm for adopting a deserted deaf-blind baby girl soon after their homecoming seems preposterous, given her age as well as her emotional and physical state. Both of her companions reported that it took great effort to convince her not to do so.[47]

Macy's ill health dominated everything. By mid-October doctors diagnosed septic poisoning and at the end of the month she entered the hospital. There she stayed for all of November, receiving multiple blood transfusions and undergoing two eye operations in hopes of salvaging some sight in her one remaining eye. The eye operations accomplished little. She returned home in December. By March 1935 she had recovered from the septic poisoning, but neuritis in her right shoulder and arm caused her great pain. Doctors wanted to perform cataract surgery but feared her general health too volatile. Helen reported that Annie found the most solace in the dogs.[48]

A few days after Annie's birthday on April 14, 1935, she returned to the hospital for cataract surgery. Helen ordered her a Lakeland terrier from England for a present and, according to the *New York Times*, brought it to the hospital for a visit. When she was discharged in mid-May newspapers reported that "nothing less than a miracle" had happened and that she would be able to see "better than ever." But there was no substantial improvement. In July and August Helen referred to Annie's eye as a "jobitical demon." The household spent part of the summer in a lodge in Arkansas, but it failed to cheer Annie. Doctors suggested another surgery but Helen (probably understating the case) wrote that Annie "is not in a frame of mind to consider [doing so]."[49]

We have no words from Annie during this period. Determining the primary source of her infirmity is difficult: emotional malaise, physical pain from her eye, other illnesses, overwork, sorrow over her growing blindness—everything blended together. Decades later Keller wrote that her dear friend believed "old age was more difficult than to die." Macy "mourned over what seemed to her her increasing decrepitude, and in her blindness thought of herself as old."[50] Keller's words express sympathy, but also subtle frustration—*seemed to* and *thought of herself* subversively hint that the decrepitude, the old age, were partly of Macy's manufacturing. Macy's equation of blindness with decrepitude and old age denied all she had taught Keller.

Annie continued to seek the physical and emotional contentment that eluded her. And she did so in the way she always had—physical escape. She had found immense happiness in Puerto Rico, and tried to resuscitate that past happiness. She insisted to Helen that they find "a similar nook of delight," and in October 1935 Macy, Keller, Thomson, and their driver and handyman Herbert Haas set sail for Jamaica. They left little record of the trip, but we know it didn't accomplish the miracle that Annie desired. Helen simply reported that "for Teacher it had none of the fascination that had enchanted her in Puerto Rico, and she was oh, so tired!"[51]

In May 1936 Dr. Berens again operated on Macy's eye. He told her it would do no good, but with tears and "arms around his neck" she had begged him to try. The results were as he had predicted. At Annie's insistence, she and Helen spent part of the summer at a lodge outside of Quebec, but illness forced Annie home in early July. Helen knew her dear friend was dying. Years later, she blamed Annie's blindness for her death, more than any other physical factor: "Instinct told me that as soon as she realized she would never see again, she would lose interest in living." Always searching, the two found a cottage on the Long Island shore after returning to New York in August. "That was our last desperate attempt," Keller later wrote, "to strengthen her so that her life might be tolerable."[52]

Annie had to leave the cottage by ambulance. "We are still living through a period of anxious waiting," Helen wrote to a friend in late September. "Teacher has alternating comfortable and difficult days, and must be guarded against all excitement." Thomson reported privately to Lenore Smith that doctors diagnosed "coronary tuberculosis." Doctors did all they could but eventually sent her home to die.

In her 1956 biography of Macy, Keller described Macy's last month as extremely agitated. She went "from mood to mood," "yield[ing] to despair."[53]

Helen, perhaps simply the eternal optimist, insisted that during the last week of life Annie's "unconquerable, generous soul" once again emerged. She spelled to Helen a funny story about a rodeo. Helen treasured the fact that "she fondled my hand!" "Her dearness," Helen remembered, "was without limit, and it was almost intolerable. Beautiful was her touch." Helen promised her that they would once again travel to Scotland in the spring.[54]

On October 15 Anne Sullivan Macy fell into a coma. Polly Thomson shouldered the task of dealing with the press. Annie died at home on October 20, 1936. After a funeral in New York, her ashes were interred at the National Cathedral. More than thirty years later, in 1968, the ashes of Helen Keller would join hers.

Conclusion

ANNE SULLIVAN MACY did not want to be remembered as a worker of miracles. Miracles required luck or divine intervention. She wanted to be remembered as a skilled and innovative educator, and to be remembered with compassion, with understanding, and with honesty. In "Foolish Remarks of a Foolish Woman" she left a subtle directive to future biographers to avoid idolization. "I have met a number of famous men uneventfully," she wrote, "but I have learned something about them. They are Human like the rest of us, they are not gods or even sacred cows as their biographers would have us believe." Drawing conclusions about her, however, was and is difficult. After her death, newspaper headline writers did not even know what to call her. The labels she posthumously earned ranged from "Lifelong Friend and Teacher" to "Mentor," "Companion," and "Instructor," all the way down to "Aide."[1]

Conclusions about Anne Sullivan Macy are difficult because she expressed and lived out both passionate optimism and dire pessimism. She had experienced, and experienced profoundly, the worst of what human beings do to one another as well as the very best they are capable of. This left her a complex and seemingly contradictory woman.

Near the end of her life she characterized herself as the "prey of the vultures of circumstance." Because of those "vultures of circumstance," her life had been spent "always straining at my chains, again and again beaten to my knees by forces stronger than my human will." Despite forces stronger than her will, however, she had prevailed. "I am not beaten with my forehead in the dust," she wrote. "Clinging to the skirts of faith, I climb upwards to heights where I glimpse bright worlds of thought, of love, and liberty."[2]

What made Anne Sullivan Macy the woman she was, however, was that she did not and could not rest on the glorious visions of "thought, love, and liberty." She could neither run away from, nor shake off, the traumas of her past and the knowledge that others continued to live similarly traumatized lives. For, she explained, "through the midnight stillness of my soul I hear the loud insistent moans of others in bondage and like me disinherited, creatures who sigh and sleep and wake to sigh again." She lived surrounded by, immersed in, and constantly aware of both beauty and ruin.[3] Prominent among the beauties of her life was her extraordinary friendship with Helen Keller.

Macy once said, "I'm spending my days in experimenting."[4] As she remarked, these experiments could be costly, and she paid the price in full. Sometimes, however, she succeeded beyond her wildest dreams.

Acknowledgments

WHEN HELEN KELLER made plans to write a biography of Anne Sullivan Macy, a friend assured that her the dead Macy would "appear" to her as "a sacred fire—not consuming but warming, cherishing and enlightening" (*Teacher*, p. 36). Perhaps Macy appeared to help Keller along with her book, but I had no such luck. I did, however, have the assistance of librarians, colleagues, friends, and family members and the kindness of strangers to help me as I made my way through this book. Early in my thinking about this project Cathy Kudlick kindly and gently told me I was all wrong. She was right. I appreciate her forthrightness and friendship.

The National Endowment for the Humanities and the University of Wisconsin System provided valuable funds that made this project possible. As readers, as taxpayers, and as citizens who care about the world, we must remind our legislators that funding historical scholarship matters to today's world.

The questions and insights of my students at the University of Wisconsin–Green Bay make me a better scholar and teacher. The world would be a better place if they and their parents, and the state legislature and Wisconsin voters, recognized their skills.

UWGB librarians Debra Anderson, Jeff Brunner, Emily Rogers, and Mary Neumann made it possible for me to (most of the time) combine scholarship and teaching with sanity. Illene Noppe educated me on children and parental death. Dr. Al Uniacke helped me to understand trachoma better. Sarah Miller provided enthusiasm and detail skills. Helen Selsdon of the AFB bestowed cheer and the expertise of Super Archivist Girl. Jan Seymour-Ford of the Perkins School for the Blind answered probably repeated questions, provided a welcoming library space, and offered air-conditioned rides on hot July days.

Gayatri Patnaik of Beacon Press believed in this project, and I am thankful to her for giving me a chance. Her enthusiasm, excellent editing skills, and sense of humor made this process pleasant. She, Joanna Green, and the rest of the Beacon staff expertly combine kindness with professionalism.

I am a lucky woman. Deb Anderson provided the long conversations that made chapter 7 bearable. Susan Burch is tiara worthy. Debbie Furlong is compassionate and wise. Andy Kersten is the most ideal colleague and friend imaginable. Jerry Podair generously gave advice without strings attached. Catherine Rymph provided smart comments, and she helps to make history conferences humane. Sister Caroline Sullivan listens to me and makes me listen to myself. Psychologist Kristin Vespia shared her wisdom on trauma, friendship, and loss, and on top of it all is a great friend. The staff at Green Bay's wonderful Baird Elementary School—especially Nancy Hess, Doug Boss, and Gini Mitchell—made my personal life manageable. The members of the Really Very Boring Adult Book Club—Martha Ahrendt, Karlyn Crowley, Regan Gurung, John Pennington, Joan Thron, Mike Thron, and Carrie Thoms—and the bored children who named it make me happy and keep me entertained.

As always, my thanks go to my family. David and Florence Tuff share support and love. Ron and Kathie Nielsen provide cheerleading and childcare—simultaneously when needed—and Friday lunch companionship. Morgan cheerfully bears my historical comments, questions, and barely restrained lectures with only a smile and a dramatic eye roll. Maya often prepares my breakfast, asks the smartest questions, and makes me laugh. I love them very much. Nathan Tuff makes it all possible, has done so for over twenty years, and for that I am ever so grateful.

NOTES

ABBREVIATIONS:

AAS	Anne Sullivan Collection, American Antiquarian Society
AFB	American Foundation for the Blind
AGB	Alexander Graham Bell
ASM	Anne Sullivan Macy
ASM Notes	Notes by Anne Sullivan Macy, in Notes of Nella Braddy Henney, Nella Braddy Henney Collection (Hayes Research Library, Perkins School for the Blind, Boston, Massachusetts)
Bell, LOC	Alexander Graham Bell manuscript collection, Library of Congress
JDS	Johannah Dunnivan Story, ASM Notes
JH	John Hitz
KK	Kate Keller
MA	Michael Anagnos
MCM	M. C. Migel
NBH	Nella Braddy Henney
NBHC	Nella Braddy Henney Collection
NBH Notes	Notes for *Anne Sullivan Macy*, NBHC
PAR	Perkins Institution and Massachusetts School for the Blind, annual reports
PIL	Perkins Institution Letters, Perkins School for the Blind

INTRODUCTION

1. ASM Notes. These note pages are largely unnumbered. If numbers or other indicators are given I refer to them.

2. Ibid.

3. ASM to HK, 1917, AFB.

4. "Teacher Whimsically Sketches Her Life and Philosophy, Calling Them 'Foolish Remarks of a Foolish Woman,'" ASM Notes.

CHAPTER 1—FEEDING HILLS, 1866–1876

1. Notes, January 26, 1928, NBHC. Variably spelled Cloissey, Cloesy, Clohesy. I use the spelling adopted by NBH, as that is what Macy approved for her biography.

2. 1860 U.S. Census; Hasia R. Diner, *Erin's Daughters in America: Irish Immigrant Women in the Nineteenth Century* (Baltimore: Johns Hopkins University Press, 1983), 16; Nella Braddy Henney, *Anne Sullivan Macy: The Story Behind Helen Keller* (New York: Doubleday, 1933), 3.

3. Thomas Sullivan's brother John Sullivan (1833) married Mary (1830). Their children included Anne (1854), Ellen (1857), John (1861), Daniel (1862), Katie (1865), William (1867), and Mary (1870). Thomas Sullivan's other brother, also named John (1847), married Anastasia (1853). Their children included Anna (1873), Mary (1875), Maggie (1877), and Katie (1880). These dates are from 1870 and 1880 census records. Henney lists another brother named Dan (*Anne Sullivan Macy*, 3).

4. Diner, *Erin's Daughters in America*, 10; Janet A. Nolan, *Ourselves Alone: Women's Emigration from Ireland, 1885–1920* (Lexington: University Press of Kentucky, 1989), 13.

5. Nolan, *Ourselves Alone*, 2, 50; Diner, *Erin's Daughters in America*, 4, xiv, 31; notes, January 26, 1928, NBHC.

6. Guy A. McLain, *Pioneer Valley: A Pictorial History* (Virginia Beach, Virginia: Downing Company Publishers, 1991); Clifton Johnson, *Hampden County, 1636–1936* (New York: American Historical Society, 1936); Arthur Minot Copeland, *Our County and Its People: A History of Hampden County, Massachusetts* (Springfield, MA: Alfred Minot Copeland Century Memorial Publishing Company, 1902).

7. Johnson, *Hampden County*, 567.

8. JDS; notes, January 26, 1928, NBHC.

9. Notes, January 26, 1928, NBHC; ASM Notes.

10. ASM Notes; notes, January 26, 1928, NBHC.

11. 1870 U.S. Census.

12. Notes, January 26, 1928, NBHC; Howard Markel, "'The Eyes Have It': Trachoma, the Perception of Disease, the United States Public Health Service and the American Jewish Immigration Experience, 1897–1924," *Bulletin of the History of Medicine* 74, no. 3 (2000): 525–560.

13. Notes, January 26, 1928, NBHC.

14. "Memories of Mother," ASM Notes; notes, January 26, 1928, NBHC.

15. ASM Notes.

16. "Memories of Mother"; notes, January 26, 1928, NBHC.

17. Sheila M. Rothman, *Living in the Shadow of Death: Tuberculosis and the Social Experience of Illness in American History* (New York: Basic Books, 1994), 2, 7, 13; Katherine Ott, *Fevered Lives: Tuberculosis in American Culture Since 1870* (Cambridge, MA: Harvard University Press, 1996).

18. Rothman, *Shadow of Death*, 4; Ott, *Fevered Lives*, 8, 9, 20–26, 46.

19. Rothman, *Shadow of Death*, chap. 8.

20. Phyllis Rolfe Silverman, *Never Too Young to Know: Death in Children's Lives* (New York: Oxford University Press, 2000), 11, 36; ASM Notes.

21. ASM Notes; "Memories of Mother."

22. ASM Notes.

23. JDS.

24. ASM Notes.

25. Ibid.

26. Notes, January 26, 1928, NBHC; ASM Notes.

27. Notes, January 26, 1928, NBHC.

28. JDS I, IV.

29. Notes, January 26, 1928, NBHC. The exceptions to this were John Hitz and Sophia Hopkins.

CHAPTER 2 — TEWKSBURY ALMSHOUSE, 1876–1880

1. JDS, 41; Henney, *Anne Sullivan Macy*.

2. JDS, 2.

3. Gerald N. Grob, *Mental Institutions in America: Social Policy to 1875* (New York: Free Press, 1973), 276.

4. Ibid.; *The Tewksbury State Hospital and Infirmary One Hundredth Anniversary* (pamphlet, Commonwealth of Massachusetts, Department of Public Welfare, October 13, 1954); Franklin B. Sanborn, *The Public Charities of Massachusetts During the Century Ending January 1, 1876* (Boston: Wright and Potter, 1876), 49–51.

5. JDS.

6. *Twenty-third Annual Report of the Inspectors of the State Almshouse at Tewksbury for the Year Ending September 30, 1876* (Boston: Albert J. Wright, 1877), 5; *Twenty-Second Annual Report of the Inspectors of the State Almshouse at Tewksbury for the Year Ending September 30, 1875* (Boston: Wright & Potter, 1876), 13; *Twenty-fourth Annual Report of the Inspectors of the State Almshouse at Tewksbury for the Year Ending September 30, 1877* (Boston: Rand, Avery & Company, 1878), 12.

7. *Twenty-third Annual Report*, 14, 18; Frank W. Goodhue (director, Massachusetts Department of Public Welfare), letter to NBH, March 23, 1927, NBHC.

8. JDS, 43. ASM usually used the spelling "Jimmie," but I use "Jimmy" when she did.

9. Erving Goffman, *Asylums: Essays on the Social Situation of Mental Patients and Other Inmates* (Chicago: Aldine Publishing Company, 1961), ix–x; JDS, 4; ASM Notes; Henney, *Anne Sullivan Macy*, 20.

10. JDS, 4; "Notes on Teacher's Life," ASM Notes.

11. JDS.

12. ASM Notes.

13. Ibid.; "Black and Blue," *Boston Daily Globe*, April 11, 1883.

14. Henney, *Anne Sullivan Macy*, 22; JDS, IV.

15. *Twenty-third Annual Report*, 34–36; Henney, *Anne Sullivan Macy*, 26.

16. Henney, *Anne Sullivan Macy*, 26.

17. Ibid., 26–27.

18. Ibid., 27.

19. Ibid., 27–28.

20. "A Tewksbury Memory," ASM Notes.

21. Henney, *Anne Sullivan Macy*, 28.

22. "A Tewksbury Memory."

23. Ibid.

24. JDS.

25. Ibid.

26. Ibid.

27. Ibid.

28. Ibid.

29. Ibid.

30. JDS; *Twenty-third Annual Report*, 25.

31. "A Tewksbury Memory."

32. JDS.

33. Francis R. Walsh, "Who Spoke for Boston's Irish? The Boston Pilot in the Nineteenth Century," *Journal of Ethnic Studies* 10, no. 3 (1982): 21–36; "Teacher's Life, Tewksbury," ASM Notes; "A Tewksbury Memory."

34. JDS.

35. Ibid.

36. Ibid.

37. "A Tewksbury Memory."

38. JDS.

39. Ibid.

40. "Notes on Tewksbury, the Procession of the Horribles," ASM Notes.

41. Ibid.

42. *Twenty-Second Annual Report*, 23, 24; Henney, *Anne Sullivan Macy*, 32.

43. Henney, *Anne Sullivan Macy*, 31–36.

44. Ibid.

45. JDS.

46. ASM Notes.

47. JDS.

48. "A Tewksbury Memory."

49. Henney, *Anne Sullivan Macy*, 60–61.

50. "Notes on Teacher's Life," ASM Notes.

51. Ibid.

52. Helen Keller, *Teacher* (New York: Doubleday, 1956), 113.

53. "A Tewksbury Memory"; JDS.

54. ASM Notes; JDS.

55. JDS.

CHAPTER 3—PERKINS, 1880–1886: PART ONE

1. PAR, 1877, 16–17.

2. Ibid., 10.

3. PAR, 1886, 18; 1882, 37; 1877, 51; 1883, 39.

4. PAR, 1884, 54; 1882, 64; 1884, 68.

5. PAR, 1880, 104–106.

6. S. C. Wrightington (Commonwealth of Massachusetts, State Board of Health, Lunacy and Charity, Department of the In-door Poor) to MA, January 20, 1881, PIL; PAR, 1881, 132; Dr. Henry Bolton, M.D., to MA, September 27, 1880, PIL; Rev. E. C. Cummings to MA, September 18, 1880, PIL; City of Taunton, Offices of the Poor, to MA, August 21, 1880, PIL.

7. ASM Notes.

8. Ibid.

9. Ibid.

10. NBH notes for ASM book, NBHC (hereafter NBH Notes).

11. ASM Notes.

12. Ibid.

13. Ibid.

14. Ibid.

15. Ibid.

16. Ibid.

17. PAR, 1882; "Teacher's Life," detached notes, Pt. II, ASM Notes.

18. "Teacher's Life."

19. Cora A. Newton to NBH, May 23, 1927, NBHC.

20. ASM Notes; PAR, 1881, 37, 38; 1882, 39.

21. "Teacher's Life."

22. John R. Betts, "Mind and Body in Early American Thought," *Journal of American History* 54, no. 4 (March 1968): 787–805; PAR, 1883, 54; 1886, 39, 43; 1877; 1883, 55.

23. PAR, 1883; ASM Notes.

24. PAR, 1877, 68; 1881, 46.

25. PAR, 1885, 44, 46.

26. PAR, 1881, 42–43.

27. ASM Notes. Macy may have misremembered the specific Gilbert and Sullivan production in which she saw Lillian Russell. Russell appeared prominently in many Gilbert and Sullivan productions, but as far as I can discern, not in *Patience*.

28. Philip A. Jenkins, "Cape Cod's Private Miracle," unpublished essay, Hayes

Research Library, Perkins School for the Blind. NBH's notes indicate that Hopkins was there prior to Anne's first summer at Perkins, but other biographical material on Hopkins indicates she arrived in 1883. Hopkins doesn't appear in the Perkins yearly reports until 1883.

29. Henney, *Anne Sullivan Macy*, 76; NBH Notes.

30. "Brewster," ASM Notes.

31. Ibid.

32. "Teacher's Life, Brewster," ASM Notes.

33. "Brewster."

34. Ibid.

35. Ibid.

36. PAR, 1884, 58.

37. PAR, 1885, 50.

38. Elisabeth Gitter, *The Imprisoned Guest: Samuel Howe and Laura Bridgman, the Original Deaf-Blind Girl* (New York: Farrar, Straus, and Giroux, 2001), 280. Lydia Hayes, a student at Perkins at the same time as Macy, remembers this also. Notes on interview with Lydia Hayes, NBH Notes.

39. ASM Notes.

40. Ibid.

41. Ibid.

42. Ibid.

43. Ibid.

44. Deborah Pickman Clifford, *Mine Eyes Have Seen the Glory: A Biography of Julia Ward Howe* (Boston: Little, Brown, 1978), 122.

45. ASM Notes.

46. Ibid.

CHAPTER 4—PERKINS, 1880–1886: PART TWO

1. Cora A. Newton to NBH, May 23, 1927, NBHC.

2. "Notes on Teacher's Life."

3. ASM Notes.

4. Lenna D. Swinerton to NBH, June 20, 1927, NBHC; notes on interview with Lydia Hayes, NBH Notes.

5. "Self-Analysis," ASM Notes.

6. Ibid.

7. Henney, *Anne Sullivan Macy*, 76, 86.

8. "Notes on Teacher's Life."

9. Henney, *Anne Sullivan Macy*, 33–34.

10. "The Governor's Charges," *Boston Daily Advertiser*, March 30, 1883; "Shocking!" *Boston Daily Globe*, March 30, 1883; "Tewksbury Almshouse," *Boston Daily*

Advertiser, March 31, 1883; "Medical Testimony," *Boston Daily Globe*, May 22, 1883; Benjamin F. Butler, "Argument Before the Tewksbury Investigation Committee," Democratic Central Committee, July 15, 1883; Mrs. Clara T. Leonard, *The Present Condition of Tewksbury* (Boston: Franklin Press; Rand, Avery & Company), 1883.

11. "A Strong Witness," *Boston Daily Globe*, April 3, 1883; "Chapter Four," *Boston Daily Advertiser*, April 4, 1883.

12. "Better Keep Still," *Boston Daily Globe*, April 9, 1883.

13. "Further Testimony Concerning Tewksbury," *Boston Daily Globe*, April 19, 1883.

14. "The Little Ones," *Boston Daily Globe*, April 4, 1883; "A Strong Witness," *Boston Daily Globe*, April 3, 1883.

15. "Chapter Four," *Boston Daily Advertiser*; "A Strong Witness," *Boston Daily Globe*; Tewksbury Again," *Boston Daily Advertiser*, April 5, 1883; "Chapter Six," *Boston Daily Advertiser*, April 10, 1883; "Another Legal Battle," May 23, 1883; "Not all the Books Yet," *Boston Daily Globe*, May 2, 1883; "Tewksbury's Defense," *Boston Daily Globe*, May 31, 1883.

16. NBH Notes; Henney, *Anne Sullivan Macy*, 79–80.

17. "A Tewksbury Memory."

18. "Notes on Teacher's Life"; "Refused the Degree," *Boston Daily Globe*, June 1, 1883.

19. "Notes on Teacher's Life."

20. Ibid.

21. Ibid

22. Ibid.

23. NBH Notes.

24. Ibid.

25. "Teacher's Life, My Graduation," ASM Notes.

26. PAR, 1885, 125; 1886, 112.

27. PAR, 1886, 113.

28. Ibid., 131–132, 21.

29. "Teacher's Life, My Graduation."

30. PAR, 1886, 125–126.

31. Ibid.

32. Ibid.

33. Ibid., 132, 21–22.

34. "Teacher's Life, My Graduation."

35. Ibid.

36. PAR, 1886, 31; James M. Taylor to MA, May 14, 1886, PIL.

37. "Teacher's Life, My Graduation"; PAR, 1886, 23.

38. Ibid., 80.

39. Ibid., 125.

CHAPTER 5—BECOMING TEACHER, 1887

1. MA to ASM, August 26, 1886, AFB.

2. PAR, 1887, 79, 81.

3. ASM Notes.

4. Arthur Keller to MA, January 28, 1887, PIL; ASM Notes.

5. Helen Keller, *The Story of My Life: With Her Letters (1887–1901) and a Supplementary Account of Her Education, Including Passages from the Reports and Letters of Her Teacher, Anne Mansfield Sullivan, by John Albert Macy* (New York: Grosset & Dunlap, 1903), 302.

6. ASM Notes; "The South," ASM Notes; Jenkins, "Cape Cod's Private Miracle."

7. "Going to Tuscumbia," ASM Notes.

8. Ibid.

9. Ibid.

10. Ibid.

11. "Life in Tuscumbia," ASM Notes.

12. Ibid.

13. Ibid.

14. PAR, 1887, 98; Helen Keller, *The Story of My Life* (New York: Dover, 1966), 2. The 1880 Census lists Catharina Keller, though in every other reference she is Kate Keller.

15. Keller, *Story of My Life* (1966), 2.

16. This information is derived from 1880 and 1900 census reports. Those for 1870 and 1890 either don't remain or were never taken for Tuscumbia.

17. Kim E. Nielsen, "The Southern Ties of Helen Keller," *Journal of Southern History* 73, no. 4 (November 2007): 1–24.

18. Keller, *Story of My Life* (1966), 9–10. In a letter to AGB, Helen's aunt Evaline Keller thanked him for his hospitality. This letter suggests that the trio visited Bell and then saw Chisholm. Likely Kate Keller stayed home because she was pregnant with Mildred, and Evaline cared for Helen on the trip. Evaline Keller to AGB, April 20, 1887, Alexander Graham Bell manuscript collection, Bell, LOC.

19. "Going to Tuscumbia," ASM Notes; ASM to Sophia Hopkins, March 7, 1887, AFB.

20. Nina Silber, *Romance and Reunion: Northerners and the South, 1865–1900* (Chapel Hill: University of North Carolina Press), 124; "The South," ASM Notes.

21. David W. Blight, *Race and Reunion: The Civil War in American Memory* (Cambridge, MA: Harvard University Press, 2001), 171, 260. See also Gaines M. Foster, *Ghosts of the Confederacy: Defeat, the Lost Cause, and the Emergence of the New South* (New York: Oxford University Press, 1987), especially chaps. 6 and 7.

22. ASM Notes.

23. ASM to Sophia Hopkins, April 4, 1888, AFB; Keller, *Story of My Life* (1903), 304.

24. Ibid., 308–309.

25. Ibid., 307–308.

26. Ibid., 308.

27. Ibid.

28. Ibid., 309.

29. Ibid., 310; MA to ASM, March 20, 1887, AFB.

30. Keller, *Story of My Life* (1903), 311–312.

31. Ibid., 313.

32. Ibid., 309, 315.

33. Ibid., 315.

34. Ibid.

35. Ibid., 316.

36. MA to ASM, April 10, 1887, AFB.

37. Keller, *Story of My Life* (1903), 316.

38. Ibid., 317.

39. Ibid.

40. ASM to Sophia Hopkins, October 30, 1887, AFB. The full name, Lilian May Fletcher, is given in PAR, 1887, 78.

41. Keller, *Story of My Life* (1903), 331–333.

42. Ibid., 319, 324–325.

43. ASM to Sophia Hopkins, May 22, 1887, AFB; Keller, *Story of My Life* (1903), 336; ASM to Sophia Hopkins, October 30, 1887, AFB.

44. Keller, *Story of My Life* (1903), 341.

45. MA to ASM, September 1, 1887, AFB; ASM to Sophia Hopkins, March 4, 1887, AFB; "Teacher's Life in the South," ASM Notes.

46. "The South," ASM Notes.

47. ASM to Sophia Hopkins, March 4, 1888, AFB; ASM to Sophia Hopkins, March 4, 1887, AFB.

48. "Teacher's Life," ASM Notes.

49. MA to ASM, September 1, 1887, AFB; Keller, *Story of My Life* (1903), 334.

CHAPTER 6—TUSCUMBIA, 1888–1891

1. PAR, 1887, 79, 82, 86, 93.

2. Ibid., 71–72, 75–78.

3. Ibid., 80–81.

4. Ibid., 94–97.

5. Keller, *Story of My Life* (1903), 344.

6. ASM to MA, January 13, 1888, AAS; MA to ASM, January 22, 1888, AFB.

7. Keller, *Story of My Life* (1903), 346; MA to AS, January 22, 1888, AFB.

8. MA to ASM, March 24, 1888, and March 25, 1888, AFB.

9. ASM to MA, April 2, 1888, and April 6, 1888, AFB.

10. ASM to MA, April 20, 1888, AAS.

11. ASM to Sophia Hopkins, April 10, 1887, AFB.

12. ASM to MA, April 20, 1888, AAS; Keller, *Story of My Life* (1903), 347–349.

13. ASM to MA, April 20, 1888, and April 22, 1888, AAS.

14. MA to ASM, April 10, 1887, May 27, 1887, and April 24, 1888, AFB.

15. ASM to MA, January 13, 1888, and April 2, 1888, AAS; Keller, *Story of My Life* (1903), 348; ASM to MA, April 22, 1888, AAS.

16. PAR, 1888, 122–123.

17. Ibid.

18. Ibid., 126; MA to ASM, August 5, 1888, and September 2, 1888, AFB.

19. ASM to Sophia Hopkins, March 4, 1888, AFB; Keller, *Story of My Life* (1903), 355.

20. MA to ASM, August 5, 1888, and August 23, 1888, AFB.

21. ASM to MA, November 7, 1888, November 18, 1888, December 8, 1888, and January 17, 1889, AAS.

22. MA to ASM, December 21, 1888, January 1, 1889, January 6, 1889, January 10, 1889, and January 13, 1889, AFB.

23. MA to ASM, November 16, 1888, January 13, 1889, and April 9, 1889, AFB; ASM to MA, December 8, 1888, AAS.

24. MA to ASM, December 21, 1888, AFB.

25. PAR, 1888, 69–70.

26. ASM to MA, February 1, 1889, AAS.

27. Ibid.

28. ASM to MA, February 1, 1889, AAS; MA to ASM, March 5, 1889, AFB.

29. MA to ASM, March 13, 1889, AFB.

30. Keller, *Teacher*, 57; MA to ASM, April 9, 1889 (two letters dated April 9, 1889), AFB; Henney, *Anne Sullivan Macy*, 147.

31. Ibid., 154.

32. Ibid., 151–152; Keller, *Story of My Life* (1966), 30–32.

33. Henney, *Anne Sullivan Macy*, 154–155.

34. ASM to MA, July 7, 1890, AAS.

35. Ibid.

36. Ibid.

37. MA to ASM, August 5, 1890, September 18, 1890, and October 24, 1890, AFB.

38. ASM Notes.

39. "Captain Keller," ASM Notes.

40. "Teacher's Life in Tuscumbia, Mrs. Keller," ASM Notes.

41. ASM to MA, December 8, 1888, AAS; "The South," ASM Notes; "Teacher's Life in Tuscumbia, Mrs. Keller."

42. MA to ASM, October 6, 1891, and November 1, 1891, AFB.

43. ASM to MA, November 4, 1891, AAS.

44. Ibid.; MA to ASM, November 9, 1891, AFB.

45. Henney, *Anne Sullivan Macy*, 157–158; MA to ASM, November 15, 1891, AFB.

46. Bert Hansen, "America's First Medical Breakthrough: How Popular Excitement about a French Rabies Cure in 1885 Raised New Expectations for Medical Progress," *The American Historical Review* 103, no. 2 (April 1998): 382.

47. Henney, *Anne Sullivan Macy*, 159; MA to AS, December 1, 1891, AFB.

48. PAR, 1891, 53, 98, 109.

49. Ibid., 57.

CHAPTER 7—THE BATTLE FOR HELEN, ROUND I, 1891–1894

1. Keller, *Story of My Life* (1903), 414.

2. Annie Pratt to AGB, February 2, 1892, Bell, LOC.

3. Ibid.

4. Ibid.

5. Ibid.

6. Ibid.

7. Arthur Keller to MA, February 5, 1892, PIL.

8. Quoted in "Miss Sullivan's Methods, A comparison between her reports to the Perkins Institution and the statements made in the Volume entitled The Story of My Life by Helen Keller," p. 130, 131. An undated and anonymous composition held in the Perkins School for the Blind Library. Joseph Lash believes this 171-page document was likely written by lawyer David Prescott Hall, Julia Ward Howe's son-in-law. Joseph P. Lash, *Helen and Teacher: The Story of Helen Keller and Anne Sullivan Macy* (Reading, MA: Addison-Wesley, 1980), p. 134.

9. Keller, *Story of My Life* (1903), 65, 66; Fanny S. Marrett to MA, March 6, 1892, AAS.

10. Keller, *Story of My Life* (1903), 401.

11. Note, PAR, 1891, inserted between pages 94 and 95. In a March 11, 1892, letter to the *American Annals of the Deaf* (quoted in SML) Anagnos wrote that he received this testimony from an unnamed teacher after he had requested that she interview Keller. The unnamed teacher was presumably Fanny S. Marrett. Anagnos's quotations come directly from a report written by Marrett dated March 6, 1892. Presumably Marrett had earlier given an oral report, for by March 6, 1892, Sullivan was already in Brewster, according to a letter from Sullivan to Anagnos dated March 6. ASM to MA, March 6, 1892, AAS.

12. ASM to MA, March 6, 1892, AAS.

13. Ibid.

14. AGB to Mabel Hubbard Bell, March 10, 1892, Bell, LOC; Mabel Hubbard Bell to AGB, March 22, 1892, Bell, LOC.

15. Keller, *Story of My Life* (1903), 66–67, 71.

16. MA to John Macy, November 13, 1902, AFB.

17. Arthur Keller to MA, March 28, 1892, PIL; Arthur Keller to MA, April 28, 1892, AAS.

18. Arthur Keller to MA, April 28, 1892, AAS; ASM to MA, June 11, 1892, AAS; ASM to MA, June 21, 1892, AFB.

19. ASM to MA, June 11, 1892, AAS.

20. ASM to William Wade, June 28, 1892, AFB; ASM to MA, July 7, 1890, AAS; ASM to William Wade, July 7, 1892, AFB.

21. Keller, *Story of My Life* (1903), 50–54.

22. MA to ASM, August 7, 1892, AFB.

23. ASM to MA, August 17, 1892, AAS.

24. Ibid.

25. Ibid.

26. ASM to MA, November 25, 1892, and December 11, 1892, AAS; MA to ASM, December 19, 1892, AFB.

27. Mabel Hubbard Bell to AGB, March 22, 1892, Bell, LOC; AGB to MA, March 16, 1892, PIL; Michael Anagnos to AGB, March 30, 1892, PIL; AGB to MA, April 22, 1892, PIL; ASM to AGB, April 24, 1892, Bell, LOC.

28. Caroline A. Yale to JH, April 13, 1892, Bell, LOC; ASM to AGB, April 24, 1892, Bell, LOC.

29. AGB to ASM, May 7, 1892, Bell, LOC; AGB to Arthur Keller, May 15, 1892, Bell, LOC; AGB to ASM, May 16, 1892, and June 15, 1892, Bell, LOC; "The Method of Instruction Pursued with Helen Keller a Valuable Study for Teachers of the Deaf," *The Silent Educator* (June 1892). Also printed in "Helen Keller Souvenir #2 1892–1999, Commemorating the Harvard Final examination for Admission to Radcliffe College" (Washington, DC: Volta Bureau), 7–11.

30. ASM to MA, August 17, 1892, AAS; ASM to JH, November 5, 1892, AFB.

31. ASM to MA, December 11, 1892, AAS; ASM to JH, November 5, 1892, AFB. A letter from Keller to John Hitz implies that he sent them at least one clipping. Keller, *Story of My Life* (1903), 212–213.

32. ASM to MA, December 11, 1892, AAS; MA to ASM, December 19, 1892, AFB; Keller, *Story of My Life* (1903), 212.

33. ASM to MA, January 23, 1893, AAS.

34. Ibid. This is also referred to in George O. Goodhue to ASM, April 13–14, 1894, Bell, LOC.

35. ASM to MA, January 25, 1893, AAS.

36. ASM to MA, undated, January or February 1893, AAS; Lash, *Helen and*

Teacher, 167 (I was unable to find this letter at Perkins, the LOC, or the AFB);
Arthur Keller to MA, March 6, 1893, AAS.

37. Arthur Keller to MA, March 6, 1893, AAS; Lash, *Helen and Teacher*, 171;
Annie Pratt to AGB, April 29, 1893, Bell, LOC.

38. AGB to ASM, April 28, 1893, Bell, LOC; Annie Pratt to AGB, April 29, 1893,
Bell, LOC; Lash, *Helen and Teacher*, 173.

39. AGB to ASM, undated (but after March 1893 Niagara Falls visit), Bell,
LOC; Mabel Hubbard Bell to AGB, May 17, 1893, Bell, LOC.

40. Lash, *Helen and Teacher*, 174–175; Keller, *Story of My Life* (1903), 78–79.

41. Robert V. Bruce, "A Conquest of Solitude," *American Heritage* 24, no. 3
(1973): 30; Robert V. Bruce, *Bell: Alexander Graham Bell and the Conquest of Solitude* (Boston: Little, Brown, 1973), 404.

42. ASM to JH, June 20, 1893, AFB.

43. ASM to MA, November 20, 1893, AAS; ASM to MA, February 5, 1894,
AFB.

44. Hitz spoke about this as early as February 1894. JH to AGB, February 12,
1894, Bell, LOC; George O. Goodhue to AS, April 13–14, 1894, Bell, LOC; JH to
AGB, April 27, 1894, Bell, LOC.

45. JH to AGB, April 27, 1894, Bell, LOC.

46. Lash, *Helen and Teacher*, 183.

47. Lash, *Helen and Teacher*, 184; Bruce, "Conquest of Solitude."

48. ASM, "The Instruction of Helen Keller," address delivered before the
AAPTSD, Chautauqua, New York, July 1894; "Helen Keller Souvenir #2," 12–23.

49. Ibid., 12–13.

50. Ibid., 15, 16.

51. Ibid., 18.

52. Ibid., 19, 20.

53. Ibid., 22.

54. "Chautauqua Comments," *Silent Worker*, September 1894, 9.

CHAPTER 8—THE BATTLE FOR HELEN, ROUND 2, 1894–1900

1. AGB to Arthur Keller, July 20, 1894, Bell, LOC.

2. Ibid.

3. Annie Pratt to AGB, July 30, 1894, Bell, LOC.

4. Ibid.; AGB to Arthur Keller, July 20, 1894, Bell, LOC; *Silent Worker*, March
1895, 2.

5. Annie Pratt to AGB, July 30, 1894, Bell, LOC; Arthur Keller to AGB, August
13, 1894, Bell, LOC.

6. AGB to Mabel Hubbard Bell, November 15, 1894, Bell, LOC; Keller, *Story
of My Life* (1903), 80, 81.

7. *New York Times* (hereafter referred to as *NYT*), January 6, 1895.

8. *Silent Worker*, January 1896, 12; *NYT*, December 19, 1894, and January 18, 1895.

9. HK to KK, February 10, 1895, AFB; Keller, *Story of My Life* (1903), 80–82, 224–234; HK to KK, February 13, 1896, AFB; *NYT*, January 6, 1895; HK to KK, May 7, 1896, AFB.

10. HK to KK, February 10, 1895, AFB.

11. Obituary, *NYT*, January 12, 1896; Keller, *Story of My Life* (1903), 82, 232–233.

12. Lash, *Helen and Teacher*, 169–170, 195–196, 197.

13. Arthur Keller to Mrs. Hopkins, February 11, 1896, AFB; Sophia Hopkins to ASM, March 15, 1896, written on the back of Arthur Keller's February 11, 1896, letter.

14. Ibid.

15. Lash, *Helen and Teacher*, 196.

16. JH to AGB, April 27, 1894, Bell, LOC.

17. HK to KK, May 7, 1896, AFB.

18. Ibid. See: Telegram from AGB to ASM, July 17, 1896, Bell, LOC; HK to KK, May 21, 1896, AFB; HK to KK, July 22, 1896, AFB. Lash, *Helen and Teacher*, 197.

19. Lash, *Helen and Teacher*, 200.

20. ASM to JH, untitled copy of part of an undated letter written while at Wright-Humason School, AFB.

21. *Silent Worker*, September 1896, p. 7; Keller, *Story of My Life* (1903), 235–236.

22. HK to KK, July 22, 1896, AFB.

23. Keller, *Story of My Life* (1903), 138–139, 227.

24. J. E. Chamberlin to ASM, March 22, 1892, and May 6, 1893, AFB.

25. HK to J.E. Chamberlin, February 2, 1934, AFB; Keller, *Story of My Life* (1903), 227.

26. Arthur Gilman, "Helen Keller at Cambridge," *Century Magazine*, January 1897, 473–475; *NYT*, June 19, 1896, and October 14, 1896.

27. ASM to JH, September 3, 1896, AFB; Gilman, "Helen Keller at Cambridge," 473–475.

28. Ibid.

29. Keller, *Story of My Life* (1903), 84.

30. Ibid., 87–88; HK to JH, July 9, 1897, AFB.

31. Arthur Gilman to ASM, April 26, 1897, AFB; *NYT*, June 30, 1897.

32. ASM to JH, December 27, 1897, AFB.

33. JH to AGB, December 27, 1897, Bell, LOC; "Miss Sullivan's Statement," December 30, 1897, AFB.

34. Keller, *Teacher*, 88.

35. Eleanor Hutton to J. E. Chamberlin, January 12, 1898, AFB; Arthur Gilman to KK, December 8, 1897, AFB; Eleanor V. Hutton to J. E. Chamberlin, undated, AFB; KK to ASM, November 22, no year [1897?], AFB; KK to ASM, November 28, no year [1897?].

36. KK to JH, December 28, 1897, AFB.

37. Arthur Gilman to KK, December 8, 1897, AFB.

38. Ibid.; JH to AGB, December 27, 1897, Bell, LOC.

39. Keller, *Teacher*, 81; "Miss Sullivan's Statement."

40. KK to JH, December 28, 1897, AFB.

41. Ibid.

42. KK to ASM, November 28, 1897, AFB; J. E. Chamberlin to NBH, December 6, 1933, AFB.

43. Helen Keller, "A Terrible Extreme," December 28, 1897, AFB.

44. Ibid.

45. Arthur Gilman to Minna C. Smith, December 24, 1897, AFB; Arthur Gilman to Eleanor Hutton, December 11, 1897, and December 23, 1897, AFB; Arthur Gilman to J. E. Chamberlin, December 24, 1897, AFB.

46. ASM to JH, December 30, 1897, and December 27, 1897, AFB.

47. JH to Eleanor Hutton, January 15, 1898, AFB; ASM to JH, January 14, 1898, AFB.

48. Keller, *Teacher*, 85, 87.

49. Ibid., 94.

50. Ida Chamberlin to JH, June 10, 1898, AFB.

51. Ibid.

52. Keller, *Teacher*, 90–91.

53. Merton S. Keith, "Final Preparation for College," "Helen Keller Souvenir #2," 51, 55, 56.

54. HK to JH, February 3, 1899, and March 12, 1899, AFB.

55. Keith, "Final Preparation for College," 56; AGB to HK, May 28, 1899, AFB; Keller, *Story of My Life* (1903), 254.

56. Keller, *Story of My Life* (1903), 96, 258; HK to JH, October 20, 1899, AFB.

57. Ibid.

58. ASM to JH, October 29, no year given, AFB.

59. Ibid.

60. William Wade to AGB, October 31, 1899, Bell, LOC; Fred H. Wines to AGB, November 21, 1899, Bell, LOC.

61. HK to William Wade, December 5, 1899, Bell, LOC.

62. Excerpt of letter from ASM to JH, undated, AFB.

63. Ida Chamberlin to JH, December 15, 1899, AFB; HK to JH, April 22, 1900, AFB; Keller, *Story of My Life* (1903), 265–266.

64. Keller, *Story of My Life* (1903), 266–267; HK to AGB, June 2, 1900, Bell,

LOC; J. E. Chamberlin to Agnes Irwin, August 31, 1900, Helen Keller Papers, Arthur and Elizabeth Schlesinger Library on the History of Women in America, Radcliffe Institute for Advanced Study, Harvard College.

CHAPTER 9—RADCLIFFE, 1900–1904

1. Keller, *Teacher*, 96.

2. Ibid., 98.

3. Helen Keller, *Midstream: My Later Life* (New York: Greenwood Press, 1929; New York: Alfred A. Knopf 1968), 70.

4. J. E. Chamberlin to Annie Pratt, November 26, 1900, Bell, LOC; ASM to Annie Pratt, December 26, 1900, Bell, LOC.

5. Ibid.

6. Ida Chamberlin to Annie Pratt, January 12, 1901, Bell, LOC; HK to JH, March 11, 1901, AFB; AGB to Mabel Hubbard Bell, March 15, 1901, Bell, LOC; HK to JH, March 11, 1901, AFB.

7. HK to JH, April 10, 1901, AFB; Keller, *Midstream*, 73.

8. HK to JH, December 7, 1901, and October 27, 1901, AFB; Keller, *Midstream*, 19–20.

9. Keller, *Midstream*, 19–22.

10. ASM to Annie Pratt, December 26, 1900, Bell, LOC.

11. HK to KK, March 3, 1902, AFB.

12. Ibid.; Keller, *Midstream*, 4–6.

13. HK to JH, March 12, 1900, AFB.

14. Exceptions are: Helen Keller, *The Story of My Life*, ed. Roger Shattuck with Dorothy Herrmann (New York: Norton, 2003) and Helen Keller, *The Story of My Life*, ed. James Berger (New York: Modern Library, 2003).

15. Keller, *Story of My Life* (1903), 285.

16. ASM to AGB, March 12, 1902, Bell, LOC.

17. 1880 Census; the *Minneapolis City Directory* for *1889–1890* and *1890–1891* (Minneapolis, MN: Minneapolis Directory Company); 1910 Census, Wrentham, Massachusetts; 1920 Census, Queens, New York.

18. Keller, *Teacher*, 98–99.

19. AGB to John Macy, April 2, 1903, Bell, LOC; AGB to AS, April 2, 1903, Bell, LOC; Samuel Clemens to HK, March 17, 1903, PIL.

20. HK to KK, May 12, 1902, AFB.

21. AGB to ASM, December 30, 1901, Bell, LOC.

22. Keller, *Teacher*, 99–100.

23. AGB to JH, June 22, 1904, Bell, LOC; Keller, *Midstream*, 24–26; JH to AGB, July 1, 1904, Bell, LOC.

24. Keller, *Midstream*, 26.

25. JH to AGB, July 1, 1904, Bell, LOC; Keller, *Midstream*, 27–32.

26. Lash, *Helen and Teacher*, 319; "Helen Keller's Big Audience," *NYT*, October 19, 1904; "Helen Keller as Seen at the St. Louis Fair," *Atlanta Constitution*, October 23, 1904; 1910 U.S. Census, St. Louis Ward 20.

27. Keller, *Teacher*, 122.

28. NBH Notes; notes, January 26, 1928, NBHC.

CHAPTER 10—JOHN, 1904–1914

1. "Ballade of Slips," *The Century* 1, no. 4 (February 1896): 639.

2. Henney, *Anne Sullivan Macy*, 212; Keller, *Teacher*, 101.

3. Keller, *Teacher*, 100.

4. ASM to John Macy, undated, July, AFB.

5. Ibid.

6. Ibid.; ASM to John Macy, February 26, no year, AFB.

7. Lash, *Helen and Teacher*, 323–324.

8. Ibid., 325; *Sandusky Star* (Sandusky, Ohio), March 7, 1905; "Miss Keller's Teacher," *TriCity Star* (Davenport, Iowa), January 18, 1905.

9. ASM to Eleanor Hutton, March 22, 1905, AFB.

10. HK to AGB, April 7, 1905, Bell, LOC.

11. HK to Sister Mary Joseph, November 29, 1905, AFB; 1900 U.S. Census, Boston Ward 2; 1910 U.S Census, Glen Ridge, New Jersey. His parents, at least in 1910, were in St. Louis. 1910 U.S. Census, St. Louis Ward 20.

12. Lash, *Helen and Teacher*, 335.

13. ASM notes, NBHC.

14. KK to John Macy, November 11, 1905, AFB.

15. ASM to HK, September 1, no year, AFB.

16. Keller, *Midstream*, 33 46, 84; 1910 U.S. Census, Wrentham, Massachusetts.

17. Keller, *Teacher*, 125; notes from dinner with Phil and Lenora Smith, in Washington, March 10, 1927, NBH Notes.

18. Keller and John Macy are both listed as authors in the 1910 census, ASM as a teacher. 1910 U.S. Census, Wrentham, Massachusetts; Keller, *Midstream*, 35; Keller, *Teacher*, 122.

19. Keller, *Midstream*, 87–88; *NYT*, July 6, 1906; Keller, *Teacher*, 149–151.

20. Keller, *Teacher*, 149–151.

21. *NYT*, January 17, 1908; *Daily Courier* (Connellsville, Pennsylvania), January 16, 1908.

22. Keller, *Teacher*, 108.

23. *NYT*, February 2, 1909, and July 25, 1909; HK to Lenore Smith, March 28, 1909, AFB.

24. *NYT*, June 14, 1912, and September 5, 1912.

25. HK to Lenore Smith, August 27, 1910, AFB.

26. HK to KK, August 15, 1912, AFB.

27. Ibid.

28. Henney, *Anne Sullivan Macy*, 232; HK to KK, September 26, 1912, AFB.

29. HK to ASM, undated, October 1912, and October 3, 1912, AFB.

30. HK to ASM, October 7, 1912, and October 10, 1912, AFB.

31. HK to ASM, October 17, 1912, and October 14, 1912, AFB.

32. HK to KK, October 11, 1912, AFB.

33. HK to Lenore Smith, November 30, 1912, AFB.

34. HK to KK, September 26, 1912, AFB; Keller, *Midstream*, 96–98; *NYT*, February 6, 1913, and February 7, 1913.

35. Arturo Giovannitti to HK, September 4, 1913, AFB; HK to Andrew Carnegie, April 21, 1913, AFB; Keller, *Midstream*, 146–147.

36. HK to KK, May 26, 1913, AFB.

37. HK to John Macy, January 25, 1914, AFB.

38. Keller, *Midstream*, 147.

39. HK to John Macy, February 8, 1914, AFB.

40. HK to John Macy, January 25, 1914, AFB.

41. HK to John Macy, February 8, 1914, and March 4, 1914, AFB.

42. HK to John Macy, February 8, 1914, AFB.

43. Ibid.; HK to John Macy, January 25, 1914, AFB.

44. Ibid.

45. HK to John Macy, February 8, 1914, AFB.

46. HK to John Macy, April 4, 1914, AFB.

47. Ibid.

48. Ibid.; HK to John Macy, May 11, 1914, AFB.

49. HK to KK, December 1, 1914, AFB.

50. Keller, *Teacher*, 127; HK to Lenore Smith, December 27, 1914, AFB.

CHAPTER II—ON THE ROAD, 1914–1924

1. Keller, *Teacher*, 126–127.

2. Ibid., 115–117.

3. Ibid., 128.

4. Ibid., 69, 127.

5. Ibid., 107.

6. Ibid., 70.

7. Ibid., 101.

8. Arturo Giovannitti to ASM, undated, AFB; Arturo Giovannitti to ASM, August 10, year unlisted (likely 1915 or 1916), AFB.

9. Ibid.

10. Keller, *Midstream*, 177.

11. ASM to HK, undated, 1916, AFB; HK to Lenore Smith, November 22, 1917, AFB.

12. Keller, *Midstream*, 179; HK to Jon Macy, March 4, 1914, AFB.

13. *NYT*, November 19, 1916.

14. *Chicago Tribune*, June 9, 1916.

15. Keller, *Teacher*, 129; Mark Caldwell, *The Last Crusade: The War on Consumption, 1862–1954* (Atheneum: New York: 1988), 14. For more on tuberculosis, see: Ott, *Fevered Lives*; Georgina D. Feldberg, *Disease and Class: Tuberculosis and the Shaping of Modern North American Society* (New Brunswick: Rutgers University Press, 1995); Rothman, *Shadow of Death*, 198–207.

16. *NYT*, November 21, 1916.

17. HK to ASM, November 21, 1916, AFB.

18. Keller, *Midstream*, 181.

19. HK to ASM, December 1916, AFB.

20. ASM to HK, undated, 1916, AFB.

21. Ibid.

22. Caldwell, *Last Crusade*, 74, 117; Lawrason Brown, *Rules for Recovery from Pulmonary Tuberculosis: A Layman's Handbook for Treatment* (Philadelphia: Lea and Febiger, 1923), 64–65.

23. HK to ASM, November 27, 1916, AFB.

24. Rothman, *Living in the Shadow*, 212–213; Feldberg, *Disease and Class*, 94.

25. HK to ASM, November 1916, AFB.

26. ASM to HK, 1916, AFB.

27. ASM to HK (likely written December 25) 1916, AFB.

28. Ibid.

29. ASM to HK, 1916, AFB.

30. Ibid.

31. ASM to HK, 1917, AFB.

32. Ibid.

33. Ibid.

34. Ibid.

35. Virginia Woolf, *On Being Ill* (London: Hogarth Press, 1930; Ashfield, MA: Paris Press, 2002), 19; ASM to HK, 1917, AFB.

36. ASM to HK, 1917, AFB.

37. HK to ASM, January 30, 1917, AFB.

38. ASM to HK, 1917, AFB.

39. Ibid.

40. Ibid.

41. Ibid.

42. HK to ASM, February 13, 1917, AFB.

43. HK to ASM, March 23, 1917, and March 25, 1917, AFB.

44. ASM to HK, 1917, AFB.

45. ASM to NBH, June 9, 1931, AFB.

46. HK to KK, October 16, 1917, AFB.

47. HK to Lenore Smith, November 22, 1917, AFB; Keller, *Midstream*, 182.

48. Ibid., 182–183.

49. Keller, *Teacher*, 127–128.

50. Keller, *Midstream*, 186–187; Keller, *Teacher*, 145.

51. HK to Lenore Smith, May 3, 1918, AFB.

52. HK to Lenore Smith, September 13, 1918, AFB.

53. ASM to Francis Trevelyan Miller, April 16, 1919, and April 12, 1919, AFB.

54. HK to KK, July 8, 1919, AFB.

55. Ibid.; Keller, *Midstream*, 209.

56. *NYT*, August 19, 1919; Keller, *Teacher*, 154.

57. Keller, *Midstream*, 209–215; HK to KK, June 29, 1920, AFB.

58. Keller, *Teacher*, 155, 157; HK to KK, May 10, 1920, AFB.

59. HK to KK, June 29, 1920, AFB.

60. HK to KK, July 7, 1920, AFB.

61. 1910 U.S. Census, Wrentham, Massachusetts; 1920 U.S. Census, Queens, New York.

62. Lash, *Helen and Teacher*, 324.

63. HK to Harry Weber, August 15, 1920, AFB; Harry Weber to HK, August 20, 1920, August 23, 1920, and August 28, 1920, AFB. See schedules in the Vaudeville File, AFB, box 95, folder 10.

64. Keller, *Teacher*, 126; HK to KK, August 15, 1912, AFB.

65. Keller, *Teacher*, 165–166.

CHAPTER 12—THE AMERICAN FOUNDATION FOR THE BLIND, 1924–1930

1. Ida Hirst-Gifford to Board of Trustees, AFB, April 15, 1924, AFB.

2. AFB box 22, folder 3.

3. Charlie Campbell to ASM, HK, and Polly Thomson, March 13, 1924, and May 27, 1924, AFB; JCN (full name unknown) to ASM, June 9, 1923, AFB; MCM to ASM, April 18, 1924, AFB.

4. AFB, box 22 folder 4; Robert Irwin to C. S. Glover, November 6, 1924, AFB.

5. HK to Mildred K. Tyson, June 7, 1924, AFB; ASM to MCM, August 6, 1924, AFB; F. E. McKay to Robert Irwin, December 30, 1924, AFB.

6. ASM to MCM, November 10, 1924, AFB.

7. ASM to MCM, December 24, 1924, AFB; Charlie Campbell to ASM, March 20, 1925, AFB.

8. ASM to MCM, June 25, 1925, AFB.

9. Ibid.

10. ASM to MCM, October 25, 1925, AFB.

11. ASM to MCM, undated, AFB.

12. Robert Irwin to MCM, November 30, 1925, AFB.

13. *NYT*, January 11, January 12, and January 13, 1926.

14. Report of Organizing for Helen Keller Meetings, June 10, 1926, AFB.

15. HK to Walter Holmes, September 1925, AFB.

16. *NYT*, October 25, 1925; John Albert Macy, *The Story of the World's Literature* (New York: Boni & Liveright, 1925).

17. Keller, *Teacher*, 185.

18. Ibid., 177, 181.

19. Ibid., 58.

20. Ibid., 79, 169, 201.

21. Ibid., 159.

22. Ibid., 159, 221.

23. Ibid., 159–160.

24. *NYT*, October 21, 1936. Whether this came from an interview or from a written statement is not clear.

25. Keller, *Teacher*, 89, 163.

26. HK to Mildred Keller Tyson, January 20, 1927, AFB.

27. ASM to MCM, April 30, 1927, AFB.

28. ASM to MCM, May 18, 1927, AFB.

29. HK to NBH, undated letter from "late 1920s," AFB.

30. Keller, *Teacher*, 185, 186; Polly Thomson to NBH, July 3, 1927, NBHC.

31. "Teacher Whimsically Sketches."

32. ASM Notes.

33. "Teacher Whimsically Sketches."

34. Carolyn G. Heilbrun, *Writing a Woman's Life* (New York: Ballantine, 1988), 23–24.

35. "Teacher Whimsically Sketches."

36. Ibid.; ASM Notes.

37. "Teacher Whimsically Sketches"; Mrs. Mary Sullivan Hannan to NBH, November 14, 1928, NBI IC.

38. Henney's materials are unclear, and largely based on unnoted conversations, but ASM's sister Mary appears to have been dead by this time.

39. NBH to Dan J. Murnane, October 2, 1928, NBHC; Mary Sullivan Hannan to NBH, November 12, 1928, NBHC.

40. Henney, *Anne Sullivan Macy*, 321; MCM to HK and ASM, June 19, 1929, AFB; HK to MCM, June 24, 1929, AFB; *NYT*, June 14, 1929.

41. HK to MCM, June 24, 1929, AFB.

42. ASM to MCM, October 1, 1929, AFB.

43. Ibid.

44. ASM to MCM, November 20, 1929, AFB.

45. HK to MCM, January 18, 1930, AFB.

46. Ibid.

47. Keller, *Midstream*, 6, 33, 34, 36, 317–319.

48. Ibid., 343–344.

49. Ibid., 345–346.

50. HK to MCM, February 4, 1930, AFB.

51. Henney, *Anne Sullivan Macy*, 322.

52. Keller, *Teacher*, 190–194; Henney, *Anne Sullivan Macy*, 322–323.

53. Ibid.

54. HK to NBH, July 27, 1930, NBHC; "Cratloe," ASM Notes.

55. "Limerick," ASM Notes.

56. "How Ireland Disturbs," ASM Notes; "Ireland," ASM Notes.

57. "Ireland, the bogs," ASM Notes.

58. Keller, *Teacher*, 195.

59. HK to NBH, July 27, 1930, NBHC.

60. Polly Thomson to Amelia Bond, May 22, 1930, AFB; Amelia Bond to Polly Thomson, July 3, 1930, AFB; Polly Thomson to Amelia Bond, July 9, 1930, and July 31, 1930, AFB.

61. *Boston Transcript*, May 17, 1930; John Macy, "Equality of Woman with Man: A Myth," *Harper's* 153 (November 1926): 705–713; John Macy, "Logic and the Ladies," *Harper's* 157 (November 1928): 722–730; John Macy, *About Women* (New York: William Morrow & Company, 1930), 18, 45.

62. Macy, *About Women*, 311–312.

63. "Teacher Whimsically Sketches."

64. ASM Notes. Though the non-visual and spiritual language suggests this may have been written by Keller, this was likely written by ASM.

65. Keller, *Teacher*, 113–114.

66. Ibid.

CHAPTER 13—CONCLUDING, 1930–1936

1. *New York World Telegram*, May 18, 1931.

2. Charles Beury to ASM, December 9, 1930, AFB; ASM to Charles Beury, December 17, 1930, AFB; Edward Newton to ASM, December 23, 1930, AFB; ASM to Edward Newton, December 27, 1930, AFB.

3. *NYT*, February 17, 1931,

4. Henney, *Anne Sullivan Macy*, 341; MCM to HK, February 17, 1931, AFB.

5. HK to Mrs. Felix Fuld, April 7, 1931, AFB.

6. ASM to Charles Beury, February 23, 1931, AFB.

7. HK to Mrs. Felix Fuld, April 7, 1931, AFB; A. Edward Newton to ASM, March 11, 1931, AFB.

8. Charles Buery to ASM, February 17, 1931, AFB; ASM to Charles Beury, February 23, 1931, AFB.

9. "Teacher Whimsically Sketches."

10. Keller, *Midstream*, 346; Henney, *Anne Sullivan Macy*, 341.

11. HK to Mrs. Felix Fuld, April 7, 1931, AFB; HK to Carolyn Lyons, April 2, 1931, AFB.

12. Keller, *Teacher*, 203; ASM to Lenore Smith, September 7, 1931, AFB; *NYT*, October 11, 1931; ASM to NBH, June 9, 1931, AFB.

13. ASM to Lenore Smith, September 7, 1931, AFB.

14. Keller, *Teacher*, 203.

15. ASM to Lenore Smith, September 7, 1931, AFB.

16. ASM to NBH, June 9, 1931, AFB.

17. ASM to Lenore Smith, September 7, 1931, AFB.

18. Ibid.

19. ASM to NBH, June 9, 1931, AFB; ASM to Lenore Smith, September 7, 1931, AFB.

20. ASM legal file, AFB.

21. HK to Mildred Keller Tyson, January 21, 1932, AFB.

22. *NYT*, December 26, 1931.

23. ASM, "Education in the Light of Present-Day Knowledge and Need," Temple University Address, February 16, 1932, AFB.

24. Henney, *Anne Sullivan Macy*, 341.

25. Rush Rhees to ASM, March 15, 1932, AFB.

26. ASM to Lenore Smith, March 16, 1932, AFB.

27. Keller, *Teacher*, 207.

28. Ibid., 208; Henney, *Anne Sullivan Macy*, 345; HK to Lenore Smith, June 8, 1933, AFB.

29. *NYT*, August 26, 27, and 28, 1932; NBH to ASM, August 30, 1932, NBHC; NBH to Mrs. Mrs. Julian L. Harris, October 6, 1933, NBHC.

30. "Teacher Whimsically Sketches."

31. Ibid.

32. Ibid.

33. Ibid.

34. HK to Mildred Keller Tyson, June 9, 1933, AFB; *NYT*, September 2, 1932.

35. Keller, *Teacher*, 209–210.

36. HK to Mrs. Felix Fuld, May 10, 1933, AFB; HK to Lenore Smith, June 2, 1933, AFB; Keller, *Teacher*, 210.

37. Henney, *Anne Sullivan Macy*, xii; NBH to Blanche Colton Williams, September 18, 1933, NBHC.

38. NBH to Ned Holmes, March 1933, NBHC.

39. Mildred Keller Tyson to NBH, April 4, 1933, NBHC.

40. HK to John Finley, May 6, 1933, AFB; HK to Mildred Keller Tyson, June 9, 1933, AFB.

41. HK to NBH, September 24, 1933, NBHC; HK to MCM, August 21, 1933, AFB; Keller, *Teacher*, 215.

42. HK to NBH, September 24, 1933, NBHC.

43. Ibid.; Polly Thomson to NBH, undated, 1933, NBHC.

44. NBH to "Beloved Trio," undated, 1933; *NYT*, December 16 and 17, 1933; NBH to ASM, March 19, 1934, NBHC; NBH to Amelia Bond, March 15, 1934, NBHC; NBH to ASM, March 27, 1934, NBHC; ASM to NBH, April 11, 1934, NBHC.

45. NBH to "Beloved Trio," undated, 1933, NBHC.

46. HK to MCM, June 30, 1934, AFB; Keller, *Teacher*, 215; Polly Thomson to MCM, January 16, 1934, AFB; HK to NBH, January 17, 1934, AFB; HK to MCM, January 29, 1934, AFB; HK to Carolyn Lyons, June 14, 1934, AFB; HK to MCM, June 3, 1934, AFB.

47. Henney, *Anne Sullivan Macy*, 347; Keller, *Teacher*, 217.

48. HK to Carolyn Lyons, October 14, 1934, and October 27, 1934, AFB; NBH to Alexander Wolcott, November 12, 1934, NBHC; HK to MCM, December 20, 1934, AFB; HK to Lenore Smith, March 5, 1935, AFB; HK to Charlie Campbell, March 13, 1935, AFB.

49. *NYT*, April 14, 1935, and April 29, 1935; *NYT*, May 18, 1935; HK to MCM, July 23, 1935, and August 23, 1935, AFB; Keller, *Teacher*, 220; HK to MCM, July 23, 1935, AFB.

50. Keller, *Teacher*, 220.

51. HK to Charlie Campbell, March 13, 1935, AFB; HK to MCM, July 23, 1935, AFB.

52. Walter Holmes to Polly Thomson, May 13, 1936, AFB; HK to MCM, July 10, 1936, AFB; HK to ASM, July 7, 1936, AFB; Keller, *Teacher*, 222, 224.

53. HK to Robert Irwin, September 29, 1936, AFB; Polly Thomson to Lenore Smith, September 8, 1936, AFB; Keller, *Teacher*, 225–226.

54. Keller, *Teacher*, 226–227.

CONCLUSION

1. "Foolish Remarks"; *Winnipeg Free Press*, October 21, 1936; *Charleston Daily Mail*, October 21, 1936; *Kokomo Tribune*, October 20, 1936; *Reno Evening Gazette*, October 20, 1936; *Times and Daily News Leader* (San Mateo, California, October 20, 1936.

2. "Teacher's Sayings," NBH Notes.

3. Ibid.

4. ASM Notes.

Oc 01/10
Ctat 5/10
CG 10/10
Icc 12/10
Tap 2/11
OK 9/12
TER 10/12
CG 7/14
TAP 11/14
SOR 60/15
OM 5/14
CG 9/17